D0597082

# Jews and Money

*Other Books by Gerald Krefetz*

Investing Abroad:
A Guide to Financial Europe

Money Makes Money and the
Money Money Makes Makes More Money:
The Men Who Are Wall Street

The Dying Dollar

The Book of Incomes

The Smart Investor's Guide:
How to Make Money
in the Coming Bull Market

# Jews and Money

## The Myths and the Reality

### Gerald Krefetz

*New Haven and New York*
TICKNOR & FIELDS
1982

*Library of Congress Cataloging in Publication Data*

Krefetz, Gerald.
Jews and money.

Bibliography: p.
1. Jews — United States — Economic conditions.
2. Jewish capitalists and financiers — United States.
3. Jews in the professions — United States. 4. United
States — Ethnic relations. I. Title.
E184.J5K846          305.8'924'073          82-5639
ISBN 0-89919-129-0                          AACR2

*To Marcia*

# Contents

# Preface

Writing about money is never simple, and writing about Jews is fraught with dangers. Writing about money and Jews together is inflammatory no matter how cautiously handled. While I have tried to be judicious in the selection of material, there is no guarantee that some readers will not be perturbed, irritated, or surprised. This work may confirm some readers' prejudices, it may shock some readers' sensibilities. The author offers no apology for anyone's discomfiture. Among their virtues, books are meant to clarify and perhaps illuminate the human condition. I hope the reader will accept this work in that spirit.

As an observer of the financial scene, I have long been intrigued by economic conundrums and fascinated by ethnic differences. However, the trigger for this work was a statement about Jews made by the then Chairman of the Joint Chiefs of Staff, General George S. Brown, in the mid-seventies: "They own, you know, the banks in the country, the newspapers. Just look at where the Jewish money is." Whether the general's military intelligence was better than his economic intelligence remains moot. It was clear to most onlookers that the general was plumb wrong, though Jews were represented in modest ways in both industries.

But Brown certainly raised an interesting question, however wrong his information and deplorable his connotations. As I examined the available literature on the subject, it became clear to me that in recent years no one had scrutinized the scope of contemporary Jewish economic activity in America. The reason for this neglect was not hard to find: one of the oldest and most virulent anti-Semitic myths holds that Jews are driven by mercenary motives that the rest of mankind is innocent of. Moreover, the Jew, it was believed, as the gentile's economic man, was responsible for all financial woes; conversely, no sanctions against them were too severe, and no punishment was unmerited. The subject of Jews and money was best not discussed for fear of raising the anti-Semitic ghost again.

It is undoubtedly this defensive reasoning that caused the disregard of this fascinating and important subject. But catering to other people's irrationality serves no purpose, and obscuring one's achievements is self-defeating. Jews have strived mightily to improve their economic status while at the same time contributing greatly to America's economic success. Those contributions are only now appreciated. Assuredly, they should be the source of pride. The Jewishness of Jews has made a difference, as have the intrinsic natures of every other ethnic group.

I have surveyed some of the areas in which Jews have succeeded, indeed have excelled in ways that might have shocked their forefathers, but undoubtedly would have pleased their foremothers. This veritable implosion of achievement in the last generation or two has not occurred in every area of enterprise: there were and still are too many obstacles for that. But Jews have filled in those economic interstices, the spaces between traditionally entrenched interests. Through hard work, innovation, and creative license, they have cut out a piece of the business firmament for themselves.

Quick to appreciate new trends and developments, Jews have exploited novelty and manipulated chance. Equipped with the time-honed talents of the trader and the heightened awareness of continual persecution, Jews have frequently opted for portable professions and businesses that fill a need somewhere between supply and demand.

Today Jews can be found in a variety of businesses and running some of the largest of them — from movie studios and communications corporations to oil companies and investment banks. Jews have used any leverage they have had in an open society, as well they should, to advance their skills and capitalize on their traditions. For a small minority comprising less than three percent of the population, they represent four percent of the vote and perhaps five percent of the national income. Indeed, they have achieved so well that their income is probably a third higher than the American average.

This book is not a census of Jewish wealth, but rather a survey of the contemporary scene, warts and all. In preparing this work, the inevitable question arose: Is it good for the Jews? It would be disingenuous of me to believe that some information herein cannot be used in noxious ways. However, the answer to darkness is light, and fuller disclosure surely is a better guide than half-truths, fabrications, and illusions. Fantasies have so dominated the subject of Jews and money, to the detriment of all, that some facts can do no greater harm. Perhaps they can shed some of that light.

My thanks to all those who contributed to this endeavor, but especially to Elisabeth Scharlatt for her skilled and perceptive editing, and to Ticknor & Fields for the courage to undertake a sensitive subject.

GERALD KREFETZ
April 1982

# Jews and Money

# 1. Introduction: The Jewish Question

The real 'Jewish Question' is this:
From what can a Jew earn a living?
— Sholom Aleichem

It is better to live rich, than to die rich.
— James Boswell, *Life of Samuel Johnson*

Jews and money — the subject has been a conversation piece for a millennium, perhaps longer. Everyone is intrigued by Jewish money: the clergy decried it while kings coveted it; anti-Semites are enraged by it while Jews are both proud and secretive about it. People have paid an inordinate amount of attention to Jewish wealth. Most of the comments and observations have been pejorative, wide of the mark, and wild as well.

Moreover, the study of Jewish attitudes toward money — both historic perspective and a present-day evaluation — has been curiously neglected. It is, as it were, a subject *infra dignitatem*, beneath one's dignity. Jewish money — its purported influence and power — is one of the oldest canards of anti-Semitism. Therefore, the topic is usually dealt with in the softest of voices by Jews for fear of raising the specter of anti-Semitism; and by non-Jews for fear of being tarred by the brush, of being called anti-Semitic for even ventilating the subject. The omission is startling since money — its use and abuse, its acquisition and disposition — was and is a central element in the Jewish experience.

Though the connection between Jews and money has been apparent for a thousand years, the experiences of Jews did not motivate them to speculate and theorize on their economic conditions even at the height of Jewish financial power. For an introspective, analytical people, this is a monumental oversight. Jewish communities are undoubtedly aware of their special roles in finance, international trade, merchandising, and brokerage. And their host societies acknowledged their functions, though sometimes this acknowledgment was demeaning or hostile. Nevertheless, Jews did not consider their situation significant enough to write about. Apparently, they did not think it worthy of comment: according to one historian, Salo W. Baron, "no ancient or medieval Jewish scholar devoted himself to the detailed interpretation of these economic facts and trends. . . . No Jew wrote economic tracts."

In some ways, all that has changed — and dramatically. Though no Jews wrote about business and finance in the ancient or medieval period, David Ricardo wrote several treaties in the 19th century that started a torrent of economic speculation, which has not ceased. In the United States, a number of leading economists are Jews: Peter Bernstein, Edward M. Bernstein, Arthur Burns, Otto Eckstein, Solomon Fabricant, Milton Friedman, Alan Greenspan, William Haber, Robert Heilbroner, Lawrence Klein, Simon Kuznets, Leon Kyserling, Robert Lekachman, Wassily Leontief, Allan Meltzer, the late Oskar Morgenstern, Paul Samuelson, Anna J. Schwartz, Robert Solomon, and Murray Weidenbaum. They have covered the subject from business cycles to input-output analysis, from microeconomics to macroeconomics.

The economic role of Jews in contemporary America is just about the only topic with which these economists have not concerned themselves. This omission may be a professional lapse. However, they have a great deal of company in social scientists, historians, sociologists, and theologians. Only in the last decade or two have ethnic identity and religious factors become acceptable subjects of debate. The melting pot was a much-honored concept, but a little scratching beneath the surface exposed pluralism. Indeed, between fifty and seventy-five million citizens consider themselves ethnics or hyphenated Americans, an unmeltable image they wish to preserve.

Jews, perhaps more than any other group, paid lip service to the notion that for the American experiment to succeed, each ethnic nationality and each denominational sect had to subsume its identity, values, and idiosyncrasies to the whole. It was not so much a question of assimilation, but of homogenization. To stress the differences, many Jewish leaders thought, would be negative: it would intensify diversity, and in a Democracy one should accent similarities.

And, of course, in the back of their minds was the fear that enumeration or census would set them apart. Their history was full of head counts that later became tools for head hunts. Inevitably, after a census, their assets were calculated and subsequently expropriated. Understandably, Jews have grown wary of body counting.

In recent years, some Jews have succumbed to that all-American tendency to compound braggadocio and vulgarity in touting their ability to make it. Leaving discretion and taste aside, they boast of their abilities, vanities, and riches. One observer noted that after generations of oppression, "it is not simply that living well is the best revenge but rather that living well is an obligation." And telling about it is a compulsion. Jewish leaders, particularly those of the old school, feel called upon to ask followers to avoid ostentatious display, fearing that it might create antagonism.

Most Jews, however, still harbor a European mentality when it comes to personal money: they treat it seriously and soberly; they speak of it in hushed tones, rarely joking about it. For Jews, money has stood between life and death. It was central to their existence. Money was not worshiped, but they considered it just as essential to their material being as one God was to their spiritual being. In a sense, money had an existential reality for the Jews, for it gave them substantiality in alien eyes.

Without their financial usefulness, they would have been obliterated long ago. Naturally, Jews understood this fact of life better than anyone else, but it was formalized by an anti-Semite in a roundabout fashion. Edouard Drumont, a nineteenth century Frenchman, declared that "anti-Semitism is an economic war." Throughout history, Jews have realized that they must not lose this war. To put it another way, whenever Jews were not economically successful and financially indispensable, they were dismissed, expelled, or murdered. It has been incumbent upon them to succeed.

During the English Counter-Reformation, the Catholic Church tried to recover its ascendancy by presenting a stark truth to royalty: no bishop, no king. For scattered Jews, the watchword was just as simple: no money, no Jews. Of course Jews have been oppressed, expelled, and murdered even when they were integrated into the economy — witness the Nazi period. Now, however, economic success is the law of survival — to exist Jews must prosper. And nowhere have they prospered better than in the United States.

Still, to this day, many Jews feel a marked ambivalence toward money — aware of its power, but at the same time choosing to withdraw from the limelight. For too long, the Christian world has held up the image of the Jew as archetypal financier, as omnipotent manipulator of money. The Jew was accused of being the source of Christian economic problems, the plague of monetary health. Many inexplicable economic and social events have been attributed to the Jews, from the fall in agricultural prices to the rise of prostitution; no connection has been too farfetched; no fiscal arrangement too bizarre to implicate the Jews.

The idea of the Jew as moneychanger, pawnbroker, or banker became indelibly etched into the popular psyche — often in the most pejorative and contemptible terms. Every language had its own disparaging slurs and proverbs that associated Jews and money:

"A real Jew will get gold out of straw." (Spanish)

"The Jew-tax (interest rate) and the whore's hire are both very high." (German)

"A bankrupt Jew searches his old accounts." (Greek)

"Bargain like a Jew but pay like a Christian." (Polish)

"A Jewish miser will regret nothing more than having had to part with his foreskin." (Russian)

"Mammon is the God of the Jews." (Hungarian)

"A Jew at a fair is like a fish in water." (Yiddish)

One specialist in ethnophaulisms — slurs against other peoples — has found more of these derogatory sayings in Spanish and German than in any other language. The reason, he suspects, is due to the fact that these two countries "sinned most against the Jews."

The theme was elaborated on by writers of both popular works and belles lettres. The classic image, delineated by Shakespeare in the character of Shylock in *The Merchant of Venice,* has haunted Jews ever since. Never mind that Jewish bankers could not compare to the great Italian and German banking families and that the populace hated and feared Christian bankers far more than the petty Jewish moneylender: the Jew made a convenient scapegoat.

While the Second Vatican Council (1962–65) attempted to alter Catholic teaching and thinking, no single pronouncement, no conclave of the Church, no parliamentary decree can swiftly change the image in the popular mind of the medieval trinity of Jew–heretic–usurer. Since Vatican II, religious anti-Semitism has decreased, but the economic type has not. Indeed, anti-Semitism in the United States now seems less concerned with whether Jews are to blame for Christ's death than with their ostensible control of money and power.

And this "Jewish Question" does not disappear. After two hundred years of American history, public opinion polls find that, year after year, close to a third of the population has anti-Semitic leanings. Little wonder then that Jews are extremely touchy about the subject — they are happy and proud of their achievements, but their accomplishments are misinterpreted, and something is lost in translation.

Most balanced discussions of the economic contribution of Jews to American society are met with profound distrust. At one time Jews would have paraded their poverty, but now that they have so much more to be discreet about, questions on the subject are met with silence. Jewish wealth cannot be compared to newly acquired wealth, like the oil riches of the Arab world. But in the context of American private wealth, the Jews stand out as *prima inter pares,* the first among equals. They have taken to heart the free enterprise system and the spirit of capitalism. After a fashion, they have out-Protestantized the Protestant Ethic.

Today the Jewish community in the United States is said to be the most fortunate by far in terms of assets, income, occupational prestige, and educational status. Jews have made the most of their opportunities and, in a curious way, their disadvantages. A Catholic priest and sociologist, Andrew M. Greeley, has noted that Jews "have become in every measure one could care to choose the most successful group in American society, a fact which no one at this point would presume to deny." Economist Thomas Sowell of Stanford University has reached the same conclusion:

> Jewish family incomes are the highest of any large ethnic group in the United States — 72 percent above the national average.... Among families headed by males with four or more years of college and aged thirty-five to forty-four, Jews still earn 75 percent higher incomes.... Among families headed by males with less than nine years of school and aged thirty-five to forty-four, Jews still earn higher incomes than others with the same characteristics.... A smaller proportion of Jewish families today have multiple earners than is true of American families in general. Even Jewish families with no one working have higher incomes than other families with no one working. Earnings from investments of one sort or another are apparently greater among Jews, as are other advantages built up on the past.

# 2. Success and Survival

One's religion is whatever he is most interested in, and
yours is Success.
— James M. Barrie, *The Twelve-Pound Look*

The transformation of Jews in a couple of generations, from people without money to people with money, is a fascinating story. The figures are remarkable — even astounding. They are skewed so sharply from national norms as to be virtually unrecognizable in terms of the American experience. Whether it is called intestinal fortitude, operation bootstrap, moxie, social striving, or upward mobility, American Jews have fought mightily for financial security. For the most part, they have found it, though perhaps at a substantial cost.

As a group, Jews have attained a higher standard of living and earn more money than any other religious group in the United States. Though the reasons may be complicated and the motivation complex, the evidence seems incontrovertible, though hardly complete. Americans, who count everything from ball bearings to baseball scores, have shied away from religious enumeration. Eighty-five nations in the world record denominational affiliation, but the United States does not. In the 1950s, the Bureau of the Census did one such survey, but it met with so much misinterpretation and opposition from established religious organizations that it has not subsequently pursued this line of investigation.

Other surveys, though not as complete as the Census Bureau's inquiry, have confirmed what many suspected: in this affluent society, Jews are the richest of the rich. The prevailing notion that Wasps make the big money — are really the American wealthy — must be reinterpreted in light of new evidence.

While there are a number of surveys of wealth, two of the most extensive and authoritative bear close scrutiny, for their findings reinforce each other: one sponsored by the Council of Jewish Federations and Welfare Funds (CJFWF), and the other, by the Center for American Pluralism's National Opinion Research Center (NORC) at the University of Chicago. Both indicate, directly or indirectly, that the average family income for Jews far exceeds the national average, and surpasses that of most other religious or ethnic groups.

In the early 1970s, the CJFWF's National Jewish Population Study found that the median family income for all Jewish families was $12,630, while the national average at that time was $9,867. Jews had median family incomes that were over twenty-eight percent higher than the remainder of the country. Compared with other ethnic groups, the differences are even more startling. While the median Jewish family income was $12,630, the median family income for Puerto Ricans was $4,969; for blacks, $5,074; for Mexicans, $5,488; for Irish, $8,127; and for Italians, $8,808. The average median income for these five ethnic groups is $6,493, or just about half of what Jews earn.

These figures were confirmed by the NORC in 1974. At that time, the average Jewish family earned $13,340 — thirty-four percent more than the national average of gentile white ethnic groups' $9,953. In relation to other religious groups, the average Jewish income of $13,340 compared with an average of $11,374 for Catholics; $11,032 for Episcopalians; $10,976 for Presbyterians; $10,103 for Methodists; $9,702 for Lutherans; and $8,693 for Baptists. Jews earned an average of $3,000 more than the members of any other major denomination.

These figures tell only part of the story, for the income distribution curve for Jews is considerably different. Over forty-three percent of Jewish households earn more than $16,000 a year. In New York City, where a plurality of the nation's Jews live, only 27.3% of all families have incomes over $15,000. In the nation, only 25.5% have incomes over $15,000. In other words, at the high end of the income scale nearly twice as many Jews make middle and upper class incomes — more than $15,000 a year.

Jews find themselves in an enviable position with close to half their households sitting in the lap of bourgeois luxury. In fact, they make up a notable part of the upper class. Of the fifty-three million American families (as of 1972), 13.5 million can be considered middle and upper class; of the two million Jewish families, nearly nine hundred thousand can be so considered. Jews do not compose three percent of the affluent income earners, as might be expected if they were proportionally represented, but they do make up close to seven percent of the middle and upper classes.

Naturally, there are other ways of measuring personal wealth, liquid assets, property, but the few surveys that do exist say nothing about religious affiliation. Nevertheless, some observations, though lacking in statistical precision, seem reasonable. Though Jews have propelled themselves into the upper income brackets, and a number have corralled a great deal of capital in the equity markets, no American Jews have reached the fabled ranks of the Hunts, Rockefellers, Mellons, or Du Ponts, that is, no American Jews are billionaires, though a few come close. Still, there are scores of multimillionaires and hundreds of millionaires. With the present limited information, it is impossible to say whether there are more Jewish millionaires than millionaires of other religions. A reasonable guess might find that Jews make up a fifth of the very rich in America.

Whether or not there is a connection between being self-consciously Jewish and achieving financial success, there does seem to be a connection between the collective Jewish experience and economic achievement. A group's livelihood — especially its business activities — is influenced by historic, social, cultural, and religious factors. For example, their experience did not predispose them to finance capitalism, though they had a number of outstanding models in the past. It did predispose them to independence and self-sufficiency since they lived in a hostile or indifferent society; to professionalism, where the practice was as important as profit; to scholarly pursuits, where long preparation meant a lengthy postponement of gratification; to progressive industries, where innovation was rewarded; and to peripheral enterprises, which allowed for expansion without direct competition with basic or mainstream corporations. Consequently, the Jewish entrepreneurial spirit and tradition of risk-taking has led them into the peripheral and the marginal, creative, and novel areas of existence. Whether it was the nomadic restlessness of Jewish life, its insecurity, or its frontierlike existence compounded by the feeling that they were under siege, Jews were forever involuntarily experimenting with the most basic problems: how to exist, how to earn a living.

Finally, this entreprenurial spirit or capacity for risk-taking allowed, or perhaps provoked, Jews to find new businesses and new business forms. In the past, they had introduced some basic economic concepts such as fair profit and a just price. They had developed the idea of fiat money and were among the first to use negotiable instruments of credit. At the height of nationalistic resurgence in the nineteenth century, the Rothschilds were developing international syndicates, a form of international banking. In twentieth century America, Jewish businessmen were developing investment banking expertise to finance consumer-oriented businesses — department stores, Alaskan fisheries, movies, theatres, copper mining and smelting, airlines, and clothing factories.

In the 1960s, Jews were again in the forefront in creating a new business form — the conglomerate, a multi-purpose holding company whose disparate profit centers were purportedly synergistic — greater than the sum of its component parts. It was not a Jewish invention — that honor probably belongs to Royal Little of Textron — but Lehman Brothers, Lazard Freres, Loeb Rhoades, and Goldman Sachs were forceful in selling the new notion. Besides the self-interest of these investment banking houses (the major interest in conglomerates was only partially due to new products, market penetration, increased revenues, balance sheet growth, and rising price-earnings ratios), mergers and acquisitions generated volumes of new corporate issues that Wall Street underwrote, sold, and traded. And a number of Jewish businessmen were quick to see the potential of the new financial form. Prudent and conservative money managers were skeptical of the conglomerate: it had a striking resemblance to earlier overblown, credit-created pyramids, which had appeared earlier and milked unsuspecting investors before collapsing. Business history was littered with square cannon balls, rotten tulip bulbs and burned-out matches from Ponzi-like operators of the John Laws and Ivor Kreugers.

Besides the investors in conglomerate shares and debentures, the people who had the most to lose were the staid managements of victim companies. For the most part, the takeover candidates were old industrial companies with secure if unexciting markets, substantial assets, little debt, underutilized capital, high dividends, diverse ownership, and no immediate growth prospects. In brief, they were old-line, quasi-somnambulant corporations.

The conglomerate era of the sixties, abetted by a high-flying stock market and a prolonged boom, was really a none-too-subtle attack on establishment corporations. Though the accounting was devious and the newly issued paper of dubious value, the conglomerate posed a substantial threat to the corporate status quo. By the late sixties, stalwarts of American industry and finance such as Chemical Bank, Goodrich, Great American Insurance, Jones and Laughlin, and Pan American were under the gun. And naturally, in the spirit of free enterprise, they ran to the government for protection.

James Ling of Ling-Temco-Vaught, Roy Ash of Litton, and Roy Little of Textron were joined by Ben Heineman of Northwest Industries, Howard Newman of Philadelphia and Reading, Saul Steinberg of Leasco, Charles Bludhorn of Gulf & Western, Mishulam Riklis of Rapid American, Laurence Tisch of Loews — each practicing the "highest form of creative capitalism." These Jewish conglomerate-builders, from the flamboyant to the conservative, spearheaded the attack. Aided by clever investment bankers, a permissive Democratic president, and a credulous public, they shook up old managements, created anomalous corporations and provided Wall Street with a string of dazzling investment vehicles. Just about every one was a star of the go-go years, and just about every one suffered grievously when reality in the form of recession and a strict Republican administration returned in the seventies.

The battle was, of course, between "the old establishment and the nouveau riche." The old establishment's financial structure was Republican to the core, while the Jewish investment bankers and conglomerate builders were strongly represented in the Democratic party, though they often hedged their bets with campaign donations to both sides. Even so, the Nixon administration immediately directed the Justice Department's antitrust division against what has been called the "Jewish-cowboy connection," that is, the Wall Street financiers and Texas oil men. The Jewish-cowboy connection, according to G. William Domhoff, who coined the term, contains some oil companies (e.g., Amerada-Hess, Tidewater, Kerr McGee, Halliburton), airlines (American, Braniff, Continental), movies (Paramount, 20th Century Fox, Metro-Goldwyn-Mayer, [MGM], and "best of all, . . . consumer goods and merchandising where Sears, Jewel Tea, Gimbel's, Macy's, City Stores, Allied Department Stores head a star-studded list."

The Nixon attack cut the conglomerates to the quick and the stock market reappraised their values. Within the first couple of months of the new administration, thirteen conglomerates lost $5 billion in market value. It was not the end of the conglomerates, but their "creative capitalism" was to become more prudent in the seventies.

For the Jews, the fall of the conglomerates marked the end of an era. On the whole, they emerged relatively unscathed, but it seemed clear that there were limits to their financial power. While the theory of a free enterprise system welcomed competition, mergers, acquisitions, and a to-the-wall attitude, the reality proved different. When the central or core establishment started to hurt from the exercise of those doctrines, especially when exercised by outsiders who were considered aggressive and pushy, cease and desist was the order of the day.

Most Jews are not concerned that their reach may exceed their grasp, for never in modern history have they been in such an enviable position of wealth and power. As a group, they have risen to the top, and as individuals, their existence is freer, happier, and more productive than it has been for a thousand years. It may not be a Messiah's dream, but it may be the next best thing.

## Occupation: Middle Class

The job pattern of the Jewish work force is as unlike the national pattern as the Jewish education experience is unlike the American model. In part, the occupational patterns reflect higher education, but other elements also enter the picture. Regardless of the motivation or the constraints, American Jews have worked through a series of stages on the road to economic freedom and maturity. The rapid transition from cottage industry to post-industrial society is remarkable: it has been compressed into a few generations.

The following table compares Jewish and national job patterns:

|  | Jews | | National Averages | |
|---|---|---|---|---|
|  | Male | Female | Male | Female |
| Professional and technical | 29.3 | 23.8 | 14.3 | 14.9 |
| Managers, officials, proprietors | 40.7 | 15.5 | 14.0 | 4.8 |
| Clerical workers | 3.2 | 41.7 | 6.8 | 36.3 |
| Sales workers | 14.2 | 8.3 | 6.6 | 7.8 |
| Craftsmen, foremen | 5.6 | 1.5 | 21.2 | 1.3 |
| Operatives | 3.9 | 2.3 | 17.8 | 12.9 |
| Nonfarm laborers | 0.3 | 0.2 | 6.8 | 0.9 |
| Service workers | 1.2 | 3.6 | 7.3 | 19.3 |

To put the figures in more general terms: 87.4% of working Jewish males and 89.3% of working Jewish females are white-collar workers, while only 41.7% of the white male work force and 63.8% of the female work force are in this class.

A Gallup survey from the mid-sixties compared employment patterns among religious groups. There is no reason to think that the findings would be markedly different now. On average, fifty-six percent of the national work force did not do manual labor. For Protestants, the figure was fifty-two percent; for Catholics, fifty-three percent; for nonbelievers, sixty-two percent; and for Jews, ninety-five percent. The last figure seems somewhat high, but close to recent observations.

The number of blue-collar jobs is slowly shrinking throughout the country, but Jewish blue-collar workers are rapidly disappearing. In 1910, probably eight out of ten males were manual workers, but now, only five out of ten work with their hands. However, for Jews the change was faster. Shortly after the first mass migrations from Eastern Europe stopped, in 1930, thirty percent of Jewish males were manual workers. In 1950, it was down to twenty percent, and by 1970, it was down to little more than ten percent.

At one time, the Jewish working class was obliged to take those jobs because of discrimination, lack of other opportunities, and because there was a great demand for manual workers. Since laborers were poorly paid, without job security, and of dubious social standing, Jews found such work distasteful, unremunerative, and déclassé. Though economic circumstances forced them into such jobs, their basic discontent spurred their rise to the leadership of several labor unions. Today, with the noticeable decrease of Jewish labor members, such as in the International Ladies Garment Workers Union, Jewish leadership will undoubtedly wane. As the Jewish work force becomes nearly 100 percent college-trained, the number of Jewish manual laborers will fall to statistical insignificance — rather like the present situation of Jewish farmers.

Though Jews come from a tradition that is close to the soil, in today's world they are not of the soil. A mystical attachment to the land, both spiritual and primeval, was a major stimulus for Zionism. The ancient concept of the Promised Land was as much agrarian and pastoral as it was territorial and theological. Jews have sung praises of Zion, but few move to Israel. Jewish poets and philosophers have sung of the fertility of the soil, but very few Jews are farmers. In Israel, only 2.7 percent of the Jewish population live in farm communities. In the United States, the percentage is far less — only 20,000 of the 1.7 million American farmers are Jewish. Much lip service is paid to what Amos Elon, an Israeli writer, terms the "agrarian ritual," but not many Jews are tillers and hoers. American Jews, at one time or another, set up agricultural settlements in Louisiana, New York, and Oregon. While these were interesting experiments in utopian living, none of the settlements survived though the participants were amply supported by Jews outside of these communities. Judaism began as a pastoral religion, but today the vestiges of its rural origins remain only in its rituals, for Jews are decidedly a city people with urban concerns and livelihoods.

In recent years, there has been a significant shift in occupations among Jews: the younger ones have left manufacturing and wholesale trade, and have lessened their participation in retail trade and the civil service. Young Jews are increasingly interested in the professions, entertainment and recreation, communications, education, and construction. In finance, business, and in transportation, the employment patterns have remained relatively constant between generations.

More younger Jews are working in the service industries, having lost some of their parents' interest in government service, an interest born from the dismal employment prospects of the 1930s. The younger generation is aware of civil service job security, but perhaps also senses the lack of challenge in bureaucratic work. Furthermore, they understand that government employment, after a long period of growth, may now be in a long period of decline. Indeed, the drop in government employment presaged a traumatic blow for New York City's civil servants. The city's bankruptcy was only averted by drastic steps — one of which was the layoff of sixty thousand city employees in two years. Probably half of those civil servants were Jews. When New York City's first Jewish mayor, Abraham Beame, himself a career civil servant, caused such massive firing, the irony was not lost on the electorate.

The demographic shift seems to indicate that Jewish youth were quick to understand the subtle changes that take place in the modern industrial state as it moves from hardware society to software society, from accumulating goods to demanding services. However, it would be a mistake to attribute too much prescience to Jews in predicting changes in the economy. While many enter professional and technical areas — indeed twice as many as their fathers' generation — the boom is in the field of education. There has been a three-fold increase from father to son. With close to twenty percent of the Jewish work force presently in teaching careers, the supply is rapidly exceeding the demand. And there is a strong possibility of a glut of teachers in the 1980s.

The occupations that young Jews are now engaged in or preparing for have become the areas that are most appealing to the rest of the population. Besides the surplus of teachers, the increase of professional and technical people will also put pressure on

Jews. For example, in the field of education, the government projected that the number of doctorates needed between 1972 and 1985 was twenty-seven thousand. But the number of graduates with Ph.D. degrees in education will come close to 149,000. Similar projections find the same pattern in almost every discipline. For the same period, the country will produce six-hundred thousand Ph.D.s, but may have jobs for only two hundred thousand. Thus, Jews are facing greater economic competition.

Moreover, since the Nixon recessions, the unemployment picture has changed. Not only did the 1970s witness higher unemployment rates, but the people losing jobs came from executive, administrative and technical ranks — heretofore exempt from the threat of layoff. This new phenomenon of white collar unemployment has hurt Jews in unforeseen ways.

Regardless of what Jews do for a living — and they seem to do everything from running the largest chemical company in the United States to operating three out of every four retail establishments in New York City — they seem to think that their activities are prestigious. This pride is perhaps deceptive, but it serves Jews well. By thinking highly of themselves, they stretch their abilities and embellish their conceits. Humility is not a Jewish trait.

At one time, it was thought in sociological circles that members of a minority were less class conscious. It is now understood that this view was incorrect — ethnic minorities are as class conscious as everyone else. A survey of families with similar average incomes found that nine out of ten Jewish families thought of themselves as middle class, while only five out of ten black families saw themselves in that class, and seven out of ten Protestant and Catholic families came to the same conclusion. In a parallel survey based on college education rather than income, the results were quite similar: Jews consistently placed themselves in the middle class nine out of ten times, somewhat above the white Protestants and white Catholics, and considerably above blacks. This self-concept is of course part hubris, but it is also a reflection of economic mobility, of how far they have come.

Jews were perhaps middle class before there was a middle class. Historically, they have been the people of the middle, a buffer between rich and poor, landlords and peasants, rulers and taxpayers, northerners and southerners, orient and occident, and buyers and sellers. If the rise of the middle class is a relatively recent event in the West, middle class endeavors of commerce, trading, and exchanging were ancient practices for Jews in the Middle East, North Africa, and Europe. A mobile people, they moved throughout these areas establishing themselves at important crossroads and villages, preferably near centers of local power. Jews populated the centers of the civilized world's oldest cities, and in a sense, the cities grew up around them. Two functions were thus served: settled on trade routes, Jews acted as traders and distributors for goods in transit, buying and selling whatever passed their way. The local patron — king, duke, lord, or mayor — was just as important since he could maintain order, a requisite for trade. At first, Jews depended on the centers of power; later the cities, the centers of power would depend on the Jews.

The visibility that resulted from living near the trade routes and the power establishment gave the impression that Jews were everywhere and that they were more numerous than they actually were. The impression was also created that they were important since they consorted with the powerful.

The long attachment to urban dwelling and commerce imbued Jews with characteristics that would bloom in a newly industrialized, free-enterprise-oriented, frontier-motivated society. America was ripe for the exercise of talents that had been honed for a millennium. Many Jews in the great waves of migration did not come from strictly urban centers, but from Central and Eastern European villages. Nevertheless, their humble origins diminished only the scope, not the spirit, of their abilities.

If Jews eluded the European obstacles of second-class citizenship and third-class life styles by immigrating, they found other constraints when they settled in the United States. But these were far more manageable. Simon Kuznets, the 1971 Nobel Laureate in economics, has noted five factors that kept Jews (and other minorities) from fully participating in the economy. These restrictions change as the minority adapts to society; some disappear, others take new shapes. The first three constraints come from within the group: the affiliation constraint — the desire to remain within the minority rather than assimilate into the majority; the heritage-equipment constraint — the tradition and training of the minority; the recent-entry ("greenhorn") constraint — the time it takes minority members to adapt to the custom of the majority.

Two other constraints come from established society: the majority-bias constraint — the attitude of the majority toward the minority group and the economic-growth constraint — the availability of jobs for the new workers.

Each of these factors shaped the Jewish labor force, reduced its parameters and channeled its energies. The affiliation constraint kept Jews in small organizations, often run or owned by other Jews, where they could observe their traditions and be free of discrimination. It also forced them to find such jobs in large- or medium-sized cities where, if it was necessary to work in non-Jewish occupations, they could assume the protective covering of a large population. Finally, it led to self-employment, professional practices, independent trades, single or small proprietorships — ways of maintaining independence if affiliation with other Jews was neither practical nor possible. Though affiliation was preferred, it was not a strictly determining factor. Except for a very small ultraorthodox group, religion did not control the choice of occupation for most Jews.

In tradition and training, most other immigrants tried to do what the Jews had done. They worked primarily in mechanical and industrial jobs, small crafts, textile, or tailoring. Initially, most of the Jewish labor force was blue collar, but within a few years one third of the immigrants were operating their own shops and stores. For instance, of the 241 clothing factories in the United States, Jews owned 234 of them by 1885. By 1915, the ready-made clothing industry was the chief employer of Jewish labor: one out of ten Jews was employed in the needle trades. The heritage-equipment constraint was transitional for it provided fertile grounds for transforming jobs. In a general sense, the comparatively broad educational backgrounds of Jews made it easier for them to adapt to new opportunities..

The greenhorn constraints are simply the restrictions that arise from cultural shock in a new environment. Recent immigrants are denied some jobs because they do not speak the language. Since there was no obligation to speak English for American citizenship before 1907, many immigrants never did become bilingual.

Two restrictions on employment for Jews came from their surroundings. The first — majority-bias — became perceptibly worse in the twenties and thirties before it became better. As long as Jews filled blue collar jobs and other jobs without competitive social status, anti-Semitism was not an issue. But the scarcity of jobs during the Depression, combined with earlier right-wing rantings of Henry Ford, Father Coughlin, and other superpatriots, increased the bias and discrimination against Jews.

Finally, the rapid expansion and growth of the country conjoined with the mass migration of the Jews. The new immigration laws of the 1920s stanched the flow of immigrants shortly before the economy went into a decade-long tailspin. The jobs that were available when the Jews came ceased to be available when they stopped coming — a coincidence of timing. After 1930, when the economic-growth constraints made life more difficult, especially at the bottom of the laborpool, the Jews moved into areas where previous restraints were less potent. There were fewer things to hold them back. The decrease in manual work by Jews was matched by an increase in managerial, executive, sales, technical and professional services. Jobs in large corporations and government agencies became available — opportunity for talent, skill, and expertise. The Second World War perhaps quickened the changing job structure, but the changes benefitted Jews. The demands of the American economy matched the availability of trained Jews to meet those demands. The vast growth of industry carried the Jews to new economic heights — like a surfer on a wave.

Success or fortune are relative terms, but on every level, Jews have realized a formidable ascendancy. In the last fifty years, they have caught up on centuries of deprivation. A few Jews have always been rich. At the turn of the century, one survey calculated that within New York City there were sixty Jewish millionaires out of a total Jewish population of 900,000. Perhaps there were a few more in the rest of the country. Jews then constituted about

1.25 percent of the entire population, or about half of today's representation. In 1922, another survey found that of 151 millionaires, 23 were Jews — seven of these were Guggenheims.

A few Jews enjoyed wealth, but for the overwhelming majority there was abysmal poverty. Most Jews, especially those arriving between 1880 and 1925, remained poor and oppressed, with high hopes but few prospects. During the Depression, their condition was at its nadir. One writer summed up the experience of the Jewish immigrants in an autobiographical novel, *Jews Without Money*, which was something of a success when it was published in 1930. Michael Gold, a leftist journalist and member of the radical magazine *New Masses*, wrote of the hard and cruel conditions in the Lower East Side, the rites of passage for these immigrants. Though it portrayed an earlier period, the realistic, Zola-like images of unemployment, sweatshops, landlords, petty tyrannies, illness, greed, backbiting, and adolescence were all empathic scenes of life during the Great Depression.

Gold's Marxist viewpoint somewhat distorted his vision. But the picture of poverty among the Jewish masses that he recorded apparently struck a particularly sympathetic and realistic cord. "There are enough pleasant superficial liars writing about America," Gold said. "I will write a truthful book of poverty; I will mention bedbugs."

Through "vermin," "mud puddles," and "manure heaps," Gold indicted the whole economic system. His mother, reportedly, was mortified when her son went public with the family cockroaches. But many Jews and non-Jews easily identified with Gold's class warfare: in six years, through the worst of the Depression, the book went into fifteen printings — no mean record for a novel of protest.

But *Jews Without Money* was more than social commentary and protest: it was an educational novel with an overriding message. Toward the end of the work the father sums up his life:

> "Ach, Gott, what a rich country America is! What an easy place to make one's fortune! Look at all the rich Jews! Why has it been so easy for them, so hard for me? I am just a poor little Jew without money."
> "Poppa, lots of Jews have no money," I said to comfort him.

"I know it my son," he said, "But don't be one of them. It is better to be dead in this country than not to have money. Promise me you'll be rich when you grow up, Mickey!"

"Yes, poppa."

But even as Jews suffered through the 1930s along with everyone else, they continued to lay a base for future success — in a sense to fulfill that promise. The indictment of capitalism was fashionable and understandable among Jewish intellectuals, but somewhat irrelevant. Even then there were Jews, far from rich, who were making the system work for themselves. In a retrospective article of 1936 on the Jewish community, *Fortune* spoke of the perennial theme of Jewish influence, power and money. The motivation was less to deflate Gold's pessimistic view than to counter some of the absurdities published about Jews. True, a few years previously, Henry Ford had recanted and apologized for his sponsorship of anti-Semitic tracts and newspapers, but the country was still rife with prejudiced pamphlets.

*Fortune* addressed itself as much to Nazism as to domestic anti-Semitism. In the introduction to one of his editions written that year, Gold told the story of a German friend who was arrested while translating *Jews Without Money*. When the German police arrested her, they read what she was working on and burst out laughing: it was incomprehensible to them that poor Jews actually existed. Gold went on to write: "No, every Jew is not a millionaire. The majority of Jews belong to the working class and to the bankrupt lower middle-class. . . . Jewish bankers are fascists; Jewish workers are radicals; the historic class division is true among the Jews as with any other race."

The Germans had, of course, been drinking at the well-head. Hitler had read the bogus *Protocols of the Learned Elders of Zion* which was first published in Germany in 1919 and he incorporated some of that fiction into his new fiction, *Mein Kampf*, published in 1924. In a sense, Hitler began where Ford had left off. Hitler provided the new set piece for the "international Jewish conspiracy." The future Führer wrote:

Jews first enter communities as importers and exporters. They then become middle men for internal production. They tend to monopolize trade and finance. They become bankers to the monarchy. They lure monarchs into extravagances to make them dependent on Jewish money-lenders. . . . They seek popularity by a show of philanthropy and political liberalism. They promote the development of joint-stock companies, stock speculation and trade unions. . . . By control of the press they create turmoil. Both international finance and international communism are Jewish tricks to weaken the national spirit.

*Fortune* attempted to present a balanced analysis of the subject. Specifically, the editors asked if there were any facts to support a charge that Jews have monopolized or are monopolizing economic opportunity in the United States. They concluded: "There is no basis whatever for the suggestion that Jews monopolize United States business and industry."

They reached that conclusion by surveying the major sectors of the American economy. After systematically examining owners, directors, and chief executive officers of virtually every industry, the magazine turned up a few rare birds: three prominent Jews in the exectuive ranks of auto-makers, but none in auto distribution; in the steel industry, Republic — the seventh largest producer — was partially owned by the Block family of Chicago; in oil distribution, American Oil of Baltimore — owned by the Blausteins — controlled five percent of the national distribution. For the rest of industry, except for occasional directors from investment banking houses, Jews were either absent or well hidden, for none could be found in coal, rubber, chemicals, shipping, shipbuilding, railroads, bus companies, aviation, utilities, telephone and telegraph, engineering and construction, heavy machinery, lumber, or dairy products.

Jews were, however, prominent in scrap and waste product businesses — they controlled iron and steel, paper, cotton rag, wool rag, and rubber. There were some Jewish interests in light industries, for instance the production of wool, silk, cotton, and rayon weaving. Meat packing was a significant sector for Jews since it entailed preparing meat under the dietary laws, and they controlled about ten percent of the industry. Jews were well represented in furniture manufacturing, shoe and boot construction, tobacco purchasing, cigar production, and alcohol — they controlled half of the important distilleries in the country. Jews were particularly prominent in merchandising, but in only a few, highly visible, major department stores in the East. The mass merchandisers and mail-order companies were largely in gentile hands — even Sears, Roebuck, which had been founded by the Rosenwalds, was run by an acknowledged anti-Semite, Robert Wood.

Perhaps the only industry that Jews dominated was clothing. Jewish firms produced eighty-five percent of the men's clothing and ninety-five percent of women's. The fur trade was also a Jewish industry and Jews were well represented in Hollywood.

But what of the traditional Jewish occupation — the money trades — how did they fare there? Apparently, they were no better off in the world of finance than in a number of other fields. In New York City, where half the Jews in the country lived, constituting nearly a third of the city's population in the early thirties, of the 420 directors of banks belonging to the New York Clearing House, thirty were Jews, or seven percent. A few years later, another survey found that of the 93,000 commercial bankers in the country, 0.6 percent or 550 were Jews. In insurance companies, *Fortune* found only two chief executives who were Jews, and few Jews throughout the industry. Jews, however, were prominent in retail insurance sales. Of 1375 members of the New York Stock Exchange, 252 or eighteen percent were Jews. Of the 637 stock exchange firms, fifty-five were Jewish, twenty-four half Jewish and thirty-nine were Jewish-dominated — again about eighteen percent of the exchange firms.

While the figures hardly indicate control of the country's financial structure, the standard argument emphasizes that Jewish control occurs behind the scenes, that is, through the board of directors. In the 1930s, the majority of directors in American corporations were gentiles. Of the eighty thousand directors listed in the 1934 edition of *Poor's Register,* 3,825 were Jews, or 4.8 percent. In their seminal work, *Corporations and Private Property* (1932), Berle and Means found that of the two hundred largest nonbanking corporations, ten had Jews as chairmen of the board or as presidents, again about five percent. In short, neither in front or behind the scenes could Jews be charged with dominating, controlling, or monopolizing the American economy.

If it was obvious to all but the most adamant anti-Semites that Jews were but a small force in the American business and financial world, why have they attracted so much attention? *Fortune's* answer is valid even today:

> The Jews *seem* to play a disproportionate part for two reasons: the Jews ... are the most urban, the most city-loving, of all peoples, and the favored occupations bring them into most direct contact with the great consuming public. ... The proclivity of the Jews for finance, trade, and exchange has been frequently noticed ... and the concentration of Jews in the cities is a present as well as an historical fact.

More recent observers noted much the same thing — that the high economic profile was part real, but also part mirage, for in the three branches of industry where Jews were prominent in the mid-thirties, "clothing manufacture, department stores, and entertainment ... [were] enough to support the illusion of Jewish economic significance. The ordinary American who bought at a Jewish-named department store, saw the movies of Goldwyn and Mayer, and had heard of Jewish bankers might presume Jewish financial power was extensive if he wished."

But back in the thirties, *Fortune* was surprised not to find a greater input from the Jewish community.

> Who can lay a better claim ... for the creation of the present economic order, [but] are less well represented in many directions than they should be? The Jews and the English were the chief designers of finance capitalism in the last century but only the English have profited correspondingly. The Jews have seen themselves surpassed in one business or banking province after another by upstarts who were still swinging swords or pushing plows when the Jews were the traders and the bankers of Europe. It is one thing for a non-Jew to say "Oh, the Jews own everything." It is another for an impartial observer to see exactly what they do run.

Clearly, most of the contemporary Jewish fortunes are not in the basic, smokestack industries of America. They have been made not so much outside the mainstream of big business, but rather alongside it. Whatever the historical connections, social circumstances, or predispositions, entrepreneurial sense has led Jewish businessmen to peripheral areas where innovation, experimentation, and knowledge could make the real difference. In addition, it was the Jewish acceptance of risk that enabled them not only to succeed but to thrive.

However well Jews have progressed financially, they don't seem much closer to controlling and manipulating the economy today than they did when *Fortune* undertook its first investigation. Of course, today the economy is far more diverse and much larger: it accommodates whole industries that were unknown forty and fifty years ago, and it has boosted the importance of marginal or peripheral enterprises. Jews still do not have much of a representation in basic industry, but their presence in peripheral areas has grown.

For instance, any survey of automobile, steel, coal, rubber, glass, chemicals, oils, paper, agribusiness, heavy construction, or machine tools business will find few Jews, as before. Indeed, a new *Fortune* look at the composition of chief executive officers in 1976 concluded that top corporate officers are overrepresented by Protestants, especially Episcopalians and Presbyterians, and are underrepresented by Catholics, Baptists, and Jews. The magazine found Jews overrepresented only in retailing — accounting for roughly thirty percent of the top posts in merchandising.

There is one significant difference, however, from the old days: now there are quite a few industrial czars of national importance who happen to be Jewish. Some of them are self-made men, others have climbed the career ladder, and some have inherited their companies and their cash. For instance, some of the more prominent Jews or men of Jewish extraction in business are Edwin Land of Polaroid; Armand Hammer of Occidental Petroleum; Leon Hess of Amerada, Hess Petroleum; William Paley of CBS; Ben Heineman of Northwest Industries; Walter Annenberg of Triangle Publications; Nathan Cummings of Consolidated Food; Irving Shapiro recently of Du Pont; Michel Fribourg of Continental Grain; Lewis Wasserman of MCA; Mishulam Riklis of Rapid American; Victor Posner of his family holding company;

Charles Bludhorn of Gulf + Western; W. Michael Blumenthal of Burroughs, the Treasury Department, and Bendix; Edgar Bronfman of Seagrams; and Leonard Goldenson of ABC.

In addition, a few noteworthy Jews recently departed such as Lewis Rosenstiel of Schenley; David Sarnoff of RCA; Charles Revson of Revlon; Gustave Levy of Goldman, Sachs; Samuel Newhouse of the Newhouse newspaper and broadcasting chains; and Andre Meyer of Lazard Freres. And there are a number of Jewish millionaires who have successfully evaded the public eye or whose enterprises are perhaps so banal as to go virtually unrecognized. While many of these figures are ardent Jews, some are converts to other religions, and some are Jews in name only, for they do not practice Judaism and, in fact, abjure any relationship with it. Under David Sarnoff, for example, Jews were not in evidence at RCA, and within the Newhouse newspaper chain only non-Jews were employed as editors and publishers, a scene not unlike that at *The New York Times* under the Adolph Ochs-Arthur Hays Sulzberger regime. In other companies and professional organizations founded and headed by Jews, there is a distinct effort to reduce the Jewish tone. This only suggests what many Jews have long known, that Jews are sometimes their own worst enemies in the effort to blend into society.

# 3. A Monetary Imperative

I have never known much good done by those affected to trade for the public good. It is an affectation, indeed not very common among merchants, and few words need be employed in dissuading them from it.

— Adam Smith, *The Wealth of Nations*

*Defense Mechanisms*

Jewish hypersensitivity to money has been gathering momentum throughout modern times. And every time there is a shock to the Jewish central nervous system or communal body — an inquisition, ghettoization, pogrom, "crystal night," Holocaust, or war — Jews realize once again the necessity of money. Critics of Jews invariably put the cart before the horse: Jews, they say, are genetically greedy and it is second nature to them to acquire wealth. The cash nexus is a central Jewish concern, for without money the Jew is naked before his enemies and perhaps, according to historian Leon Poliakov, damned in the eyes of his God.

With the start of modern history Jews found that a reverence for money [was] a source of all life. Increasingly, each action in the Jew's daily life was subjected to the payment of a tax. He must pay to come and go, pay for the right to pray with his coreligionists, pay to marry, pay for the birth of his child, even pay for taking a corpse to the cemetery. Without money, Jewry was inevitably doomed to extinction. Thus the rabbis henceforth view financial oppressions (for example, the moratorium on repayment of debts to Jews . . .) as on a par with massacres and expulsions, seeing in them a divine curse, a merited punishment from on high.

Thus, the acquisition of money has become a reflexive action, as instinctive as blinking when a hand menaces the eye and as sure a response as the flight of an antelope on the Serengheti plain. For the Jew, money does not represent security, for he seems constitutionally insecure, nor is it a form of camouflage, for Jews often choose to stand aside and stand out. For the Jew, money is safety, a tool of survival. Over the years, the manipulation, earning, creation, and saving of money has been raised to a fine art — the result of defensive social conduct, which is passed from generation to generation. The Jews are a wonderful example for the new science of ethology — the biological study of paradigms, patterns, and gestures as a clue to understanding character.

Any review of the social evolution of Jews in recent times must concentrate on the mightiest defense mechanism — the acquisition of money — since it is so central to their existence and survival.

Having assumed this adaptive technique, some Jews refuse to believe that their economic expertise is anything special — particularly since one of the founding fathers of modern ethology, Nobel Laureate Konrad Lorenz, is suspect for writing ambiguous essays, which smack of Nazism to some critics. Nevertheless, social evolution appears as valid as physiological evolution. It's only man's spiritual pride, Lorenz has said, that allows him "to accept that his intestinal tract is a product of evolution, but resent the suggestion that his standards of social behavior are also in some way the product of an evolution."

Perhaps money is to Jews what aggression and territoriality is to other national, religious, and ethnic groups. And conversely, perhaps, with the establishment of a Jewish state, which at times is both aggressive and territorial, the reliance on money will abate. In the American context, however, it continues to exert a magnetic attraction, for Jews seem to make much of it and to hold it in high regard.

It is not only as a group activity that money-making is a specialty of the house: in the last generation or so, individual Jews have done some of the most profound and creative thinking on business and finance. Modern Jewish economists got a running start with David Ricardo and Karl Marx in the nineteenth century, and have really flourished in contemporary times.

For example, since a Nobel Memorial Prize for economic sciences was established in 1968 by the Central Bank of Sweden, to be awarded under the auspices of the Nobel Foundation, a dozen Nobel Memorial Prizes in economics have been awarded — over a third of them to Jews or persons of Jewish extraction. Considering the fact that Jews make up less than a third of one percent of the world's population, the representation is more than coincidence. Jews have been generously represented in all the Nobel awards: indeed, of the 513 Nobel Prizes awarded since 1901, Jews have won 88, or seventeen percent. But economics appears to be their forte.

The ability of Jews to make money may also prove to be their undoing. Success is something of a double-edged sword, for it stirs resentment, jealousy, and hate — emotions that are never far below the surface. In the past, anti-Semitism was a mass phenomenon, a lower-class happening, often induced by upper-class leaders. One socialist, August Bebel, once remarked that "anti-Semitism is the socialism of the lower middle class." In the United States, as elsewhere, the most virulent form seemed to appear in places that were the least populated by Jews. The fear of Jews arose, and still arises, from the assumption that they will ascend too high in the economic and social structure. Jewish manipulation, social engineering, dominance, and control might result. Jews have always seemed foreign and alien to native populations. It was perhaps best summed up at the time of the Eichmann trial in Israel, when Robert Servatius, chief defense attorney, asked Salo W. Baron, professor at Columbia University and the most prominent Jewish historian of the twentieth century: "Can you explain the causes of that negative attitude which has existed for so many hundreds of years and of that war against the Jewish people?"

Baron responded, "The answer is: dislike of the unlike."

This combined fear of foreigners — "the unlike" — and of economic control was never as potent in the United States as it was in Europe, so American anti-Semitism has been mild by historical standards. After all, Jews were doing what everyone else was doing, or trying to do — board the train of economic mobility. If the Jew was the traditional economic man, he was joined by innumerable materialistic neighbors — the economic man was a respected factotum in society. Not all Americans saw free enterprise, wheeling and dealing, and capitalism as positive virtues: indeed, the counter-cultures of the thirties and the sixties were particularly hostile to business. But for the most part, Jewish ambition fell within the mainstream of society.

Nevertheless, Jews continue to feel uneasy. In fact, there is a curious anomaly: the more successful Jews are, the more attuned they become to anti-Semitic vibrations. Their antennae are now so sensitive that anti-Semitism is detected in any criticism of Israel, any praise of the Arabs, or mention of Jewish lobbying pressure. And, of course, negative observations about Jewish money. However, the Jewish establishment has not recognized one of the most insidious of modern evils, a condition that in the past was a forerunner of anti-Semitism — inflation. It is an economic disease that should have particular and sinister meaning for Jews.

In almost every serious economic crisis, there is a rise in the level of anti-Semitism, though Jews usually have nothing to do with precipitating the problem at hand. In the twentieth century, the cardinal economic illness is inflation, hardly a Jewish disease, but one that occurs when a central bank pumps up the money supply beyond the productive capacity of the economy. Ironically, every large industrial nation has had recent bouts of double-digit increases in their consumer prices. In the past, the price increases signaled disaster for governments and had a devastating effect on democracies. In a none-too-subtle fashion, inflation is class war on a massive scale. Unlike other economic maladies — depression or recession, high unemployment, or booms and busts — inflation pits elements in society against each other. And the consequences of this kind of internecine warfare undermine the body politic, as each contending group feels its financial security ebbing. For instance, capital assets shrink, depriving those who have them of property — without due process — and of the right to deploy those assets as they see fit. Naturally, those without capital assets — about a fifth of the country — are not affected by this process. However, depreciation certainly reduces the wealth of the middle class. The rich and the clever — the entrepreneurially minded — easily contend with that side of inflation, borrowing and expanding with money of value, and repaying the loans with money of far less value. The sharpies — the borrowers — take money from the suckers — the lenders — in a classic squeeze play on the middle class.

Inflation also turns things topsy-turvy on the income side. The highly skilled or strongly unionized wage earners are able to raise their wages almost without regard to the state of the economy. This scramble for more pay tends to disemploy the unskilled or semi-skilled, the same thing that happens when the government raises the minimum pay rate. In other words, the skilled and the organized redistribute the wealth to their advantage by suppressing the nonunion, the unskilled, and the marginal workers — the very young and the very old. Furthermore, as a larger part of corporate earnings go to labor, less of the income pie is left as capital. When profits fall, less money is left to replace used and worn-out plants and equipment, items that cost much more to replace during inflationary periods.

Social dislocation is the political result of economic mismanagement. And social unrest has never been a welcome state of affairs for Jews for they have always been on the receiving end of scapegoat treatment. It was inflation, after all, that led to their greatest tragedy, the Holocaust. The disabling of the Weimar Republic was a direct result of 1923 hyperinflation, which at its worst found an egg selling for eight billion marks and a loaf of bread for two hundred billion marks. The German experience was a landmark in the annals of political economy:

> Towering frustrations, bitterness and hatred were part and parcel of the inflationary process. To see hard-won savings disappear, to have the purchasing power of weekly wages constantly deteriorate, to be forced to exist on a perpetually falling standard of living, to scavenge and barter for food — all undermined the citizen's confidence in the economy and, more importantly, in the government. A

disstable society is the first to welcome a man on horseback, and it is no coincidence that Hitler's beer-hall putsch took place at the very crest of the hyper-inflation. Uncontrolled inflation is a deadly social disease, and in Germany it was directly responsible for the fall of the Weimar Republic and the rise of Nazism.

Hitler told his audiences that the economic mess was the work of the Jews. Everything was blamed on them — the defeat of the military during World War I, the Versailles Treaty, immorality, social corruption, unemployment, parasitic capitalism — all were the work of international Jewry. It was an idea that obsessed Hitler until his death.

Therefore, it is surprising that Jews are not more alarmed about recent spells of double-digit inflation in the United States and around the world. An issue that should be of major concern to the Jews is not, while far less important events, such as the marches of isolated bands of self-styled fascists or the opening of Nazi-oriented bookstores, cause fear.

There are, of course, a number of serious economic issues which have concerned American Jews. Would another Arab oil boycott, which would result in higher gasoline prices, turn gentile Americans against their Jewish neighbors? Would towering oil prices be the cause of a new wave of anti-Semitism? Many Jews think so, but then many Jews think that the non-Jewish population of the country is far more anti-Semitic than it ostensibly is.

For Jews, education continues to be the way to success. Though their passion for learning is an old one, it blossomed in America. In America, secular education was substituted for religious indoctrination. Jews eagerly attended the free public school systems of the United States, which contrasted with the state-dominated, church-oriented school systems of Europe that either kept them out or provided alien information. There was no greater boon to the Jews' fortunes than open education.

Immigrant parents were dedicated to keeping their children in school. At the turn of the century, the United States Industrial Commission found that Jewish mothers had lower employment rates than other "nationalities" — they stayed home to look after their children, making sure they attended classes. The working class parents took every measure to ensure that their children —

at least the males — would not follow in their footsteps. What was good enough for them was not good enough for their offspring. Consequently, the children remained in school well past the minimum requirements and past the normal age for entrance into the work force.

The Commission observed that "in the lower schools, the Jewish children are the delight of their teachers for cleverness at their books, obedience and general good conduct."

Nevertheless, Jews were not seen by all as intelligent, clever, or particularly smart. Probably half the immigrants from Eastern Europe, regardless of their tradition for being people of the Book, were illiterate. Various studies in 1910 and 1911 of Polish and Russian Jewish children found a significant number (sometimes a majority) of them below grade level. Army induction examinations during World War I found that Russian Jews ranked at the bottom of all ethnic groups in mental comprehension. In brief, there were more than a few signs of backwardness in the early part of the century and it is an anachronism to credit the past with the achievements of the present.

In the early part of the century, an economic base, which was not to reveal itself for a generation or more, was laid. Its emergence was still further delayed and stymied by the Great Depression. But if the changes in social mobility and class status did not show, Jews were already beginning to fill the colleges. Before the Great War, Jews were overrepresented fivefold in institutions of higher learning. The unseen economic takeoff was well underway.

If the aim was to leave the ghettos behind, to get out to the anteroom and into the living room of America, the approach could not have been more apropos. The allure of education had a cumulative effect: the higher achievements of parents acted as a staging ground for children. Very quickly, national educational norms were passed as more Jewish children went to school for a longer period than any other ethnic or denominational group.

Today eighty-four percent of the American Jewish population has had four years of high school, compared with only thirty-five percent of the general population. It is perhaps even more significant that in a technically-oriented society, thirty-two percent of

Jewish adults have had a college education, compared with seventeen percent of the nation's adults. To put it another way, Jews average fourteen years of education, while non-Spanish whites in the United States average only eleven and a half years.

While Jews presently obtain more education on average than the most well-educated religious groups — Episcopalians and Presbyterians — the older generation in these Protestant denominations still have more education than older Jews. However, this is likely to change since Protestant educational achievements appear to have reached a plateau while Jewish achievements keep increasing. The comparison is illuminating in one respect: Jews have caught up with remarkable speed despite their educational heritage — they provide the best return on their educational investment.

Nearly ninety percent of all young Jewish males and sixty-five percent of all females have had some college training. Moreover, three out of five Jews that start college complete it. They are less likely to drop out than any other group. Or to look at it from the other side, less than a quarter of Jewish youth do not attend college. Projections suggest that within a decade, sixty percent of young Jews will be college graduates.

Over thirty percent of Jewish males obtain professional or doctoral degrees. Jewish women, on the other hand, have only recently thrown off the yoke of perpetual maternity. Their educational achievements already surpass national averages, but are still minimal when compared with professional and doctoral degrees attained by their male counterparts.

With all that education, are Jews smarter than everyone else? They are certainly schooled longer, but that does not necessarily mean that they are more clever. Does the Jewish gene pool contain an abundance of "smart" protein molecules? Until science is better able to define intelligence — to discover if it is transmitted, and if so, how — this is an area of great speculation, colored by pride, passion, and prejudice. There are limitless theories explaining the preponderance of Jews in intellectually oriented activities.

One of the more provocative theories suggests that for the last one or two thousand years, Jews gave the best and the brightest of each generation the optimum chance to reproduce. The ideal match in a Jewish community — whether in ancient Cairo, Iberian Toledo, Republican Venice, or a Middle European shtetl — was between children of the rabbis or the learned community and children of the richest merchants. Just as the ideal French marriage for generations was between two peasant families with contiguous land, thus maintaining a stable, orderly, and tightly knit society, so Jewish devolution concerned itself with propagating the most successful and the most astute. Whether the decision was conscious or unconscious, instinctive or rational, this "law of succession" was a model of natural selection. The shrewd and the scholarly would be most able to cope with the uncertainties of Jewish existence.

Of course, this program would have been of no avail if other religious groups were doing the same thing. But Christian Europe's survival plan was more concerned with the hereafter: its scheme contrasted sharply with the Jewish attitude. Both spiritually and pragmatically, a place in the mother Church assured salvation, a place in the beyond, and a comfortable existence in present life. Indeed, the priesthood was the only way out of the peasantry for an ambitious and intellectually talented youngster. It was not only an escape for the peasantry, but an avenue for all estates throughout Catholic Europe. But the demand of ecclesiastical celibacy prevented some of the cleverest Christians from passing on their genetic traits. A portion of the most intelligent gentiles, generation after generation, kept breeding out the very qualities that Jews encouraged.

Environmental factors must also be considered in attempting to understand Jewish intelligence. Only recently, scientists have come to understand the connection between malnutrition and mental retardation. The old and honored Jewish tradition of charity most likely reduced the incidence of starvation and subsequent brain damage. This was particularly true for expectant mothers who were given special consideration: the household would go hungry so that she would not; small children were also enjoined to eat well. How much this socioreligious consideration raised intelligence, or perhaps more specifically, protected it from the ravages of malnutrition, is impossible to say. But it must be noted that Jews were administering this type of preventive health technique long before the Western world knew of the correlation between intelligence and nutrition. This survival skill did not do much for their waistline — obesity has been a constant health problem among Jews — but it probably added to their IQ.

Jews also paid special attention to their children's emotional and psychological needs, thus preventing what has been termed "sociogenic brain damage." This is damage caused by lack of adequate mental stimulation, physical play, and human contact. Social deprivation, a more recently acknowledged factor in human intelligence, was rarely a problem in Jewish households. Children were and are forever taught, instructed, talked with, talked to, and occasionally badgered. This form of contact, intended to give Jewish youth a predisposition to scholastic religious study of the Torah, was enormously stimulating. It pervaded every class and permeated every family. Certainly, it was responsible for the famed verbal facility of Jews and for their high performance on intelligence tests. As one author has noted, "The Jewish home, more than the Gentile home, is a place in which learning is highly valued. This single factor underlies all the other differences."

There are other hypotheses to explain Jewish intellectual proclivities. Whatever the theory, the evidence is overwhelming that Jews take to intellectual pursuits and use them in an inordinate fashion to make a living. It is no secret that there is a direct correlation between number of school years completed and level of income attained. A high school graduate makes roughly $100,000 more in his lifetime than a grammar school graduate. A college graduate makes at least $200,000 more than a high school graduate. On this basis alone, Jewish earnings and income would be extraordinary.

Perhaps the best place to use one's education is in the academic world. In the 1930s, there were relatively few Jews on the faculties of American institutions of higher learning. Currently, over twenty percent of the tenured faculty at elite colleges and universities are Jews. Out of proportion with Jewish representation in the general population, this percentage is in line with the student population, in which one out of five students is Jewish.

Jewish faculty members have taken the proverbial "publish or perish" slogan to heart: in one survey of top schools, over half of the Jewish staff had published five or more scholarly articles — far more than their colleagues. At the same time, Jewish faculty members show the lowest attendance for organized religious services. Many of these professors no longer consider themselves Jewish. Some Jews would of course question how smart that is.

## Shared Standards

Jews, whose existence has never seemed far removed from the endangered species list, prospered in the United States because it took less of their energy to adapt. They did not dissipate their energies on assimilation, or on fighting inequality. They wasted no effort copying the core culture since their goals were compatible from the start. Most Jews were skeptical at first and sought to work with fellow Jews. If that was impossible, then they worked for themselves — a fact that accounts for the very high rates of self-employment among Jewish immigrants. But group identity enabled Jews to revive and sharpen half-forgotten skills and age-old occupations. If those talents had been in declining or dying industries or trades, there would have been no economic takeoff. At least not until new skills were developed or new resources acquired.

For many, the "ethnic community has been a useful incubator for economic skills, but once these skills were developed, it has been a confinement that has had to be transcended for any substantial economic achievement to take place," notes one economist. For the Jews, this was only half true since their skills were in a sense compatible with and requisite in an expanding American economy. Other ethnic immigrant groups often had to learn new skills and new values to move up. The background of Jews gave them skills and attitudes that were remarkably similar to those of other Americans. Yankees and Jews could both be described as materialistic, shrewd, individualistic, aggressive, resourceful, thrifty, and hard-nosed.

A number of personal characteristics encourage economic advancement. But what works for one group does not necessarily work for another. For example, while matriarchies can be supportive and encouraging, they can also be emasculating and debilitating. In many ways, matriarchy seems to have worked for Jews better than it has worked for blacks. Family stability is another basic trait of economically successful groups since a tightly knit family structure provides an atmosphere well suited for work, education, and thrift. These conditions encourage the development of skills in planning, abstraction, system building, perseverance, and postponement of gratification — which lead to jobs in medicine, law, academic work, science, and other professions. They do not necessarily foster the intuitive, inspirational, or emotional capabilities that are prerequisites for jobs in popular entertainment, athletics, sales, and the arts.

In other words, Jews, along with Chinese and Japanese Americans, West Indians, Northern Italians, Scots, and other minority groups believe in self-denial, tend to work and plan for the future, and are career-minded to a great degree. Of course, it is as absurd to think that a great deal of training and discipline is not needed for prize fighters, jazz musicians, or other performing artists as it is to think that doctors, lawyers, and scholars lack intuition and imagination. But occupational choices are sometimes conditioned for generations and will only change slowly.

Certainly, many Jewish immigrants worked as laborers and blue-collar wage-earners, reflecting both their previous employment and their opportunities. However, their business heritage, up to the rapid expansion of industrialization in the nineteenth century, was largely in retailing, trade, petty business, and the professions. Industrialization resulted in proletarianization as workers were drawn into factories and mines. Jews in Eastern Europe and the Pale — the area in Russia where they were permitted to live — were deprived of traditional occupations. They were forced to exist as soldiers or workers.

After immigrating, they could revert to the livelihoods of parents and ancestors. Consequently, they arrived in their new countries with no capital, no tools, and no money, but with a potent image of what they had been, and could be again, in an atmosphere of freedom.

Though Jews were no wealthier than other immigrants, they had higher expectations. They were equipped with a retrospective vision, a memory of things past. They were ready to take advantage of opportunities and techniques to boost themselves up the ladder. In brief, they came with a far different mind-set than other immigrating ethnics, and they quickly took advantage of economic freedom. Jews were familiar with trading and exchanging, commerce, city living, property rights, family stability, self-control, planning, delayed rewards, and accumulation of funds for future investment — all characteristics of the growing American middle class. These were Jewish traits before the rise of capitalism. This has led to the speculation that Jews were the first capitalists.

The notion that Jews are closet capitalists is not new, but it hasn't been studied recently. It needs reexamination in light of the overwhelming economic ascent of Jews in America. In the traditional view, capitalism was the natural consequence of economic development, expanding trade, growing population, and demand for goods — basically, material factors were responsible. At the turn of the century, the German economist and sociologist Max Weber gave the conception of capitalism a new focus: he did not deny the material factors, but suggested that there was an intimate relationship between Protestantism and Capitalism.

The Protestant Ethic preceded the development of modern capitalism, setting a spiritual tone and giving it an ideology. Marx saw history the other way around. Protestantism was a stepchild of capitalism — the result not the cause of economic determinism. But Weber thought that the attitudes and habits of Protestantism — a worldly asceticism of hard work, self-discipline, thrift, and organization of time — could be attributed to two fundamental Protestant doctrines — predestination and the calling. Though these verities would not assure salvation, they were a definite sign of inner grace. Protestantism encouraged a way of life that encouraged economic development by producing more and consuming less.

The Protestant Ethic — the work ethic — was the moving spirit behind capitalism. Earlier commercial transactions lacked a rationale for making money and desiring to accumulate more than was immediately needed. Weber's theory was a little short on examples — he used Benjamin Franklin as his prototype of a modern capitalist. Franklin was not the best example of a thrifty capitalist, Poor Richard's admonitions to the contrary. While a penny saved might be a penny earned, Franklin apparently "regularly overdrew his bank account."

Most non-Marxist social scientists and historians accepted the Weber explanation of capitalism. However, another seminal German thinker, Werner Sombart, challenged Weber's ideas in a highly provocative book of 1911 entitled *The Jews and Modern Capitalism*. Weber did not go far enough, Sombart asserted, for the essential parts of Puritanism that accounted for the capitalist spirit were "borrowed from the realm of ideas of the Jewish religion."

As with most innovative ideas, Sombart's work was immediately scorned. It gave Jews a history that was at odds with contemporary Germany's growing anti-Semitic attitudes. Though Sombart was of Huguenot descent and his work was in no sense an apologia, critics found that his philo-Semitic attitudes somehow smacked of socialism.

Sombart put the Jewish contribution to finance and business development in a new light. It was the first generally positive statement about Jews and money for hundreds of years — and the first in the twentieth century. There had been occasional monographs and learned articles about specific Jewish businesses by Jewish historians, but the popular understanding of Jewish activities was extremely negative and derisive. The rise of nationalism and communism — both anti-Semitic movements — had painted the most perverse and bizarre picture of Jews. That carbuncled miscreant, Marx — though descended from a long line of rabbis — in an apparent act of self-flagellation, wrote one of the most venemous anti-Semitic tracts of his day. In *A World Without Jews,* he wrote:

> Let us look at the real Jew of our times . . . What is the Jew's foundation in our world? Material necessity, private advantage. What is the object of the Jew's worship in this world? Usury. What is his worldly god? Money.

Money is the zealous one God of Israel, besides which no other God may stand.

The bill of exchange is the Jew's real God.

Sombart, faced with these hostile public opinions, suggested that Judaism was a religion favorable to capitalistic development. Not only was Judaism a stimulant to economic growth, in some areas, Jews were originators of necessary first steps. Indeed, they made capitalism possible. He credited Jews with a significant role in international trade, "the first to place on the world's markets the staple articles of modern commerce." Besides basic commodities, Jewish traders specialized in luxury items, precious stones, and bullion. They were especially involved in the colonization of Latin America. Sombart also highlighted some of the economic institutions that Jews initiated or developed, such as the stock exchange, negotiable instruments, public bonds, and bank notes. Furthermore, Jews pursued free trade, advertising, and competition — all factors that undermined precapitalistic societies.

Sombart next looked for the elements in Judaism that were responsible for these activities. He cited commentaries from the Pentateuch, the Talmud, and other sources on interest, usury, commercial law, legal transactions, and property. This tour de force attempted to establish that the "Jewish genius" for modern capitalism arose from a contract with God, a bilateral covenant. Holiness meant obeying the Law, the responsibilities from the legal agreement — a rational approach to existence that cautioned against the snares of sensuality, beauty, art, and, of course, sex.

This middle-class respectability also led to capitalism. For it was Jewish marital relations, childhood education, and family life that were the essential factors that prepared Jews for capitalism. But Jewish law had limited sexuality by insisting on monogamy, forbidding extra-marital relations, and even limiting sexual relations between spouses. Sombart saw the limiting of sexuality and the postponement of pleasure as necessary ground work for capitalism. Thus "it is possible to prove that, quite generally, restrained sexual desires and the chase of profits go hand in hand." (Later, Alfred Kinsey, in his study of male sexuality, found that postponement of sexual gratification was a typically middle-class trait.)

All this was pretty heady stuff. On one hand, Christianity was the religion of poverty, and condemnation of material wealth was part of its creed. On the other hand, Judaism was the rational basis for wealth, the home of the modern economic spirit — free enterprise.

Sombart's thesis was, of course, too sweeping and too simple, but his views were a welcome change from the writings of Marx. Capitalism is a nebulous creation of many forces. The development of navigation, the growth of the centralized state, the spread of the money economy, the art of keeping business records, the harnessing of power, and the discovery of industrial inventions are all components in the creation of capitalism — and most of them had very little input from Jews or Judaism. Still, Sombart had insights about the role of Jews as a pariah people — their catalytic influence in trade, finance, the professions, administration, and their history as city dwellers. But by identifying Judaism as supremely rational, he neglects its strong mystical tradition.

Nevertheless, Sombart's work was the first appraisal of the economic contribution of Jews and also furthered the understanding of capitalism. Ironically, his book met with silence from Jews, for two reasons: His stress on "racial" characteristics is more fantasy than fact, a fantasy that has cost Jews dearly. Moreover, it conceivably led Sombart to his final indignity, his membership in the Nazi party, from the early 1930s until his death in 1941.

The question that Sombart raised has yet to be answered. He assumed that Jews, rather than Protestants, were the forefathers of free enterprise. It is probably as accurate to suggest that capitalism made Jews what they presently are as vice versa. There is no simple answer to what is, after all, a vast exercise in psychology, economics, history, and religion. Though Jews did not necessarily initiate capitalism, their experience prepared them for modern capitalistic societies that needed their special talents. By dint of effort they could adapt, for change was central to their existence. Had they not evolved this survival technique, they would be a vestigial remainder, an historical anachronism.

# 4. The Bankers

Know that wherever there is money, there is the Jew.
— Montesquieu, *Persian Letters*

Jews are members of the human race — worse than that
I cannot say of them.
— Mark Twain

*The Economic War*

The major economic myth to pursue the Jews is simply stated: they control the banks, the money supply, the economy, and the businesses — of the community, of the country, and of the world. Understandably, Jews have countered with another myth — that they control nothing, that their holdings are so small as to be insignificant. Naturally, the truth lies somewhere in between.

Historically, Jews have shown remarkable talent for manipulating money. Over the years, this proclivity has led them to the world of banking and finance. And nowhere have they so brilliantly exercised their financial talents as in Ameria. Free enterprise and political emancipation allowed them to exercise and sharpen these skills — skills that have been evolving for a thousand years.

For most of those years, Jews were not bankers in the modern sense, but moneylenders more akin to pawnbrokers and foreign exchange dealers. At first they lent money when no one else could or would, because of either a lack of liquid funds or injunctions against lending money at interest. Later, when money became more plentiful and Christian prohibitions were ignored by some, lending became popular and Jewish moneylenders were left with only poor clients. By then, Jews were restricted from almost every livelihood that had any appeal to gentiles. The injunctions were enforced by deportation or by restriction to ghettos. A few Jews who became rich and powerful as adjuncts or administrators for rulers — the Court Jews — were precursors to modern financiers. Their jobs included raising revenues by tax farming, negotiating loans, and supplying the military as one-man quartermaster corps.

Modern banking started in the nineteenth century with the rise of the House of Rothschild. They were not the only important Jewish bankers in Europe: indeed, a surprising number of continental banks were founded by Jews. The old Court Jew had primarily raised money for local rulers to cover his expenses, his personal diplomacy, and his extravagances. The new bankers floated state loans to finance emerging industries and railroads. While the five Rothschild brothers had banks in Frankfort, London, Paris, Vienna, and Naples, Bleichroder in Berlin, Warburg in Hamburg, Oppenheim in Cologne, and Speyer in Frankfort were operating their own banking houses. Individual Jews founded banks from London (Hambros) to Bombay (Sassoons) to St. Petersburg (Guenzburg), and a number of points in between.

Besides these personal or private banks — roughly equivalent to merchant banks or investment banks today — Jews helped to establish a number of important joint stock banks or commercial banks: the Deutsche Bank and the Dresdner Bank — two of Germany's big three, Credit Mobilier, Banque de Paris et des Pays-Bas, Banca Commerciale Italiana, Credito Italiano, Creditanstalt-Bankverein, and Banque de Bruxelles, among others.

There were a few Jewish bankers in the United States: Haym Salomon of revolutionary fame and Isaac Moses who, with Alexander Hamilton, was one of the founders of the Bank of New York in 1784. It was not until the Jewish-German immigration of the 1840s that the presence of Jewish bankers was felt in America. Some of the established German banks sent representatives, but for the most part, the German-Jewish bankers rose from the ranks only after they arrived. Between 1840 and 1880, a dozen first-rate banking houses were started: Bache; August Belmont; Goldman, Sachs; J.W. Seligman; Kuhn, Loeb; Ladenburg, Thalmann; Lazard Freres; Lehman Brothers; Speyer; and Wertheim. Influential, conservative in life-style, but unorthodox in financial matters, and inbred (like the Rothschilds, their children married each other), Jewish bankers projected an image of concentrated power because they often acted in concert, collaborating on financial deals.

But in size and power, they could not compare with the Protestant bankers — Morgan, Drexel, Gould, Fiske, Harriman, and Hill. Still, because of their clannishness and presumed power, they were objects of scorn among the Populists at the end of the nineteenth century.

Until then, Jewish moneylenders were derided for miserliness and antisocial activities, and were berated for having Shylock mentality and a Fagin temperament. Jews were cast in the invidious role of "economic man." It mattered little that they had long ago been stereotyped in that role by Christians. The Jew was perceived as the archetypal financier, however petty his practice.

The rise of Jewish bankers reinforced this image. Previously, the Jewish moneylender was a single character presumed born with certain "racial" traits. His activities were every Jew's activities. With the development of systematic anti-Semitism in Europe, and the rise of xenophobic nationalism, the wealthy Jew was seen as an alien financier, in collaboration with Jews abroad. The collection of Jewish bankers and banks in both Europe and America convinced many people that Jews were out to dominate and control the world. The public's perception of Jews changed: formerly, Jews were thought to be scurrilous, stupid, and tight-fisted individuals with a penchant for dealing in money. Now, they were perceived as an international group of clever, devious, and manipulative financiers out to dominate and, somewhat contradictorily, destroy the old verities.

The gentile notion of an international Jewish conspiracy was not so much born as revealed — made clear in the most notorious anti-Semitic document of the fin de siècle — the *Protocols of the Learned Elders of Zion.*

The *Protocols* was the capstone, of all the misbegotten ideas about Jews — a reaction to Jewish success. For a spurious document, it has had a remarkably long and influential life. The *Proto-*

*cols* first surfaced in Russia in 1903, but was not widely disseminated until after the Russian Revolution. It was then frequently reprinted in England, Germany, France, Poland, Italy, Japan, and parts of Arabia. In the United States, it was circulated through the efforts of Henry Ford. Apparently, the plagiarized concoction of a Russian religious mystic, the *Protocols* reputedly reported on a series of meetings in 1897 at the First Zionist Congress in Basle, where the plans of preexilic days of the Sanhedrin were discussed. Jewish leaders, along with leaders from the Freemasons, supposedly had updated an ancient conspiracy to undermine the Christian world and pave the way for domination. Past examples of Jewish treachery were cited, present actions were detailed, and the future conspiracy, revealed. Through liquor, sex, economic depression, and explosive detonations, Jews were to seize power in the capitals of Europe.

It was silly nonsense, but proving that was not easy. Finally, in 1921, a correspondent for the *London Times* pointed out its resemblance to a French satire and historians concluded that the *Protocols* was a forgery by the Russian secret police based on the French novel and other works. Subsequently, the *Protocols* was formally condemned in South African and Swiss Courts. But it had set the stage for hysterical anti-Semitism. Both the political right and left used the tract as proof of their theories about Jews. The Bolsheviks denounced international capitalism, and the fascists damned the Jews as a social menace. The antifascists cursed the Jews and the anticommunists cursed the Jews. Everyone found something in it to confirm his or her irrational fears. All in all, the *Protocols* might be the most successful piece of propaganda in the twentieth century.

The belief in the *Protocols* continued long after it was dismissed as a fabrication. In contemporary America, the conception of the Jew as an economic man still prevails. Misguided and benighted souls still see Jews dominating banking and finance, manipulating the world to their own advantage and causing everyone else's failures. Along with this inaccurate and mischievous assessment, there is a widespread positive perception of the economic man. An overwhelming number of Americans identify with economic success and find positive values in the success of Jews and others — there is virtue in materialism. Perhaps it is not too much to suggest that the absence of broad-based anti-Semitism in the United States is due to Jewish financial success.

Consequently, Jews are perceived not as foreign and alien, but as another patch in the American quilt. And their acceptance is due less to any growing spirit of brotherhood or ecumenicalism, than to their ability to make the system work for themselves. It is difficult to hate your neighbor if he succeeds with the values you profess. Economic success then has served Jews well in America.

## The Fall and Rise of Lehman Brothers

Andrew Carnegie, one of the shrewdest American capitalists, once remarked that it took only three generations to go from shirt-sleeves back to shirtsleeves. The Jewish-German American banking families managed better than that. Though somewhat eclipsed, decimated, and converted, many are present in financial circles today. Some are gone, while others survive through transfusions of new money and talent. After a long and quiet period, there has been a renaissance in Jewish banking houses. But there are differences: many of the new people are not Jews and most of the Jews are not German. Regardless of the number of atheists and gentile partners in a particular house it may still be regarded as Jewish. Many partners feel that the vestigial designation is neither an advantage nor a disadvantage in doing business: it is just a tag line.

Which Jewish banking house is preeminent is a matter of dispute — some say Goldman, Sachs; some say Salomon Brothers; and some say Lehman Brothers. Lehman Brothers, a firm that is over 125 years old, emerged from the recession of the early 1970s debilitated and confused. It was in serious danger of collapse, like other old-time Wall Street firms such as Francis I. Du Pont, Walston, Smithers, Heinz, and Goodbody. Considering that Lehman was one of the top three underwriting firms, contending with Morgan Stanley and First Boston for the volume of issues handled in a few years previous, the decline was rapid and painful. By 1973, the firm's capitalization had drastically shrunk, the partners were at odds with each other, the strong leadership of the late

Robert Lehman was gone, and the firm had lost $9 million in one year. Lehman was in the worst shape of its long history. It had come a long way from what a business journal once called "one of the biggest profit makers — many believe the biggest — in the business."

Lehman had always made its money by dealing in money, commodity contracts, bonds, notes, loans, stocks, and mutual funds. The underlying assumption of buying for a penny and selling for two cents, thus being satisfied with a one *cent* profit (in the words of an old saw) was cherished by the early Lehmans.

In 1844, Henry, the son of a Wurzburg cattle dealer, was the first Lehman to come to America. An itinerant peddler in the south, he soon settled down in Montgomery, Alabama with his two younger brothers, Emanuel and Mayer, as grocers. In the land of cotton, many of their customers paid for their goods with cotton, which the Lehman brothers turned around and sold: profiting on both ends of the deal was firmly fixed in family history. Soon cotton brokerage became their main business. During the Civil War, the Lehmans supported the Confederacy, selling Confederate bonds in London and cotton on the Continent. After the war, they opened a New York office, became members of various commodity exchanges, and acquired a seat on the New York Stock Exchange in 1887. In fact, the New York Telephone Guide of 1878 listed forty-five "Banks, Bankers, and Brokers," classifying Lehman Brothers as "Produce, Cotton, Oil and Commission Merchants."

When the second generation of Lehmans inherited the business, the firm's interest spread to transportation — motor vehicles and rubber tires. Its first underwriting issue in 1899 for a trust of five pump companies called the International Steam Pump Company violated antitrust laws. For a while, the house stayed out of the new issue business, though it had a penchant for the technology-oriented, high-risk issues of the day, such as Electric Vehicle Company and the Electric Boat Company. Furthermore, a number of marriage alliances were made with other wealthy Jewish families such as the Lewisohns, who brought their copper interests into the fold. But Lehman did not become a Wall Street power until after it joined with Goldman, Sachs; then, as now, a leading dealer in commercial paper, in a public offering of a company owned by Sachs' cousin-in-law, Julius Rosenwald. Rosenwald wanted to borrow $5 million for his Chicago mail-order house — Sears, Roebuck & Company. The two bankers insisted that he take $10 million through a public underwriting. After the success of that issue — one that the more conservative, capital-equipment oriented brokers would not touch — the two houses underwrote a series of companies that were to become household words: Woolworth, Continental Can, and Studebaker. The relationship between Lehman and Goldman, Sachs eventually ended in the late 1920s. But Lehman went on to help finance department stores, Hollywood studios, liquor, and airline and communication companies. In the 1960s, throughout the longest boom in American history, Lehman put together the financing for that new Wall Street hybrid, the conglomerate. And for a short while, when they were fashionable, Lehman was the leader in the merger and acquisition madness.

Herman Kahn, a retired partner and merger-maker, sometimes represented both companies in a merger if they were clients, without worrying about conflict of interest. He thought of Lehman's staff as "banking clergymen." "If a couple is getting married they don't need two; one can do the job," Kahn noted. "The same applies for companies."

Kahn was instrumental in diversifying Litton Industries and building it into a conglomerate, by acquiring Monroe Calculating Machine. Kahn stressed that mergers and acquisitions were only one part of Lehman's custom-packaged services. The bank handles negotiations of any size, or, as he facetiously put it, "no deal too small, no fee too large."

Though the recession was a factor, internal problems brought Lehman's "to the brink," in *Business Week*'s words. Companies are not as quick to borrow money, float new issues of equities, expand, or merge in periods of uncertainty or business consolidation. Recessions, besides depressing industrial output, also strain the money supply. When there is too little money around, the price of money — the interest rate — shoots upward. Money leaves the equity market and is only found in fixed interest securities of the highest quality. In brief, recessions and falling stock markets eliminate the very thing that makes investment banking houses tick — money. It is rather like trying to run a blood bank when there are no donors.

Besides the internal back office problem — at one point, before it got its bookkeeping under control, the firm had nearly $700 million worth of securities that it was having trouble matching with clients — Lehman was a collection of strong-willed superstars. Partners considered corporate accounts their personal property and objected to any undue interference. Finally, Lehman was in areas that, due to its relatively small capital base, it had no business being in, such as government bond trading, real estate, and block positioning. Each required a lot of money and miscalculations could be fatal. By mid-1974, the firm's equity had fallen in eighteen months from $23.3 million to $12.7 million. The company was on the New York Stock Exchange's early warning list when equity was down to sixty-two percent to debt.

To save Lehman, the partners agreed on a new chairman, a man who was not a Lehman, Jewish, or even a banker. Peter G. Peterson, a one-time advertising executive, head of Bell & Howell, and Secretary of Commerce under Nixon, took over. He eliminated unprofitable departments, especially those trading in government paper or bidding on corporate underwritings. A dozen partners, and a number of security analysts and salesmen all went, reducing the personnel of the banking house by a third. But leanness was only partially responsible for the house's turning the corner. Peterson started to concentrate on Lehman's talent as financial and banking consultants. Equity underwritings were nice when they came along, but the "deal" days of the 1960s disappeared in the 1970s. Lehman, which had put other companies in order, finally applied some management techniques to itself. Instead of waiting for investment banking business to bail out the firm, Lehman began charging fees for advice that it used to dispense free. This professionalization, a new trend on Wall Street, is paying off today. No great killings — just nice steady business, which may, in turn, lead to investment banking relationships. In addition to aggressively pursuing business, the firm has broadened its capital base.

A senior partner and a political heavyweight, George W. Ball, an under secretary of state in the Kennedy and Johnson administrations, sold fifteen percent of Lehman's common stock plus $3.5 million of preferred shares and notes for a $7 million investment from a couple of European banks. Lehman then merged with Abraham & Company, a brokerage house, a move that brought them an additional $5 million for roughly another fifteen percent of the firm. Within a couple of years, Lehman brought its capital base from $12.7 million to nearly $50 million. After its recovery, the return on capital was running at an extraordinary eighty percent.

Once burnt, Lehman is now capital-conscious in ways it never was before. When retiring or quitting, partners no longer walk away with their capital. Their capital is paid out over two or three years. While Lehman has taken many companies public, it has not done so itself. Thus it is still possible for the fifty or so partners to strike their own private Golcondas without worrying about shareholders.

One former partner admitted that "million-dollar paydays are not unknown." With senior partners owning between three and five percent of the partnership, it is easy to see how — when recent profits have been in the order of $35 million yearly — million-dollar paydays are possible. Actually, salaries are modest, though they are enhanced by bonuses. The balance of partnership profits are plowed back into the business. After some years under Peterson, the new Lehman Brothers is "back from the brink."

To compete in a financial arena that has drastically fewer viable firms, Lehman and Kuhn Loeb & Company merged in 1977. Kuhn Loeb grew up with Lehman Brothers as one of the preeminent German-American banking houses of the nineteenth century. Two brothers-in-law, Abraham Kuhn and Solomon Loeb, started in Cincinnati selling dry goods and then, with half a million dollars, moved to New York to start the banking business. The house reached a predominant position in investment banking under Jacob H. Schiff, Loeb's son-in-law. Presently in its fifth generation, Kuhn Loeb's relatively small capital base of $20 million placed it in jeopardy. Joined with Lehman, the new firm now ranks as the fourth largest investment banker. The merger was not only historically apt; it brought together the domestic power of Lehman with the foreign expertise of Kuhn Loeb. It also brought together, in the words of one of the principals, "two of the best kitchens on Wall Street."

## Jews in the Banks

In 1969, a Jew nearly got control of a substantial American bank. It would have been something of a first, contrary to the conventional cliche, since no major money center bank is owned or operated by a Jew. In the world of high finance, Jewish interest is concerned with investment banking, a broad catchall for activities ranging from tendering advice to underwriting securities. The heart of investment banking is public offerings and private placements, the risking of capital — sometimes one's own, but more often other people's — to finance new companies or expand old ones. It is a risky business. Commercial bankers, however, try to avoid risks and are really happiest when they are riding the yield curve — that comfortable zone that lies between what they pay for deposits and what they receive for loans. To the world of high finance, commercial bankers are "green grocers," necessary for nutritional balance but not providers of haute cuisine.

It is difficult to tell who really owns commercial banks in the United States despite the legal requirement of full disclosure. Several in-depth studies by various congressional committees showed that they are primarily owned by other commercial banks. This incestuous state of affairs is not the result of planning, but the consequence of bankers' mentalities. When you are in charge of "other people's money," in the words of Louis Brandeis, what better place to put it than in shares of other banks? Invariably, this is what is done. The banks, of course, are not the sole purchasers of bank stocks: other institutions, such as mutual funds, insurance companies, and pension funds, are also substantial holders. And this is precisely how a Jew nearly took control of a bank.

Commercial banks dominate the banking system, and a few banks stand head and shoulders above their colleagues — they are *prima inter pares*. Of the fourteen thousand commercial banks, 275 hold sixty percent of all the nation's deposits. Who owns these large banks? Jews don't, however much they might wish to. One congressional report of the House of Representatives' Committee on Banking and Currency found, in an investigation of seven hundred diverse financial institutions, that they held stock in 270 commercial banks: their portfolio holdings ranged from nine percent to ninety-nine percent of those banks. And sixty major commercial banks held in their trust departments ten percent or more of the shares of 183 other commercial banks.

Another study, this time by the Senate's Government Operations Committee, found similar evidence. The large institutional investors own or control the large banks through their stockholdings. And some of the largest institutions are themselves banks. In early 1973, thirty-two institutional investors held portfolios in excess of $5 billion each. Of that group, twelve had holdings in excess of $10 billion, and eight in excess of $16 billion. These large institutions — Morgan Guaranty and Prudential Insurance, for example — control a number of corporations and banks, not only as owners of record but through nominee accounts. While Chase owns two percent or more of the stock in forty-six companies and Morgans owns two percent or more in twenty-nine companies, nominee accounts, whose true identity is usually unknown, may own additional percentages. Thus Cede & Company, a nominee for the New York Stock Exchange, holds two percent or more interest in fifty-five companies. The Committee concluded:

> The holdings of institutional investors, especially banks, are often hidden from the view of [government] regulators and the public through the use of multiple nominees. The consequences of this continuing use of nominees in ownership reports to federal regulators is a massive coverup of the extent to which holdings of stock have been concentrated in the hands of very few institutional investors, especially the banks.

Finally, another study jointly undertaken by the Senate Subcommittee on Reports, Accounting, and Management and the private Corporate Data Exchange of New York found that the power to vote stock in 122 of the largest corporations was concentrated in twenty-one institutional investors. The major American banks, led by Morgan Guaranty, were at the head of the list. Underscoring the incestuous relationship of banks was the fact that

Morgan was the largest stockholder in four of its sister New York banks: Citicorp, Manufacturers Hanover, Chemical, and Bankers Trust, as well as California's BankAmerica. "In turn, Citicorp is stockholder no. 1 in Morgan Guaranty's parent holding company, J.P. Morgan & Co. Stockholder no. 2 in J.P. Morgan & Co. is Chase Manhattan . . . " Perhaps not very imaginative, but obviously solid investments.

The report also answered questions about corporate control. It came up with a list of fifty-six major corporations that could be controlled by five percent or ten percent of the stockholders: families, corporations, or financial institutions. Of the corporations, only Loews, Dreyfus, and CBS have substantial Jewish involvement.

In New York City — where, because of their concentration, Jews might be expected to have substantial holdings — the banks are so highly capitalized and widely held that even the Rockefellers, with family and trust holdings in the order of $1 billion, barely make a dent. Rockefeller interest in Chase — the family banking house — is less than one and a half percent of the common stock. At Chemical Bank, which was nearly taken over by a Jew, seventy-four institutions (forty-five insurance companies, six commercial banks and twenty-three mutual savings banks) owned 23.3 percent of the common stock or 3,059,780 shares, a year before the unaccepted tender offer. At the time of the offer, the shares of Chemical were trading at $80, thus giving a total market value of all outstanding shares of roughly $1.05 billion. As one does not need a majority or even a plurality to control a corporation — the Rockefellers manage to dominate Chase with little more than one percent — the notion that any single person or interest could take over a major bank if the bank, its principal owners, and its institutional allies are hostile to the idea is doomed to failure.

One firm that had a meteoric rise in the 1960s was Leasco Data Processing Equipment Corporation, a computer rental company. It was run by a bright, nimble, and chubby young man named Saul Steinberg. Borrowing a few thousand dollars from his father, Steinberg hit upon the idea of leasing computers and other data processing equipment, in the era before wafer-thin semiconductors and minicomputers, when hardware was gross and price tags gigantic. It made sense to rent and Leasco did well. If imitation is the sincerest form of flattery, there was no end to the flattery. In 1964, Steinberg took the company public. In the next few years, Leasco grew synergetically, acquiring other companies, primarily in the information services field. Since conglomerate arithmetic $(2+2=5?)$ evaluated the whole as something more than its component parts, the stock's price rose accordingly. In 1968, Steinberg managed to acquire the far larger Reliance Insurance Company.

Reliance, an old-line property and casualty company, founded 150 years earlier, was particularly attractive, with $700 million in assets. In the argot of the conglomerateers of the period, it had a very "deep pocket." Steinberg was enamored of the take-over candidate's "surplus surplus," a figure he put at $125 million. He called the acquisition of Reliance his "Raquel Welch pursuit" because it was "so big and beautiful."

With Reliance came the company's portfolio: it owned stock in twenty-five different banks and, in particular, two hundred thousand shares of Chemical Bank. Here was Steinberg's chance. He decided to make a play for Chemical Bank, the sixth largest commercial bank in the country, with $7.6 billion in assets, 140 offices, foreign branches, and nine representative offices around the world. Started in the early 1800s, it was an "establishment bank." Whether it was a viable candidate for a tender offer was another matter.

A conglomerate had never acquired a bank: in fact, there were very few tender offers for banks and none for banks with substantial assets. One observer suggested that a bank was off-limits "either due to some implied gentlemen's agreement or . . . the belief that, because of government regulations and supervision, it was immune to takeover invasion." Perhaps the underlying assumption — one favored by bankers — is that nonbankers can't run banks, and if they tried to, they would do it badly, jeopardizing public interest — i.e., the people's deposits. Steinberg's attempt sharpened this argument, for it came at a time when federal legislation had allowed banks to form one-bank holding companies. If nonbankers couldn't be trusted with running banks, could bankers be trusted to run nonbank businesses? In the 1970s, the second part of the question was answered when the value of their real estate investment trusts plummeted.

But in 1969, who could run what was still an open question. Still, the banking establishment had rather strong ideas on the subject. A bank might be "the nutritional keystone in the structure of an expanding corporate conglomerate," but bankers didn't want any part of it.

Chemical wanted to have nothing to do with Leasco. In late January, 1969, the shares of Leasco started to rise from an inflated $125 per share to $139 — long before there was any public report of the proposed tender offer. Traders apparently suspected that Leasco was about to announce an acquisition. When Chemical Bank leaked the story to the *New York Times* in the beginning of February, Steinberg was deprived of the advantage of surprise.

Chemical was not the best candidate for a tender offer. Though conservative, it had a reasonable record of profitability. There was no dissension among stockholders. Moreover, the corporation had plenty of resources for the fight. The head of the bank, William S. Renchard, advised Steinberg in a letter that "we intend to resist this with all the means at our command, and they might turn out to be considerable." He went on to cite customer disapproval, antitrust problems, since the bank already served other computer leasing concerns, and regulatory problems.

Chemical's means were considerable, but the planned tender offer had caught them completely off-guard. They had virtually no defense strategy since the issue of the bank being subject to acquisition had never arisen. Who would have the *chutzpah?* However, they reacted quickly, and Steinberg soon felt the heat. Under pressure, Leasco's investment banker, White, Weld, who was to initiate the offer, quickly decided not to. Some of Leasco's customers threatened to walk away. Then Chemical hired all the major proxy solicitation firms on Wall Street, making it considerably more difficult to wage a takeover battle. Chemical even considered the idea of having another corporation acquire the bank.

Then, uncovering its big guns, Chemical showed where establishment power really lies. Within a few days of the leaked story, Renchard was having lunch with President Nixon, Secretary of the Treasury David Kennedy, and Chairman of the Senate Banking and Currency Committee John Sparkman. Within the week, the government was searching for a Treasury Department policy or a congressional act to thwart the takeover of a commercial bank. Renchard then traveled to Albany to see Governor Rockefeller, brother of David, Chairman of the Chase. A few days later, Governor Rockefeller requested legislation preventing the takeover of a commercial bank. (In 1974, when the Rockefellers revealed their family holdings during Nelson's confirmation proceedings for the vice presidency, they owned about 430,000 shares of Chase, valued at $12 million, or 1.34 percent of the bank's outstanding shares. Perhaps the Governor's motives were not totally disinterested.) After one or two more lunches with Renchard, Steinberg realized that his dream was impossible.

Finally, the ultimate weapon was brought to bear. Leasco stock began to drop as selling pressure mounted. Chemical Bank and its fellow institutions unloaded the stock, destroying the currency of the acquisition game. From a high of 139, the stock quickly dropped thirty points. Two weeks after the incipient tender offer was revealed, Steinberg was saying that "hostile takeovers of money center banks are against the best interests of the economy because of the danger of upsetting the stability and prestige of the banking system and diminishing the public confidence in it." He never had a chance to make a concrete, public offering. The rout was complete. By the end of the year, stock was down to half of the high and Leasco was out of the acquisition business for the time being. Jews might invest in banks, along with everyone else, but no Jew was going to run a major bank as his personal fiefdom — not yet anyway.

Were Chemical's actions anti-Semitic? The bank's motivation was probably more a reaction to a parvenu than a conscious act of prejudice. Still, one cannot help recalling that within a few short years OPEC princes and Japanese trusts were openly buying American banks without significant opposition. Was it the Jew that infuriated Chemical, the act of lese majesty, or the work of an outsider? Perhaps a little of each.

Considering their tradition of moneylending, it is a bit surprising to find how few Jews are bankers. Banking would seem a natural outlet. On one hand, the banks excluded Jews from management positions. These discriminatory practices have changed in the sixties and seventies, but Jewish representation is still little more than nominal. On the other hand, Jews were never attracted to commercial banking since salaries are relatively low compared with other fields, advancement was unlikely, and creative ambition and individual initiative were not encouraged or likely to be rewarded. This combination of factors results in very few Jewish platform officers.

So while Jews are generally attracted to other areas of finance, commercial banking is not one of their bailiwicks. In 1939, of 93,000 bankers in the country, only 0.6 percent were Jews. It was almost impossible to find a Jew in the large commercial banks or the mutual savings banks. By the mid-sixties, about 2.5 percent of middle and senior management in the fifty largest banks were Jews. But at the same time, in those fifty banks, forty-five had no Jews in senior management and thirty-eight had none in middle management. In 1973, a study of 377 persons in senior executive positions in twenty-five banks outside of New York City revealed that only one was a Jew. By the end of the seventies, there was slight improvement. The conclusion of one study remarked that "in fairness, we must note that the situation was worse ten or fifteen years ago. Not long ago it would have been difficult to imagine that Chase would have a kosher cafeteria or that Bankers Trust would print a Jewish calendar." But the report also noted that there was not "one Jew among the twenty-two officers who are also directors in New York's major banks. Only three of the top 86 officers . . . are Jewish; that's 3.5% When we consider 345 senior officers . . . there is a grand total of 15 Jews, or 4.3%." So while there has been some improvement, it is still a long way from equal opportunity in banking.

Are bankers more bigoted than other sections of the population? Not likely, but they operate in a highly regulated industry, which may explain the continuing discrimination. In economic terms, their profits are regulated and controlled in comparison with competitive industries. And it has been precisely those highly regulated industries, such as the railroads, which are regulated by the Interstate Commerce Commission, and the communication companies, which are regulated by the Federal Communications Commission, that were the bastions of discrimination. They cannot earn any more money by following nondiscriminatory practices, so they don't. In a sense, discrimination is cost-free. Only with a great deal of political pressure do they change their policies. This can happen abruptly, as it did in the telephone companies. However, there has been relatively little pressure from state or federal bank regulatory agencies. Perhaps everyone should have the right to be a banker, if that is a desire, but it is an issue that arouses little public indignation.

Jews had more influence patronizing commercial banks than running them. Their most significant contribution to modern banking practices, however inadvertent, took place in Switzerland. For ages, the Swiss played host to the world's insecurity, banking foreign funds in times of crisis. The attraction of Switzerland was understandable: a stable government, neutral politics, and a strong, gold-backed currency. Moreover, Swiss bankers had acquired an enviable reputation as sharp money-managers. As a result of this felicitous combination, Switzerland is now the most overbanked country in the world. Not long ago, the Swiss were fond of pointing out that there are more banking offices than dental offices: presumably your money gets better care than your teeth. The influx of foreign money is something of a mixed blessing for it tends to inflate the economy unless restricted or sterilized. While most of the attributes of Swiss banking can be duplicated in other money centers, there is one that stands out and accounts for the flight of money to Alpine vaults. That element — secrecy — came about at the request of Jewish depositors.

Shortly after Hitler's rise to power, some perspicacious Jews started to smuggle money out of Germany. They opened accounts in Swiss banks. Within a relatively short time, the German Treasury became aware of the transactions. Their agents in Switzerland succeeded in bribing some indiscreet bankers, to the distress of the Jewish depositors. Up to then, discretion and concealment in banking were expected, but not mandatory or guaranteed. The German actions caused a furor and the Swiss government passed perhaps their most famous piece of legislation, the Banking Law of 1934, which mandated secrecy in banking. Any banking official or government employee who violates or persuades others to violate banking secrecy may be fined twenty thousand Swiss francs or sentenced to six months in jail, or both. Since then, depositors have flocked to Switzerland for that security, to the chagrin of revenue officers around the world.

It is impossible to say how many Jews took advantage of the bank secrecy act. As German troops overran the Continent, the Swiss banks did a land-office business. The numbered account achieved notoriety during this period, though there was no special provision for them in the bank act and they received no particular attention, except that the identity of the depositor was known only by a few officers and mail never bore the depositor's name, except on the envelope.

At the end of the war, the Swiss banks were flooded with new money — but this time it was from Germans. Through a curious twist of fate, the law that was passed to protect Jews, protected Nazis. After the war, the United States pressured the Swiss to reveal their German depositors and relinquish their moneys — much of it acquired through theft, expropriation, and pure plunder. Naturally, the Swiss resisted, citing the principles of banking secrecy. However, the injustice of letting war criminals keep their booty was too much even for the steely Swiss and so a compromise was finally worked out. Under the Washington Agreement, the Swiss turned over to the United States Department of Treasury $60 million in Nazi money. They would not, however, reveal the names on those accounts: they remained secret.

Hitler's "final solution" had tragically closed the book on European Jewry. But after the Holocaust, a new set of rumors stated that Jews had spirited away vast sums of monies in those banks before meeting their doom. And the Swiss would never give up these huge assets.

Jewish organizations started a campaign to claim these hidden funds. For a long time the Swiss did nothing. Then, in 1962, the Swiss Assembly passed a law ordering all banks, financial institutions, and trustees to declare any funds from foreigners from whom they had no communication since May 9, 1945 (the last day of the European war), and who could be presumed to have been victims of racial, religious, or political persecution. In 1964, the banks reported: 961 accounts with assets of 9.47 million Swiss francs (approximately $2.4 million) fell within the scope of the law. This news was met with general disbelief for it hardly squared with the idea of "lost millions" in the flight of capital from Germany. But Switzerland was not the only recipient. Some funds went to the United States, Great Britain, Cuba, and South America. For the next ten years, Swiss authorities searched for heirs and succeeded in finally distributing most of the funds, leaving only two million Swiss francs unclaimed. In 1975, the unclaimed monies went to a Jewish community group and a refugee organization in Switzerland. Obviously, not many Jewish victims of the Holocaust had either the assets or the foresight to deposit their monies abroad: those that did managed to hide only $2,500 on average — hardly an indication of great wealth, but rather seed money if survival was possible. For most, of course, it wasn't.

# 5. The Business World: Rich and Superrich

Heresy promotes the business spirit.
— Spanish proverb

## Capital Formation

Capital formation for Jews has followed the same path as it has for everyone else, though in some instances Jews have been at it longer. Even the largest Jewish-American fortunes relied heavily on self-help, ingenuity, and opportunity to fulfill a real need. In the nineteenth century, Jewish wealth was largely the result of the success of Jewish-German immigrants, who brought with them great ambitions, little capital, and few skills. Consequently, peddling and petty retailing were the start of Goldmans, Guggenheims, Lehmans, Loebs, Sachses, and Kuhns. Later, it became a point of pride and family honor whether one's ancestors "started with a wagon" or started on foot.

By the time the German Jews were established and assimilated with earlier Jewish settlers, the Eastern European migrations were under way. The new Jews arrived as destitute as earlier generations of German Jews, and slightly poorer than other immigrants. One government report found that between 1899 and 1903 the average immigrant came to the United States with $22.78. The average Jew came with $20.43. Another study found that in 1900, the average immigrant landed with $15, while the Jewish immigrant came with only $9. Naturally, a few Jews came with greater than average resources: thirteen percent came with capital of more than $30. Though their largest employers were the clothing and needlepoint trades, a substantial number, as before, became peddlers: "Becoming a fullfledged peddler required a total investment of some ten dollars: five for the license, one for a basket, and the rest for one's wares. More than a few avoided the first expense and cut down on the last," noted one observer — hardly an auspicious start for capital accumulation, but a start, nevertheless.

Though the image of American Jews at the turn of the century was predominantly one of poverty, wealthy Jews were beginning to appear. In 1892, the country could boast of 4,047 millionaires in a population of sixty-three million. In New York City, of 250,-000 Jews, sixty were millionaires. Jews became wealthy in the nineteenth century through businesses like investment banking, commodities, brokerage, merchandising, and clothing. Once established, fortunes remained intact and are still alive and well in the twentieth century: Lehman, Loeb, Wertheim, Klingenstein, Rosenwald, Lowenstein, and Straus money has survived for nearly a century.

Modern Jewish wealth has, of course, a broader base. Finance, investment banking, brokerage, and commodities are still the fastest routes to amassing wealth quickly. Even with the drastic consolidation of stock exchange firms in the 1970s, the older Jewish firms are still doing business at their old stands, but have fewer Jews in personnel or purview. As Donald Regan, ex-chairman of Merrill Lynch and now Secretary of the Treasury, said when the Arabs attempted to boycott Jewish banks, "Here on the Street, it has never really occurred to anybody what the religion is of a particular house." The reason it does not, is not because of any wave of ecumenical sentiment on Wall Street, but because most houses are multidenominational.

Nevertheless, today a number of Jewish financiers have created businesses every bit as impressive as those of the Schiffs or Seligmans, or for the matter, of the Drexels, Stillmans, Harrimans, or Morgans. Along with Bache, Lehman, Lazard Freres, Kuhn Loeb, Goldman Sachs, Loeb Rhoades, some relatively recent successes, in a way, have replaced the old stars in the investment firmament. With the passing of Sidney Weinberg and Gustave Levy of Goldman Sachs, Andre Meyer of Lazard Freres, and Robert Lehman of Lehman Brothers, a more potent set of Jewish houses and entrepreneurs have emerged. Though barely known outside financial circles, and not known for their Jewishness (none of the principals are listed in the *Jewish Who's Who*), these entrepreneurs have played a prominent role on Wall Street in the last decade — a down decade by any measure. Salomon Brothers has risen to the top as traders and investment bankers, with investment capital approaching $231 million — second only to Merrill Lynch. Under the leadership of William Salomon and John Gutfreund, Salomon Brothers has grown by conducting business only with institutions. Putting all of its partners' capital on the line, the firm takes part in $20 billion worth of underwriting annually, and maintains an inventory of $2.4 billion. For the four dozen partners and twelve hundred employees, pretax earnings of $100 million and bonuses of twenty-five percent attest to the profitability of making markets for large blocks of securities.

In 1981, the partners finally sold out to a publicly owned commodity company, Phibro Corporation. Phibro, the descendant company of a nineteenth century German-Jewish metal trading house from Hamburg, had opened its American doors in 1914 as Philipp Brothers. A house where metal-brokers wore yarmulkas and ate kosher bag-lunches, it developed into one of the shrewdest global traders. In 1960, the company merged with Minerals and Chemicals Corporation of America, a match sponsored by that eminence gris, Andre Meyer of Lazard Freres. He sold part of the new company to Charles Engelhard (a colorful character on whom Ian Flemming reportedly modeled his fictional villain, Goldfinger), and the two were eventually merged to form Engelhard Minerals & Chemicals. Phibro split from Engelhard in 1981 as a separate public company. A few months later, it agreed to buy Salomon Brothers for $300 million in cash, plus $250 million in Phibro's convertible notes. That worked out to $7 million for each general partner and $32 million for John Gutfreund. It is a natural combination, remarked David Tendler, Phibro's head and a City College graduate, since money is "the ultimate commodity."

While Salomon Brothers started earlier in the century, and reached its present stature by dealing mostly in fixed-interest obligations, another dynamic investment house arose after the Second World War. Started by Charles and Herbert Allen, Allen & Company had a flair for wheeling and dealing based on intelligence and foresight. Starting with the purchase of a Philippine gold mine, Benguet, which was still under Japanese occupation, the Allens have backed a number of diverse companies: from a bankrupt utility holding company, Ogden, to a small Mexican pharmaceutical house, which was doing some unusual work in oral contraception, Syntex. Many of the Allen deals — usually highly leveraged situations that give them a maximum return if they work out — have been so successful as to create a number of fortunes several times over. Allen & Company is not only one of the best capitalized investment houses on Wall Street, with a net worth in excess of $70 million, but it has achieved a reputation and a following as a venture capitalist par excellence.

At the opposite end of the financial spectrum from Salomon Brothers is the investment boutique — the small special-situation firm. One of the shrewdest ones is Unterberg Towbin, which is small by Wall Street standards, but solidly conservative. Started in the thirties, the house developed a taste for financing new small and unique companies. Many of these companies were in advanced technology, or such specialized and risky areas that large underwriters passed them by. It was an area that "Bobby" Towbin exploited, providing working capital for over seventy-five companies in thirty years. The firm furnished seed money for such businesses as Franklin Mint, High Voltage Engineering, and Diner's Club. It became one of the foremost underwriters, and recently merged with L. F. Rothschild.

If finance has proven a congenial place for Jews, though not always in the back offices, the known houses owned to some degree by Jews such as Bear Stearns, Drexel Burnham Lambert, Emanuel, Josephthal, Ladenberg Thalmann, Lebenthal, Carl Marks, M. A. Schapiro, Weeden, to name but a few of the more significant ones, do nothing which is specifically Jewish. And this is the case with most of the substantial Jewish interests and businesses in America. While there are areas of Jewish business concentration that in part result from exclusionary policies and prejudice, and from a penchant for certain kinds of business, substantial Jewish wealth in the United States does not rest on the ethnic community or a special interest group of Jews. Certainly there are Jewish businesses, just as there are Kosher meat-packers, which make up approximately ten percent of that industry and specialize in distinctly Jewish needs. But unlike the largest black companies, which specialize in black cosmetics, black publishing, and black music, the most successful Jewish companies have produced for and serviced everyone.

Contrary to the popular image emphasized on stage, screen, and in literature, Jews are not peddlers of nostalgia. Indeed, in the modern world, nostalgia could get in the way of survival. It has been a tragic mistake to believe in old claims, or tender memories of things past, for all too often the promises proved hollow and the hyperbole full of devious fantasies.

It was a hard lesson for the Jews — one they have only recently come to understand. In their study of New York City, *Beyond the Melting Pot,* Glazer and Moynihan caught the essence of this new Jewish appreciation of the ways of the world:

> Jews broke with the most orthodox and traditional of religions to become open to everything new; . . . they seized upon everything new because the old things were so often tied up with social snobbery, anti-Semitism, obscurantist conservatism.

It was perhaps easier for Jews in America to jettison the ancestral baggage of predetermined occupations, for the United States welcomed risk-taking and provided fertile ground for an open and competitive economy. The Jewish entrepreneurial spirit could find any number of outlets: though it made no frontal attack on the economic establishment it did take Jews into novel areas, businesses that were on the periphery of established industries and into areas of innovation where creative intuition counted for something. Jews stayed away from highly regulated industries, sensing that government interference was not advantageous for Jews, and that regulated industries were also riddled with far more prejudice than other types of business.

The financial world, with its lure of wealth, cerebral involvement, and independent decision-making, was always a magnet for Jews, both in the old world and the new. The high profile of the financial world, and the Jews within it, reinforced some of the stereotypes of Jews as greedy manipulators of wealth.

In modern America, the charge lacks substance or validity, since the scramble for success is something of a national passion of pandemic proportions. It is no more a Jewish trait than it is a Catholic, Anglo-Saxon, conservative, radical, Armenian, or Mormon characteristic. But it can be said that Jewish wealth is generated from the financial side of business rather than the operational side. Many wealthy Jews have climbed the corporate ladder through law, accounting, and investment banking. Apparently, they are more at home massaging numbers than dealing with technical or substantive problems of production. An inordinate number of prominent Jewish businessmen are asset managers — that is their forte and sometimes their failing. For instance, a few of the better known who fall into this category are Irving Shapiro of DuPont (by profession an accountant); Charles Bludhorn of Gulf + Western (a securities analyst); Meshulam Riklis of Rapid-American (a stockbroker); Howard Newman of Western Pacific Industries (a financier); the Pritzker family of Cerro-Marmon (lawyers); the Milstein brothers (financiers) and the late Eli Black of United Brands (investment banking); Victor Posner of Sharon Steel/ NVF (real estate); Laurence Tisch of Loews (garment manufacturer); Henry Crown of general Dynamics (financier); and the late Joseph Hirshhorn (investments and uranium mining).

If many Jews are drawn to the financial side, it is probably due to the fact that in the last decade or two, the financial tail wags the industrial dog. Thanks to mergers and acquisitions, conglomerates, size, and diversity, the executive suites were peopled with business-school types rather than line operators. It became imperative to have professional management training. It is no accident, then, that over fifteen percent of all business school alumni are Jews. Again, it is a matter of survival as well as status. Discriminatory practices against Jews are not past history but, in some ways, current practice. And this, in turn, calls into play the defense mechanism of overtraining and overachieving — attempting mightily to succeed in the areas most open to talent. In recent years, those areas are in management, but even here, Jews have found roadblocks.

These obstacles start at the very beginning of a career. One recent report of recruitment practices of the leading five hundred corporations in the United States found a general reluctance to send recruiters to colleges that had thirty percent or greater Jewish enrollment. Based on a survey of the first five years of the seventies, the author of the report noted:

> When we look at the total of 467 corporations which sent so few recruiters to the 'Jewish' colleges, an all-pervasive pattern of avoidance becomes evident. Whether intentionally or not, it seems the present system of corporate recruitment effectively excluded Jews from most sectors of the economy.

This emphasis on the cult of management — the high priest of which is Peter Drucker, an Austrian-born Jewish scholar — may give renewed life to another old anti-Semitic canard. In the past, an erroneous distinction was made between industrial capitalism ("good") and finance capitalism ("bad"): Jews were always accused of the latter. This simplification — a notable example of economic naivete — has resurfaced in recent years. Jews are charged with being middlemen — parasites in the production line. This school of economic anti-Semitism argues that value only results from original producers. Distributors, shippers, wholesalers, brokers, financiers, and retailers (all notably Jewish occupations) add nothing of value to the product. If the middlemen — the Jews — were removed from the system, the argument goes, prices would be cheaper and the masses would be served better.

According to this theory, there would be an additional benefit as well: since the middlemen were always responsible for the rise and fall of the supply of commodities, their disappearance would end the instability of prices. No more soaring meat, sugar, and coffee prices. This conspiracy theory of economics is always revived in periods of shortages — whether of nylon stockings or oil. And occasionally there is some evidence of a plot. But for every Organization of Petroleum Exporting Countries (OPEC), not a notably Jewish cartel, there are others, like the Union of Banana

Exporting Countries, which would like to conspire but cannot organize sufficiently to synchronize their watches. Until the business cycle is repealed and natural forces are domesticated, shortages and spiraling prices will be endemic to market economies. They may be more or less successfully managed, but they will remain part of the picture for the foreseeable future. Nevertheless, some Jews always feel uncomfortable in times of commodity scarcities because the conspiracy theorists always seem to be blaming them.

*Facts and Fantasies*

Another corollary to the conspiracy theory is that Jews control the press and the communications industry. In modern times, the theme is often repeated: from Charles Lindbergh in 1941 — "The greatest danger to this country lies in their large ownership and influence in our motion pictures, our press, our radio and our Government" — to General George Brown in 1974 — "They own, you know, the banks in the country, the newspapers" — and ex-Vice President Spiro Agnew in 1976 — "I do think the media are sympathetic to the Zionist cause . . ."

There is no question that Jews have played a formidable role, indeed, a catalytic role in the media. However, Jews are far from dominant and, certainly, too contentious to furnish a unified policy on any topic, even in the few instances where they do run, own, or operate a major company. The fantasy of Jews conspiring to promote, promulgate, or propagandize in unison could only be conjured up by people who have had no contact with Jews. A religion with three major branches, a political state (Israel) with ten parties, and an American Jewish establishment that at last count had "no less than 340 national organizations," is far too diverse for such simplistic analysis.

Nevertheless, the myth continues that Jews control the media. There is no question that Jews are well represented in some areas: recently, the three television networks were headed by Jews — the Sarnoffs (father and son) at NBC, William S. Paley of CBS, and Leonard Goldenson of ABC. Since all are publicly owned companies, even the autocratic Mr. Paley, who owns 6.9 pecent of CBS's twenty-eight million shares, could easily have been ousted when he was chief executive officer by the institutional investors, who collectively own thirty percent of the company. Indeed, Robert Sarnoff was apparently forced to resign due to lackluster performance in this highly competitive field. A 1975 RCA proxy statement revealed that he owned seventy-nine thousand shares and options to purchase seventy thousand additional shares — in all, roughly a fifth of one percent of the outstanding stock. When both Sarnoff and Paley gave up leadership of their networks, they were succeeded by non-Jews. And neither were noted for an interest in things Jewish. So, while Jewish control of the communications industry has been widely touted, no one has yet explained the composition and content of this purported influence.

In the newspaper field, there is not even the intimation of Jewish dominance, though a few Jews have had great success. Samuel I. Newhouse was by far the most successful Jewish publishing magnate, with his chain of thirty dailies, six magazines, six television stations, four radio stations, and twenty cable television systems. No one, except the immediate Newhouse family, knows just how big or how valuable the empire is, for the companies not only abjure publicity, they remain privately held. Estimates place the chain first in profits and third in size, after Time Incorporated and Times Mirror Company, with annual revenues of over $750 million and a net profit close to $50 million. Though tightly knit through family ties (at one time, sixty-four relatives were employed), the management of the chain is decentralized, with a great deal of editorial and operational freedom. In fact, the late Samuel I. Newhouse, called by *Business Week* "America's Most Profitable Publisher," maintained no corporate headquarters and no regular office, and he excelled in managing by instinct, with the aid of a prodigious memory. His business has been called "a management consultant's nightmare." He never called on Peter Drucker, the archdruid of management sciences, to organize his operations.

Newhouse's background was typical of the Jewish child born on the Lower East Side, of Russian and Austrian parents. His father was a suspender-maker who was handicapped and had difficulty earning a living, so the son went to work after grade school. Later on, by going to school days and working nights, at the

*Bayonne Times,* he eventually received a law degree. But he never practiced law, since by that time, he was part owner of the newspaper, having been paid in stock instead of salary. From the acquisition of his first paper in 1922 to the purchase of the whole Booth chain of eight papers for $305 million in 1976 — the largest transaction in American publishing up to that time — Newhouse has left the edtiorial and managerial functions in local hands. The corporate infrastructure, however, is based on family ties — a very Jewish trait.

But the Newhouse chain has apparently gone out of its way to avoid the employment of Jews. One *Washington Post* reporter recently wrote that the papers employ "only non-Jews as editors or publishers except for members of the immediate Newhouse family." It is, of course, a curious policy in a field where there are many talented Jews. The Newhouses have stuck to their position, for, as the founding father noted, "I'm not trying to save the world."

Two papers — the *New York Times* and the *Washington Post* — once owned by Jews, are models of journalistic excellence and are extremely influential in political and cultural circles. However, there is not much that is Jewish about them. Eugene Meyer, the financier and owner of the *Washington Post,* left the newspaper to his daughter, Katherine Graham. She is a Lutheran, as was her mother, even though she considers herself her father's daughter. The Ochs-Sulzberger family has always been sensitive to the *Times* appearing as a Jewish journal. Objectivity, in the eyes of the world, was better served if there were fewer Jewish editors and publishers.

This compensatory leaning against the wind probably accounts for rather less Jewish influence than more in the national press. Jewish press lords own roughly three percent of the 1,760 daily newspapers in the country, or just about their proportional representation.

In other publishing areas — magazines and books — Jews have made significant contributions, but again their power is much overrated. Walter Annenberg's Triangle Publications publishes a number of mass market magazines — *TV Guide,* for example — with circulation over twenty milliion. His father, Moe Annenberg, entered the publishing field by starting a line of horse-racing tout sheets in the 1920s to help improvers of the breed in their morning selections. Triangle, a private corporation, has made Walter Annenberg an extremely wealthy man and a force in Republican politics. In the Nixon administration, he was appointed Ambassador to the Court of St. James. But wealth has its limitations, as he found out when he attempted to fund a communications center. Having been the prime mover in the new Mt. Sinai Medical Center — the Annenberg Tower — he apparently wanted to make an architectural contribution a little lower on Fifth Avenue.

In a generous gesture to the Metropolitan Museum of Art, Annenberg offered to finance a $40 million communications center in a wing that lay between the Rockefeller and Lehman wings. It would have aided the museum's capital building program, but it might have moved the institution further into education and away from art. The direction to be taken became academic, for New York City politicians raised so many issues that the philanthropist took his gift elsewhere.

In book publishing, the Jewish presence is felt because the Jew is prominent in a literary genre developed in the last generation by Bellow, Mailer, Roth, Malamud, Singer, Heller, Perelman, and a host of other talented poets, playwrights, and essayists. In addition, publishing has a somewhat Jewish tone due to the large number of Jewish personnel working in the Manhattan literary vineyards. Whether there is a Jewish literary mafia, comparable to the purported Jewish art mafia, is highly debatable. The publishing business, with six thousand firms, is too large to be run by intellectual cliques. Truman Capote's remark that a "clique of New York-oriented writers and critics . . . control much of the literary scene through the influence of Jewish dominated quarterlies and influential magazines" is no longer true, if it ever was. On the other hand, there are a few houses started by Jews that are important in the trade: Random House, started by the late Bennett Cerf, and Donald S. Klopfer; Alfred A. Knopf; Simon & Schuster; Viking; Bantam; and Farrar, Strauss and Giroux. Some of these founders faced problems of anti-Semitism in their early years. Klopfer recalled that "In the 20s and 30s, Bennett and I and other

Jewish publishers were looked down upon. We weren't invited to the Publishers Lunch Club ... even though we had made a mark." However, the era of publishing as a gentleman's trade may well be over as conglomerates buy up the independents, and Jewish influence at the ownership level has probably passed the high-water mark.

Indeed, some of the traditional Jewish businesses have been engulfed by other people's money. Many old-line Jewish companies were either seduced into going public or were acquired by larger firms. Thus, their Jewish ethnicity was lost or submerged — assimilated on a corporate level, perhaps presaging the trend in society.

The garment trade was at one time a Jewish business of alternating fortune and backruptcy as spring and fall lines succeeded or failed. Today, the relatively stable cloak and suit operations are maintained by larger public companies.

The garment industry still consists of many small apparel manufacturers — approximately twenty-three thousand individual companies, down from 27,500 in 1969. The large corporations have entered this business so that the top ninety-five companies now account for twenty-seven percent of the industry sales. Furthermore, foreign competition is eliminating the marginal operators: one out of four garments sold in the United States is produced abroad. Consequently, the industry continues to shrink, with large operators either moving abroad or south. Only high-priced goods, such as Halstons, can be produced in New York. Much of the cheaper merchandise comes from the Orient. And in the wake of this change, the character of Seventh Avenue has been altered: it is now a street with Greek, Spanish, Chinese, Italian, and Turkish spoken alongside Yiddish.

Still another old enclave of Jewish interest — entertainment — has changed because of television and conglomerates. An infant industry started at the turn of the century by nickelodeon operators — "glove salesmen, pharmacists, furriers, clothiers and jewelers" — in the words of economist Ben Seligman, the entertainment business has always had a strong appeal to Jews as a novel art form, a potentially lucrative business, and even a public service. And as has been the case where Jews proved the potential and the profitability of new endeavors, the established conservative money moved in after the groundwork was laid and after the processes were perfected.

Conservative businessmen and financiers stayed away from the incipient entertainment world for reasons other than lack of foresight: it was another one of the taboos, nearly as old as anti-Semitism, that association with actors and players could do little for one's reputation and less for one's pocketbook. So the movie industry got off to a rough, flamboyant start without Wall Street, financed largely by individuals with giant-sized egos. For example, Adolph Zukor, an immigrant who had $40 sewed into the lining of his coat when he arrived in the United States and initially made a living selling novelty furs, used $200,000 from the fur business to finance penny arcades that had begun to incorporate movies. Joining with Marcus Loew, a Lower East Side newsboy who also made his first money as a furrier, the two acquired peep shows and penny arcades at the end of World War I. Their association was not long-lived: Zukor moved on to form the Famous Players Company and finally took over Paramount Pictures, then a distributor of films. Controlling the theatres was more important than making movies, so Zukor issued $10 million of securities through Kuhn, Loeb to build the chain. Meanwhile Loew had moved from controlling a chain of theatres of producing movies.

In the twenties, Loew joined an ailing Metro Pictures with Goldwyn Pictures (founded by Samuel Goldfish, a Polish immigrant, who joined with his brother-in-law, Jesse Lasky and the Selwyn brothers to form a production company, which was so successful that he changed his own name to Goldwyn) and the company started by Louis B. Mayer (another Polish immigrant), to form Metro-Goldwyn-Mayer.

Warner Brothers was just as famous, started by the brothers as a nickelodeon, after they had successfully peddled their only copy of *The Great Train Robbery* from town to town. Warner Brothers, led by brother Harry, a one-time shoemaker, was the first production company to appreciate sound, a fact that helped it live through the Depression without reorganizing, a singular feat. Though it had the exclusive rights to sell Western Electric's sound system, the telephone company broke the contract and sold it to all comers after Warner's successful movie, *The Jazz Singer*. With the help of Goldman, Sachs, Warner Brothers entered a number of entertainment businesses, from music publishing to radio manufacturing.

This story could be repeated for each movie company: William Fox, a New Yorker who began his career as a cleaner and dyer for $17 a week, started his chain with the purchase of his first movie house in Brooklyn; for Lewis Selznick, Irving Thalberg, and Daryl Zanuck, the ascent was very similar. From a crude beginning, to exploitation of movie chains for their distribution, to concern with quality films, to the entrance of talkies, and to the reorganization of the film companies in the thirties and their consolidation in the sixties, Jews played a leading role in producing and financing films. When it was thought to be both safe and profitable, the movie companies then became reputable investments for finance companies, conglomerates, and even bank trusts.

The entertainment industry still is a markedly Jewish business, even though the old studio gurus are gone: Paramount's nominal head is Gulf + Western's Bludhorn, and Transamerica's United Artist was run by Arthur Krim before he started Orion, which bought Filmways. Loews Theatres, a part of the hotel real-estate insurance company, is controlled by the Tisch family, M-G-M chairman is Frank Rosenfelt (the highest-paid American in 1979 with compensation of $5.2 million), and one of the largest studios, Universal, is part of MCA.

While MCA goes back to the salad days of movies, it only recently became one of the heavyweights in the industry. In a way, it is an exemplary Jewish organization: it started as a talent agency for brokering high-priced stars, and then entered television production when the home screen showed signs of a rapacious appetite. As an agency it stood halfway between the creative and the commercial worlds, a stimulant to both. The company was founded by the late Jules Stein, a one-time eye doctor who retired to pursue philanthropic works in eye research, but is presently run by Lew R. Wasserman and Sidney J. Sheinberg.

Though MCA did well in television — for example, with the crime series *Kojak,* Stein and Wasserman attempted to diversify to bring some stability to a high-risk business while still courting new and challenging ideas. MCA was one of the first to use outside directors, most notably for *Psycho* and *Jaws,* the latter being one of the highest grossing hits in movie history. In addition, the company has a record and music publishing division, a tour operation of the Universal lot, a chain of gift stores, and a book publishing arm, G. P. Putnam's Sons. Finally, in an industry that is constantly changing, MCA entered into an agreement with the General Electric of Europe — Philips N.V. of Holland — to market a novel home video disk that would exploit its large film library. Not a bad mix for a billion-dollar corporation. Stein had a nineteen percent interest in the company, while Wasserman owned ten percent of the company stock, which enables him to take home close to a million dollars a year in dividends.

There is, of course, nothing inherently Jewish about movies, or garments for that matter, but again the nature of these businesses — rapid change, high-risk, the leverage attendant with the rewards — apparently has an appeal to Jews. If one were to look for the one industry in the United States that Jews do have a lock on, it would not be the communications industry, but the toy industry. In this $3 billion industry, Jewish families are heavily represented, from the largest company, Mattel, founded by Elliot and Ruth Handler, to the newest, Mego, founded by David Abrams, but run by his son, Martin Abrams. There is a strong Jewish presence in Hasbro by the Hassenfeld family of Rhode Island, in Ideal by the Weintraub family of New York, in Marx by Louis Marx, and in Gabriel by Jerome M. Fryer.

### Black Gold, Yellow Gold, and Tradition

Of course, Jewish business interests have changed with the times. When department stores were slow to move to suburbia after World War II, a vacuum was filled by the discounters, or "underselling" stores, which specialized in low-expense and low-markup policies. They established themselves in the greenbelts around cities and provided ample parking facilities and long shopping hours. The established stores reacted with the arrogance one might have expected. Discounting was dismissed as "nothing more than selling inferior merchandise on Sundays." But the discounters did offer some special advantages even when their stated policy was to offer no services, only bargain-basement prices.

If he was not the first discounter, Eugene Ferkauf of Brooklyn surely started the ball rolling in 1948 with a second-floor luggage store, which he named E. J. Korvette. After it had grown to fifty-odd stores nationwide, it experienced financial trouble and merged with Charles C. Bassine's Spartan Industries, a clothing manufacturer. Spartan eventually merged with Arthur G. Cohen's Arlen Realty and Development. Korvettes was acquired by some French interests and finally went bankrupt in 1981. Other discounters followed: Two Guys (now part of Vornado, which also filed for bankruptcy in 1981), started by the Hubschman brothers, a series of chains run by Sol Cantor's Interstate Stores; and the Levitz Brothers of Levitz Furniture, to name only a few of the more prominent ones. Of course, Kresge and Woolworth soon followed with K-Mart and Woolco, dwarfing the original discounters. Perhaps there should be nothing surprising about the Jewish presence in retailing; it is, after all, a very old connection. But the contemporary leadership certainly proves that Jewish merchandising talents did not end with Gimbel, Straus, Altman, Filene, and Bamberger.

Another traditional Jewish business is jewelry and rare gems. In no other industry is Jewishness so obvious since many of the cutters, grinders, and polishers, shuttling along Manhattan's 47th Street in the full formal black garb of an eighteenth century Polish merchant, are Chassidic. No one knows what the sales volume is for New York's diamond center, but educated guesses place it in the vicinity of $1 billion annually. (For comparison's sake, the De Beers Consolidated Mines of South Africa, controlled by Harry Oppenheimer, has sales in the neighborhood of $2 billion of new output, or about eighty-five percent of the world's total.) For the most part, it is a highly secretive business, but one of the largest diamond cutting companies in the world, Lazare Kaplan International, is a public company. At the other end of the business is jewelry retailing, also a heavily Jewish occupation. The largest retailer is Zale, a Dallas chain of seventeen hundred stores, plus a series of fancy boutiques in other large cities. The firm was started by Morris Zale in Wichita Falls in the 1920s, when the sudden discovery of nearby oil fields brought him more business than he could handle. He changed the earnings from black gold into yellow gold.

Finally, any brief look at Jewish business interests would have to note some of their successes in real estate and construction. William Levitt, the creator of massive tract developments of single family homes, which became known around the world as Levittowns, created a new genre of housing. He provided basic shelter at minimum prices for young families, nothing grand or glamorous, but of sufficient diversity to appeal to working class families wishing to flee the inner cities. In a fashion, he shaped the American dream, a house of one's own for a small downpayment and an endless mortgage. His success was duly noted in the business community with the highest compliment: an offer to buy his construction company. In 1968, Levitt sold his firm to International Telephone and Telegraph (ITT) for $92 million, but he remained chief operating officer.

After the sale was made and Levitt became extremely wealthy, the company entered a new phase, which was to bring it down. With ITT's blessing and backing, the company started to build high-rise apartments, shining office buildings, mobile homes, and modular, prefabricated housing. The construction company became less and less profitable and eventually went deeply into the red. Meanwhile, the Justice Department filed an antitrust suit against ITT, forcing it to divest itself of the building company. But by then, the company was bankrupt and no one would purchase it, at least not until a court-appointed trustee could put it back in shape.

William Levitt finally left the company to set up a new one to do business outside the United States. He complained that government-imposed restrictions made it too difficult to build. When last heard from, Levitt was undertaking a large housing complex in Teheran, Iran.

Other Jewish builders and real-estate operators have also added color to the construction industry: the late William Zeckendorf, who put together the property for the United Nations site; the Uris brothers, with their endless glass boxes; the late William

Kaufman, who built futuristic and fanciful office buildings in New York, decorating them with works of noted artists; the West Coast Kaufman and Broad organization, presently one of the largest builders of single-family homes; and the late Henry F. Fischbach, a Rumanian-born electrical contractor whose company, Fischbach and Moore, lit up the Holland Tunnel, Lever House, the new Metropolitan Opera House, and Chicago's Prudential Building.

Last, but hardly least, in any rundown of the building industry, is Samuel J. Lefrak, a private developer who has run his "mud flats" — six story apartment houses — into a vast real-estate empire. Taking over from his father's effort to construct homes in Brooklyn, Lefrak built his "money machines" in suburban Queens, culminating in Lefrak City. Besides owning several office buildings, Lefrak owns and operates fifty-five thousand apartments in New York City and thirty thousand elsewhere in the country: the rent income alone exceeds $100 million a year. Lefrak's organization is made up of 350 companies, owned solely by his immediate family, with estimated assets of $500 to $700 million. The latest jewel scheduled to join the Lefrak tiara is Battery Park City, a landfill development of offices, stores, and apartments, located somewhere between the World Trade Towers and the Hudson River in Manhattan. However, the raison d'etre of Battery Park City is fascinating: after building all those bedrooms in the greenbelt, Lefrak is now trying to lure the very same people back to the inner city to be near their jobs. If anyone can pull off that trick, it will certainly be Samuel Lefrak.

Jewish business interests are not limited to specific industries, though the Jewish involvement obviously appears far greater in some of the previously mentioned areas. If representation in some basic industries — such as oil — is still scant, it is not altogether missing. While none of the major international oil corporations — the seven sisters — could be accused of Jewish ownership or management (indeed, they went out of their way to make sure Jews were not hired for their Middle Eastern operations, where their presence might displease Arab hosts), Jews have continued to penetrate the industry, following the lead of the late Jacob Blaustein of Baltimore.

With his father, Louis, Jacob Blaustein founded the American Oil Company — Amoco. It was the first oil company to develop antiknock gasoline: Lindberg used it on his famous trip across the Atlantic. The company became a significant force in gasoline distribution with a substantial chain of service stations, accounting for as much as five percent of the national total, but it lacked the crude reserves necessary for a broad-based, integrated oil company. Indeed, in trying to acquire reserves, the Blausteins ran up against the concentrated resources of the Rockefellers. It was a battle they were to lose, but it made them wealthy in the process.

To strengthen their position, the Blausteins sold half of Amoco to Pan American Petroleum and Transport Company so that they would be able to draw on that company's crude reserves. However, Pan American Pete fell under control of Standard Oil of Indiana, forcing the company to sell its crude to Standard Oil of New Jersey, a competitor of the Blausteins. Amoco was being squeezed: it had to purchase its crude from Standard of Jersey and it was prevented from building new refinery capacity by Standard Oil of Indiana. Threatened with legal action, the Indiana company allowed Amoco to merge fully with Pan American Pete and build a new refinery, but due to lagging business in the thirties, Indiana reneged. The Blausteins went to court to reverse the restraints of trade and a seventeen-year legal battle ensued. It was finally settled in 1954 when Amoco and Pan American were merged into Standard of Indiana.

The Blausteins became the largest stockholders in the country's sixth largest oil company, with 5,250,000 shares. In 1957, *Fortune* magazine listed the Blaustein fortune as the eleventh largest in the nation, worth between $100 million and $200 million, making the Blausteins the wealthiest Jewish family in the United States. Today the Indiana holdings are worth close to $300 million, generating nearly $14 million in dividends annually. In addition, the Blausteins own half of Crown Central Petroleum Company, a small oil company, which suffers from the same problem that plagued Amoco — insignificant crude resources. The Blaustein fortune, now managed by the son of Jacob, Morton Blaustein, commands assets of $400 million, invested in everything from real estate and tankers to buildings and banks. There are now other contenders for the title of the wealthiest Jewish-American family, but the Blausteins still rank among the richest. One of the family's favorite philanthropies is the American Jewish Committee, and for many years Jacob was its honorary chairman.

Another oil fortune, of more recent vintage, is that of Leon Hess. Like the Blausteins, Hess developed an East Coast distribution network, a chain of service stations without any crude reserves or refinery capacity. Through a merger in 1969, with Amerada Pete, a more fully integrated oil company, the new company, Amerada Hess, became a sizable domestic petroleum operation. Before the merger, Hess was believed to be the twenty-first richest person in the United States, with holdings calculated at $200 to $300 million. Since the merger, Hess's holdings have increased: he presently owns or controls nearly twenty-two percent of the voting stock of the new corporation.

Some of the success of Amerada Hess was due to the company's ability to profit from the entitlement programs. After the 1973 Arab oil embargo, the federal government stepped in to manage the price structure: it attempted to even out the price differentials between domestic crude (cheap, due to regulation) and imported crude (expensive, due to the OPEC cartel). It granted entitlements to domestic refiners who did not have access to cheap crude — the entitlements were worth the difference between the two prices. Amerada Hess was able to profit accordingly: the condition became known as "the Hess advantage." Though the company obtained expensive foreign crude from Libya, Abu Dhabi, Canada, and the North Sea, it refined much of its oil in the Virgin Islands. Other American companies did the same, with refineries in Aruba, Curacao, and the Bahamas — but they received no entitlements. For Amerada Hess, the advantage had brought an additional income of $200 million per year. Until the price of domestic oil was deregulated in 1981, Leon Hess was on to a valuable government hand out.

Leon Hess was also worried about his foreign sources of expensive oil. So concerned, indeed, that he followed the examples of some other major oil companies — Gulf, for instance — which was also at the mercy of foreign crude, and proceeded to bribe foreign officials. While the practice was common enough before the government made an issue of it, hundreds of major corporations found it a necessary business expense and invariably used devious accounting practices to hide the payments from the Internal Revenue Service and the Securities and Exchange Commission.

Hess took a much more direct route: the "payments, substantial in the aggregate" came "solely from my personal funds," he wrote to his stockholders. Nor were the funds even deducted from his personal taxes as a business deduction. Thus Hess neatly avoided any implication of questionable corporate behavior. About the only misstep Leon Hess has taken in a successful business career was to purchase the New York Jets — not always a winning team.

Jewish business successes pop up in the most unexpected places: from whiskey (Edgar Bronfman of Seagram) to birdseed (Leonard Stern of Hartz Mountain), from lipstick (the late Charles Revson of Revlon) to grain trading (Michel Fribourg of Continental Grain), from defense contracting (Henry Crown of General Dynamics) to floor coverings (Jesse Werner of GAF), from precious metals (the late Charles Engelhard of Engelhard Minerals & Chemicals) to dress patterns (James Schapiro of Simplicity Patterns), from temporary personnel agencies (the Scheinfelds and Winters of Manpower) to photocopying (Max Palevsky of Xerox), from computer hardware (Simon Ramo of TRW) to computer software (H. Taub and Frank Lautenberg of Automatic Data Processing), and from hotels (the late Ben Swig of the Fairmont Hotel chain) to cheese cake (Nathan Cummings of Consolidated Foods).

Obviously, Jews have entered a wide mix of enterprises. They have not succeeded in everything they have undertaken: the most recent spectacular failure was the collapse of the Israeli-American Maritime Fruit Company, an international merchant marine operation with two-score of refrigerator ships, that went belly up in the mid-seventies. Jewish ingenuity was insufficient to save the company from liquidation. However, American Jews have succeeded to such a phenomenal degree that no one presently thinks of their interests as minority businesses though Jews constitute less than 3 percent of the population.

Jewish business genius has long been slandered by assertions that Jews were greedy money-manipulators, and that their self-interest, unlike anyone else's, was their prime concern. This anti-Semitism threw a vast cloud over their accomplishments and obscured their true talents.

Moreover, as second-class citizens, Jews have had a strong affinity for socialism though socialists have not always reciprocated the sentiment. In fact, the image of Jewish genius for business was further befogged by the efforts of socialist Jews to undermine the tradition of capitalism and free enterprise. Milton Friedman, the Nobel Laureate in Economics, reflected that after his first visit to Israel, he felt the full weight of two conflicting traditions at war with one another. "One of them was a very recent tradition — a tradition 100 or 150 years old. That's the tradition of socialism. . . . Jewish intellectuals have been strongly pro-socialist and have contributed disproportionately to the socialist literature. . . ."

The other tradition Friedman mentioned was two thousand years old — a tradition "of how you get around government regulations. How you find chinks in controls, how you find areas in which the free market operates and make the most of it. It was that tradition which enabled the Jews to survive during centuries of persecution."

This contradiction is further compounded by the modern American tendency, most noticeable in some intellectual, academic, and political circles, to downgrade business, to see the profit motive solely as aggrandizement of the rich. Besides viewing the business world with cynicism and contempt, their goal is to redistribute other people's wealth rather than create their own. Consequently, their alienation of Jewish intellectual and cultural leaders has blinded them to the unusual and unique creative drives that Jews poured into the world of business and finance. And the assumption that business is somewhat tedious and dull, lacking in creativity, imagination, and public spirit has relegated to neglect an area of endeavor in which Jews have excelled. A reassessment of the role of business will find Jewish business interests positive contributions to the American economy and the world.

# 6. International Finance: Blood Is Thicker Than Oil

"Now [that you are] here," she said to Alice, "it takes all of the running you can do to stay in the same place. If you want to get somewhere else, you must run at least twice as fast as that."

— The Red Queen in *Through the Looking Glass,* Lewis Carroll

## The Boycott and OPEC

Perhaps it is possible to separate Jewish interests from Israeli interests, but the trick is yet to be turned. What touches Israel touches global Jewry, and vice versa. Purists and theoreticians may argue about the separation of church and state, Jews and Israelis, Judaism and Zionism, but in the real world the connection is hard, fast, and seemingly indivisible. And no one does more to strengthen the links than enemies of Jews and Israelis. The energy crisis is a case in point: OPEC put together a unified cartel, but at the same time, solidified Jewish connections and, not incidentally, aroused American sympathies.

The oil embargo and subsequent tightening of the Arab boycott throws some light on the power of Jewish money. The crisis arose as a consequence of the 1973 Yom Kippur War when the Arab states, in concert, cut off the flow of petroleum to the West. Israel won the war, though not by much, and the Arab states and the oil producing countries won the peace. The cost to the rest of the world was a quadrupling of oil prices, from approximately $2.50 a barrel to $10, and later, to $40 in 1981.

While the war cost Israel $3 billion (and presumably a similar amount for the Egyptians and Syrians), the oil nations, who were noncombatants, reaped huge windfalls. The windfalls were, of course, the massive funds that have continued to flow to the petroleum exporters ever since: OPEC can now count on an additional $75 billion to $100 billion annually in their balance of payments.

The embargo did not directly affect Israel, which imported some petroleum products from the West, and had an arrangement with Iran, a non-Arab state and second largest OPEC producer, which continued to supply Israel throughout the war. But the embargo had a direct effect on the West: fuel shortages, gas lines at service stations, steeply rising prices for all petroleum-based products and a strong dose of inflation throughout every economy, which subsequently led to worldwide recessions from 1973 through 1975 and in 1980. Never before had a region or a country become so rich so quickly. Almost overnight the petrodollar became king. At first the projections of petrodollar surpluses bordered on the astronomic: the World Bank initially saw OPEC surpluses running to $650 billion in 1980 and $1.2 trillion by 1985. The first figure is approximately the value of all the assets of companies listed on the New York Stock Exchange, while the second was close to the gross national product of the United States at the time of the embargo. At that rate, there was no doubt that the Arabs would inherit the world, at least have the reserves to own everything by the turn of the century.

But the projections did not take into account the human factor or a fundamental law of economics: spending rises to meet income. The petrodollar pool could, indeed, destabilize world currencies unless some sort of recycling system was developed. While the International Monetary Fund created a facility to do just that, the Arabs created their own recycling system by undertaking vast development schemes and buying foreign property and assets.

The industrial West, after incurring initial deficits to pay for their oil imports, found that their exports to the oil producing countries had helped avert a dramatic deficit in their balance of payments. The nations most hurt by the rise in oil prices were the less developed countries — within three years, their deficits tripled. Without the ability to export to the oil producers, the less developed countries, where approximately one billion people have incomes on the order of $200 a year, are the countries suffering most from the energy crisis. The OPEC members have successfully rearranged the distribution of world wealth, with oil revenues now roughly $100 billion annually. In the oil producing countries — at least in the sparsely populated states — this redistribution allowed for amenities like free telephones and free health and educational services. Difficult as it is to believe, though, some oil producers are spending it faster than they earn it. The massive development plans — the first Saudi Arabian scheme cost $142 billion and overshot its mark by $18 billion, and the second five-year plan — 1980–85 — will cost $240 billion, or perhaps as much as $391 billion if military expenditures are included. Some states were in the embarrassing position of having to borrow money.

The huge surpluses of monetary reserves that the Arab oil producers have accumulated have led Arab oil consumers to reexamine the embargo and boycott of Israel. Everyone in business, regardless of product or nationality, wants to trade with the OPEC members. For the selling of everything from fighter planes to bathroom fixtures, a whole industry has grown up offering nothing more than the ability to sell to the Middle East. The Arabs, of course, appreciate the enormous leverage that the petrodollar affords them and have not been slow in extracting conditions of trade. The oldest condition of all, the boycott of Jews and Israel, dates back to 1946, two years before Israel's birth. Since then it has been updated, extended, and strengthened. The object of the boycott is to weaken Israel. If war is an extension of diplomacy, the boycott is an extension of war. Americans — Jews and gentiles — are now caught in the crossfire.

The Arab boycott contains two elements: one common to all economic wars, and the other, peculiar to situations where national laws are hazy and jurisdictions overlap. The first is a direct and unequivocal ban on all trade between the twenty members of the Arab League and Israel. Any number of states and peoples have used this weapon: the United States forbids trade with Cuba and Vietnam, and at one time, forbid it with a large number of communist states. Unions frequently boycott the goods of the companies they are striking against: this tool was used not long ago to organize farm workers in the grape and lettuce fields. Even American Jews have used the boycott to bring economic pressure. When Mexico voted in the United Nations to condemn Zionism in the fall of 1975, Jews and Jewish organizations cancelled tours of Mexico. The action put a major crimp in that country's tourist industry, which in turn contributed to the necessary devaluation of the peso by a drastic sixty percent the following year. Within a few weeks of the Jewish boycott, the Mexican government did a volte-face, apparently finding Zionism less objectionable than doing without Jewish money.

The Arab boycott does have loopholes — there is limited trade across the Israeli border with Jordan and Lebanon. But for the most part, the embargo is so effective that Israel has stated a number of times that there can be "no full peace until the boycott is dropped altogether."

It is the other element of the ban — the secondary boycott — that raises intractable problems and has created a storm of controversy in the United States. The Boycott Office in Damascus requires certification that goods shipped to Arab countries are not of Israeli origin. So along with the invoice, bill of lading, certificate of origin, and sight draft, the American bank must have a certificate of boycott compliance. Only then will the Arabs pay the exporter according to instructions of the Arab banks. This practice has been presumed to be perfectly legal, and every major bank in international trade participates in this aspect of the boycott. Some Arab states are also censorious about the wording on their commercial papers. Thus the United Arab Emirates warns that "the term Persian Gulf should not be used on shipping documents of correspondence. Shippers should use the term Arabian Gulf."

Furthermore, the Arab countries will not trade with companies that contribute materially to the Israeli economy. This latter point is somewhat ambiguous in its application even though the Boycott Office has issued one hundred pages of regulations. Elizabeth Taylor's films are banned because she reportedly donates

$100,000 annually to Jewish causes, but then, so is a film of Barbra Streisand's, *Funny Girl,* because in it, she kisses Omar Sharif. Sophia Loren's films are also banned because she once acted in a movie about Israel. Disney's films are likewise verboten since in *Snow White,* the prince's horse was named Solomon. Other boycott items are Jantzen swim suits, Converse tennis sneakers, Frank Sinatra's recordings, all of RCA's recordings, and Ford products — the Arab states have cast a very wide net. Companies that sell items to Israel for hard currency are not on the blacklist since this deprives Israel of foreign exchange reserves. Companies that sell Israel defense or military items may or may not find themselves on the list. But if their military material is relatively unique, and Arab nations want them — such as products of Rockwell International, Grumman, General Dynamics, Textron, and General Electric — loyalties are irrelevant, and Arab governments will also purchase from them. In reality, there is no one boycott list, since each Arab government maintains its own.

What has raised controversy is the Arab insistence that its suppliers certify that the subcontractors are also free from doctrinal error. Occasionally, the enforcement of this secondary or tertiary boycott gives the Arab embargo an air of religious discrimination, that their trading partners be *Judenrein.* The Boycott Office denies any religious overtones, but the head of the office, Mohammed Mahmoud Mahgoup, has said that "if principal officers are members of the board of a company or have a majority of its shares, and are at the same time prominent in Zionist activities, the company no doubt will be affected."

In other words, it is not sufficient for the company to be free of any Israeli business that could be deemed to be supportive, but in addition, its officers must not engage in any pro-Israel activity. Thus, companies that have no policy concerning Zionism, any more than they would concerning vivisection or vegetarianism, find themselves blacklisted because prominent owners or chief executives have personally contributed to the Jewish state. Thus Hartz Mountain Food, Bergdorf Goodman, Bulova, and Revlon were all blacklisted even though they have almost no business interests in the Middle East. While the Boycott Office denies any religious discrimination is involved, some of their actions make it difficult to believe their claim.

The late King Faisal was perhaps more candid when he lectured Henry Kissinger on his foreign policy objectives. "All over the world [the Jews] were putting themselves into position of authority ... the Jews were trying to run the world, but ... he would stop them with his oil weapon."

The boycott founders when the Arabs ask prime contractors to certify that their subcontractors are also not on the blacklist. Occasionally, the prime contractors are asked about race, religion, and national origins of directors and officers. Such certification under American law was not illegal, though under the Export Administration Act, companies were obliged to report such requests to the Commerce Department and to tell the government whether they complied with the request. In some fifty thousand transactions with Arab states between 1970 and 1975, three-quarters of the companies did not tell the government, or simply did not file papers.

There was a slight change in American policy as a consequence of the Ford–Carter presidential debates. During one exchange, President Ford declared that henceforth, all boycott reports filed by United States companies would be made public. It was the kind of step that American Jewish agencies had pursued for years, since they viewed publication of names as a way of bringing pressure on companies to stop complying with the boycott. Subsequent publication of the names of corporations yielding to the Arab boycott has had some deterrent effect, but not much. The largest bank in the United States, Bank of America, will no longer process boycott requests, but unlike its leadership in determining the prime rate, not many banks have followed its example. California, New York, and Massachusetts have prohibited compliance by state law.

However, publication of the confidential reports did reveal some quirks and inanities in preparing such a list. James Beam Distilling Company — producers of a highly potable sour mash bourbon whose president, Martin Lewin, is a Jew — complied with the boycott request, presumably enabling it to send its spirits to the whiskey-free Moslem world. Kyser Roth International, a Jewish firm owned by Gulf + Western, which is run by Viennese-born Jewish financier Charles Bludhorn, had also complied with the Arab Boycott Office. Both firms subsequently ended their obeisance.

Before the publication of the reports, the Commerce Department found that ninety-four percent of all companies consented to boycott requests. Since the publication of the corporate names, there has been change: only sixty percent of all firms continue to comply. Of course, the term "compliance" is a loaded one: as ex-Commerce Secretary Elliot Richardson noted, it may "involve nothing more than a company saying it is not doing what it had never done and never intended to do."

Jewish interests have tried to introduce antiboycott legislation for several years. They had some success with the Tax Reform Act of 1976: companies that do comply with the Arab boycott stand to lose a portion of the foreign tax credit, lose tax deferral on overseas earnings and benefits accruing to their Domestic International Sales Corporation (DISC), and receive nominal fines. While these provisions may have cost some companies tax credits, they are unlikely to deter them from the lucrative Middle East markets.

Finally, in the spring of 1977, Congress passed a bill that prohibited American corporations from complying with the Arab boycott against Israel at the secondary and tertiary levels. The bill was hammered out between Jewish defense agencies and the Business Council, a prestigious, high-powered big business organization headed by DuPont's chairman, Irving Shapiro. The bill prohibited companies from complying with the Arab boycott if compliance meant discrimination against another American corporation on the basis of race, religion, sex, or nationality. There are a number of large loopholes and exemptions: Arab states can make "unilateral selections" of goods, that is, ask the prime contractor to provide materials from specific subcontractors. So in that sense, the Arab blacklist is still very much alive. However, the act requires public disclosure of boycott requests and acts of compliance.

The knotty problems of the boycott have moved from the executive to the legislative branch of government, and finally to the judiciary. The Department of Justice brought a major antitrust suit against Bechtel Corporation, a construction company with projects in seven Arab countries. Bechtel did not deny complying with the boycott since there was nothing illegal in that. But Bechtel did deny that it acted in restraint of trade — the heart of an antitrust suit — with a legal conundrum of the first order. Bechtel responded that it could not be charged with restraining competition since the goods and services of the blacklisted firms would not be allowed into the Arab countries in any event. You cannot very well restrain what would never occur in the first place. Thus the Justice Department was guilty of illegally broadening the boycott issue from an economic one in domestic trade to one embracing foreign and political boycotts. Moreover, Bechtel went on to point out that it was doing nothing more than following the same policies as the United States Army Corps of Engineers and the United States Geological Survey when they worked abroad or contracted with nonboycotted companies.

The Bechtel case was something of an embarrassment for the government. Henry Kissinger, then Secretary of State, tried to intervene with Attorney General Levi since he thought the Arabs would interpret the action as a deliberate policy shift of the government, and that it might have "an adverse effect on the peacemaking process." However, the Bechtel case was not an example of policy decision: it was an indication of how split Washington remains over the boycott. In fact, there was no more consistency on the boycott issue than there was a unified policy on energy.

While Washington wants the Arab business, it does not want to alienate American Jews or appear to be kowtowing to foreign interests that, however friendly, are enemies of Israel.

Bechtel and the Department of Justice moved to settle the highly sensitive case in a consent agreement, but the accord did not resolve the underlying issue. Bechtel agreed to stop "what it had never done and never intended to do." The company claimed it "violated no laws and had not discriminated." The Justice Department, even though it originally charged Bechtel with "a conspiracy to refrain from dealing with persons or companies on the

Arab blacklist," was content to work out a procedure to allow Bechtel to deal with Arab trade.

The consent agreement barred Bechtel from discriminating in choosing subcontractors — they couldn't use a blacklist to make selections. The Justice Department hoped that the agreement, though not binding on any other company, would be used by them as a guide in dealing with Arab states.

Naturally, there is a way out for American firms caught between the rock and the hard place. Should the Arab country specifically and unilaterally select a subcontractor from which Bechtel would procure goods and services, the construction firm would be allowed to proceed and would not be guilty of conspiracy. Moreover, contracts signed outside the United States would be allowed to stand if they contained boycott provisions, though Bechtel would not conduct itself in any fashion to violate the consent agreement.

It was, in short, something of a Mexican standoff. At the center of the matter is the question of legal jurisdiction: whether Arab rulers will control the terms of trade within the United States (as well as abroad for American companies), or whether Washington will make the rules for American citizens conducting American business. For the most part, Washington provides little leadership. A number of states have passed antiboycott laws, though their implementation seems doubtful since states have neither the know-how nor the jurisdiction to legislate in matters of foreign commerce. The boycott dilemma puts corporations squarely in a no-win position. If they refuse to adhere, they lose business. If they comply, they may face retaliation, fines, and governmental law suits. It is a quandary most businesses could do without, but with the petrodollar pool having reached gargantuan proportions, the temptation to adhere to the boycott grows proportionately.

Arab trade accelerated in the last few years to the point where the United States sells over $7 billion of nonmilitary goods annually, and an almost equal amount of military material. By contrast, Israel buys about $1.5 billion of American goods. Considering the fact that each billion dollars of sales accounts for forty thousand to seventy thousand jobs, the pressure to maintain and expand that trade is considerable in an economy that has had substantial unemployment and plant underutilization.

Finally, due to the cost of oil, the United States has a substantial trade deficit with the Middle East. There is a difference of $5 billion between what the United States buys from, and sells to, the Arab states. Even though these sales to the Middle East are in excess of $12 billion, they are only thirteen percent of Arab imports. There is obviously room to expand. Until the OPEC cartel is broken, every administration will try to close the trade deficit by increasing American exports. The only question that remains is whether they will do it by conforming to the Arab boycott at the expense of Jews or by opposing the boycott, asserting the principles of free trade.

## Jewish Money v. Arab Money

The world has not seen a shift in wealth, like the new Arab oil wealth, since Europeans raided the Spanish Main. The transfer of so much money may well be the single most important geopolitical fact in the second half of the twentieth century. OPEC did more than simply raise the price of oil: it gave the producing nations a major say in determining production levels through participation agreements and, in some cases, through nationalization of the local oil companies' assets. OPEC nations at one time controlled over four-fifths of the oil traded in world markets.

From 1974 to 1981, these states accumulated surplus, which reached a peak of $116 billion in 1980. Major conservation efforts in the West created a glut of oil and a subsequent softening of prices in the face of reduced production due to the Iraq-Iran war. The vast financial power of OPEC — its petrodollar surplus — appears to be diminishing as the thirteen-state members are having trouble keeping revenues equal to expenditures. Whether OPEC will be running a deficit in the 1980s is impossible to say, but some countries — Venezuela, Nigeria, Indonesia, and Libya — are spending virtually all of their income on extraordinary development plans.

To one degree or another, the development plans are concerned with infrastructure, the foundation of any modern society: port facilities, airports, bridges, cement plants, aluminum smelters, roads, utilities, transportation facilities, schools, hospitals, housing, and factories. Most of the individual projects cost half a billion or a billion dollars, while some of the largest are budgeted for $3 billion or $5 billion, though in a few cases they will exceed their projections by three-, four-, or five-fold.

No doubt some of the development works are wasteful — conspicuous consumption on a grand scale. One form of conspicuous consumption, the acquisition of armaments, is being consciously indulged in. Since 1973, OPEC countries have spent in excess of $10 billion for everything from F-14 and F-16 fighter planes to the latest missiles to shoot them down, plus a whole range of electronic weaponry.

The United States had pledged to sell a minimum of $15 billion of military hardware to Middle Eastern nations in the period before 1982. And that pledge predated the sale of five AWAC reconnaissance planes for $8.5 billion to Saudi Arabia. The Saudis have been buying $2.5 billion of material from the United States annually.

Nevertheless, with all of the massive funds that have accrued to the Middle Eastern exchequers, one critical institution is still absent from the Arab world — an Arab capital market. Even with multibillion dollar surpluses, it remains true that "the Arab capital market is where the money is, not where the Arabs are."

The Arab world has only slowly developed its domestic money market, preferring to concentrate on the most obvious form of international banking: syndicate lending where the underwriting participants are listed in a plain advertisement, a "tombstone," in the financial pages. Outside of these participations, there is relatively little unity in financial organizations and the Arab Monetary Fund is not a prominent force. In brief, concerted financial power has thus far eluded the Arabs. The *Economist* noted that "Arab banking has been stunted by serious constraints. For lack of professional skills and infrastructure in the region . . . [it has relied on] 'tombstone machismo'."

From the beginning of the new oil monies, Europe has been the major recipient of OPEC funds. The Arabs plunged into the Eurobond market, bringing out a number of issues managed or comanaged by Arab institutions for borrowers, often Arab, and frequently denominated in Arab currencies.

In the first flush of enthusiasm, Arabs presumed that they could oust some of the older American and European banking houses, especially the Jewish ones. After all, oil revenues would give them a huge advantage, a step-up on the rest of the world as far as supplying capital goes. They would dictate the terms of their participation in underwritings. And many financial institutions started to curry favor with Arab ministers. "It's like plugging into Eldorado," one banker remarked.

Precisely why the Arab governments wished to excommunicate the investment banks with Jewish connections is not clear. These banks had long been on the blacklist, but the Arab states continued to do business with them. Perhaps they thought that the time had come when they could do without them. Conceivably, it was another gesture in the Arab-Israel cold war. Kuwait developed a list of international investment banks that were, in the words of the *Wall Street Journal*, "Jewish-owned, Jewish-controlled, or Jewish-linked . . . [and] have in some way given aid or comfort to Israel." Of a dozen or so banks, N. M. Rothschild & Sons, S. G. Warburg & Company, and Lazard Freres were the most prominent, but there were other banks in Belgium, France, Switzerland, and Germany as well, in which Jews held prominent positions. The Kuwait financial institutions applied pressure to force these banks out of international underwriting syndicates. After all, Kuwait had placed $1 billion dollars in long-term foreign investments in the first year of high oil revenues. With growing financial muscle, Kuwait was no longer simply a participant, but a manager or comanager in the underwritings.

The muscle flexing started in France late in 1974, when Jewish banks were asked to step aside in the underwriting of a French highway. Two subsequent issues — one for Air France and one for a government utility on the Rhone — also found Lazard and Rothschild persona non grata though they would have normally taken part in such financing. In both cases, the pool or syndicate managers were French banks and Arab banks. The Arabs contended that as comanagers they would be violating the boycott and the law of their respective states if they signed a contract with boycotted banks. After all, these banks had been on the blacklist for many years. When the Arab banks attempted the same tactic in Germany, the Germans, who were adamantly against the boycott, rejected the Arab posture. In England, they met with partial success, as an old and respected merchant banking house, Kleinwort, Benson excluded two Jewish banks from the underwriting of a Japanese firm, using Libyan and Kuwait banks in their stead.

In the United States, the Arabs were to join with Merrill, Lynch, Pierce, Fenner, and Smith in underwriting an issue for Volvo and one for the Mexican government, but pulled out when Merrill Lynch refused to dump the Jewish members of the syndicate.

The French incident was particularly embarrassing because both the syndicate organizers (the banks) and the recipients of the financing (the companies) were state-owned institutions. Thus, it appeared that the French government had given in to boycott demands. A spokesman for the French Bankers' Association stated that it was "a matter of official policy." "It's an extremely uncomfortable position."

It recalled a notorious comment of one of the Immortals of the French Academy: "I am not an anti-Semite, but I will never prevent anyone from becoming one." Perhaps the posture was no surprise since government policies were tilted against Israel from the time of the Six Day War: whether it was an embargo of ships and arms for Israel or the release of Arab terrorists, the French capitulated to Arab pressures. But then, it must be remembered that France pumps precious little domestic oil.

A compromise was eventually reached: Arab and Jewish banks can now appear in the same advertising notice of underwriting. Just as the Arabs resolved the problem of buying armaments from boycotted companies by dealing with the Department of Defense, they would do the syndicate financing with Jewish banks provided that, as comanagers, they only contracted with a nonboycotted bank, which acted as a front, effectively insulating them from the Jewish banks.

The "pro-Israeli" banks are so dominant in the field that they "cannot realistically be avoided because of their sheer size," according to *Business Week*. The net result of this financial boycott is hard to measure with precision, but it appears to have had only minimal impact. Kuwait, the Arab nation most involved in investing abroad, has entered into a wide assortment of deals, from real estate development to dental and automobile companies. The Kuwait dinar is sought after but it is not yet a "hard currency," and while Kuwait investment institutions are active, they are not a substantial factor in the Western investment banking community. A few Jewish banks have lost some business, but the demand for their services apparently exceeds the demand for Arab money. The international investment business is tightly knit: one in which business is done either with everyone or no one. Attempts to place artificial, irrational, and prejudicial obstacles in its path have not so much backfired as petered out. Money, Vespasian observed, doesn't smell. The Arabs are finding out that it also has no political ideology or religious beliefs.

The Jewish banks, apparently, can take care of themselves in their own bailiwick, at least when it comes to supplying a profitable and significant service. A combination of competitiveness, reputation, experience, and an adroit feel for the market, has ensconced them in the international banking system. They may not have vast sources of capital — the largest Jewish banking house, Salomon Brothers (now a subsidiary of Phibro Corporation) is capitalized at $231 million — but they have access to funds of a far larger order. So while they have access to massive funds, this does not necessarily translate into financial power on the government level. The boycott is a case in point.

Arthur F. Burns, former chairman of the Federal Reserve System and a Jew, issued a strong memorandum at the end of 1975 as Arab boycott pressures increased. In 1974, the Arabs had requested that only a couple of dozen firms comply, but by 1975, the number was greater than five hundred. To counteract the coercion, Burns wrote to all member banks of the Federal Reserve that "participation of a United States bank, even passively, in efforts by foreign nations to effect boycotts against other foreign countries friendly to the United States is, in the board's view, a misuse of the privileges and benefits conferred upon banking institutions." Burns' letter was an administrative outlawing of boycott compliance. Immediately, counterpressures from the banks built, and by the beginning of 1976 Burns found himself isolated. Neither the White House nor the State, Treasury, or Commerce Departments were willing to go as far as Burns. A second letter from Burns emphasized that the previous letter "was not intended to create a new legal obligation for banks." He had retreated. If there was to be government action against boycott compliance it would have to come from Congress.

For the far left, far right, anti-Semites, and those who ardently believe in the conspiratorial nature of Zionism, Dr. Burns was proof that Jews are out to control the world — what better position to do it from than as chief central banker in the free world. To those who espouse that conspiracy theory, Burns represented that clique of "international Jewish financiers" one hears so much about — a paranoid view, especially considering his views on OPEC. Burns is a conservative economist, who served Eisenhower and Nixon. He is a student of business cycles and a one-time professor of economics at Columbia University. Though he implemented Nixon's ill-founded wage and price freeze because he complained that "the rules of economics are not working quite the way they used to," his faith is in the free market.

Thus, he was at odds with then Secretary of State Henry Kissinger on how to deal with OPEC. Burns saw that the shift in financial power to the Middle East could be disastrous. America should crack the oil cartel by exerting maximum pressure — by expanding domestic and offshore oil exploration, imposing stiff conservation measures, and bringing extramonetary pressures to bear. Burns would have pursued a more aggressive attack against the rise in oil prices.

In a sense, he lost the argument to Kissinger and his policy of detente. The administration, shaken by Vietnam and impotent because of Watergate, cooperated with OPEC. Troubled by the massive surpluses destined for Arab treasuries and alarmed by bankers who thought that the petrodollar pool would destabilize the international payments mechanism, Kissinger opted for a policy of cooperation. He would make the world safe for OPEC by having the cartel and the oil-importing nations set a regulated price, which would amount to putting a floor under the price of oil. Kissinger advocated that a "safety net" fund of $25 billion be set up to aid banks in the event that Arab surpluses were suddenly withdrawn. The fund never materialized and Kissinger's solution has left money and power flowing to the Arabs in the Middle East.

It is debatable whether Burns's approach would have lowered prices peacefully. But the confrontation of the two most powerful Jews in the American government simply goes to show — if proof is needed — that influential and policy-making Jews are as much at odds over what is proper policy for America, and for Jews, as anyone else. The conspiracy of Jews in high office, of "the Jewish international banker," is a figment of imagination.

## International Conspiracies

While there is no real evidence of an international conspiracy of Jewish bankers, some Jews in banking have conspired. The money game holds a fascination for Jews that some might say is equivalent to sex to the French, food to the Chinese, and power to the politician. And since the Diaspora scattered Jewish communities, their financial concerns have always had an international flavor. But some Jews have overstepped the bounds of morality and law in the realm of international banking. It is not hard to understand why.

International finance is an area that requires something of a split personality: one has to be at home in at least a few languages and a number of currencies. The dominant firm in the United States in the field of foreign securities is Carl Marks, and many of the international arbitrageurs are Jewish. Part of the great appeal of international finance is perhaps that it is the last refuge of unfettered capitalism. National states regulate their currencies, their equities and debt markets, money supplies, and interest rates — in brief, they control, tax, and rule every aspect of their monetary existence.

But in their monetary relationships with each other, nation-states are circumspect, suspicious, cynical and oftentimes downright hostile. Currencies, to paraphrase an eminent statesman, don't have friends, only interests. International monetary relations is a jungle of conflicting claims, overlapping jurisdictions, and vast uncharted ground and most financial authority stops at the border. From "dirty" floating (the manipulation of a country's currency by its central bank) to offshore funds, tax havens, and foreign shelters, international finance is relatively unregulated — perhaps unregulatable. What is monetary vice in one country is fiscal virtue in another. Gold hoarding is illegal in some countries, but in others it is a sign of thrift. For a strong currency, each nation wants a favorable balance of payments — a mercantilistic sentiment akin to the belief that everyone can win in the Saturday night poker game.

In response to the financial restrictions of nation-states, a supranational market developed for dollars — dollars (though occasionally pounds, marks, francs, and yen) that are either owned by non-Americans or by Americans outside the jurisdiction of American monetary authorities. International banks make loans and underwrite issues in these Eurodollars, an expatriate currency not subject to the credit system of any country. Free from governmental intervention, since the dollars were beyond the reach of the Federal Reserve and the borrower was often an offshore or multinational corporation beyond the reach of any agency, the Eurodollar market reacted freely to purely commercial conditions and to the interplay of market forces.

Expanding international trade, the rise of multinational corporations, the financing of capital-short companies and new ventures around the world all called for funds. At the same time, national taxation programs became more onerous — some said confiscatory — while inflation depreciated the value of currencies. Individuals, syndicates, corporations, and banks all tried to protect themselves by buying foreign assets or by moving their funds to more secure places with higher interest rates. The era of "hot money" and tax havens was born — legitimate and illegitimate funds poured over national boundaries looking for stability, high return, and secrecy.

This freedom to manipulate, to make deals, and to broker attracted not only Jews, but other freelance financiers. The Jews involved in these affairs had a lot of company from non-Jews: Sidona of Italy, Vesco in the United States, Tanaka in Japan,

Prince Bernhard in the Netherlands, and a host of German, English, and Swiss banks.

Bernhard Cornfeld was the most prominent Jew to take advantage of the disparity of national laws in the search for financial security through his mutual fund complex, Investors Overseas Services (IOS). Cornfeld, a one-time Coney Island peddler, social worker, and salesman, created a Swiss-based pyramid through his Fund of Funds. In buying a share of his investment company, the purchaser was, indirectly, buying a fractional share of other investment companies, which in turn were invested in securities — mostly American. It was the kind of operation that the Securities and Exchange Commission frowned upon, but the Swiss were happy to accommodate, provided it had the air of respectability and violated no Swiss laws. The core service of IOS was not money management, though at its height it had access to top economic and financial analysts. What attracted investors of $2 billion, from a hundred different countries, was Cornfeld's salesmen, all familiar with the niceties of currency smuggling.

One salesman recalled that he knew forty-seven different ways to take money out of the Congo. IOS was not built on its track record, though for a while it was fair, but on its talent for evading currency controls. Cornfeld's fall from financial grace was due in a narrow sense to the downward revaluation of some underlying Canadian assets. When this became known that there was less there than met the eye, the first Nixon bear market and soaring redemptions brought down the company. In a more general sense, Cornfeld, in his brief career, had managed to alienate fiscal authorities from Argentina to Zaire, not to mention the SEC and the gentlemen along the Banhofstrasse in Zurich. His offbeat lifestyle — castles, sexy ladies, and other ostentatious behavior (he had pastrami sandwiches flown in from New York for his mother) — sullied the image that Swiss money centers hoped to project.

"They went out to cut his heart out," remarked the late S. J. Rundt, a financial consultant of Swiss ancestry. And they did, eventually jailing Cornfeld for over a year before he could make bail.

There was nothing specifically Jewish in Cornfeld's actions, though he did attract a substantial Jewish following. Jewish financiers are blessed (or cursed?) with a mystique of high finance: after all, the string of prominent Jewish financial wizards is long.

So while Cornfeld attracted some innocent investors with his audacity, cunning, and novelty, he also attracted other far less innocent figures in the world of business and finance. One of the less innocent relationships was between Cornfeld and a Genevan Jewish neighbor, Tibor Pinchas Rosenbaum, a Hungarian refugee, a Swiss citizen, and president of a small private bank, the International Credit Bank. Rosenbaum was well known to the Israeli establishment and something of an influence in Zionist circles. He had been active in the Hungarian underground during World War II, rescuing Jews and aiding their escape. After the war, he continued with resettlement and immigration work for the Jewish Agency. When the state of Israel was founded, he started a Swiss-Israel trading company, maintaining and strengthening his membership in the World Jewish Congress and the Mizrachi Movement, a religious Zionist group. As a nonpracticing rabbi, and the son of a rabbi, he was drawn to the Mizrachi organization and became influential in its political arm, the National Religious Party of Israel. Through the use of *protectzia* (the Israeli equivalent of influence peddling), his company obtained hospital contracts that were later involved in the indictment and imprisonment of the Israeli Minister of Health.

Rosenbaum continued his wartime habits, building the International Credit Bank on clandestine deposits of undeclared funds from French Jews and the United States Mafia, channeled through his offices in the Bahamas. The International Credit Bank was used to funnel overseas money into Cornfeld's IOS complex. When Cornfeld finally went to jail, Rosenbaum put up a portion of his bail.

Rosenbaum had managed to build a small but influential Jewish bank: in 1973 it had $250 million in assets. Besides a number of European deals, he provided financial services for Israel. At one point, Defense Minister Shimon Peres reportedly needed $7 million within twenty-four hours. He turned to Rosenbaum who, like Disraeli turning to Rothschild to finance the purchase of the Suez

Canal, produced the funds. Rosenbaum received, unsolicited, a substantial commission of $500,000. Rosenbaum's activities were also known to the Arab Boycott Office and his bank was on the blacklist.

The International Credit Bank took an active role in financing some Israeli companies, and Rosenbaum joined the board of the Israel Corporation, a $100 million investment company founded by a private group of Jewish millionaires, with Baron Edmond de Rothschild, steward of the French branch of the family, as chairman of the board. The Paris Rothschild was the largest investor, though Rosenbaum was on the board since he had contributed $1 million by way of a Liechtenstein trust. Between 1970 and 1974, the Israel Corporation was run by Michael Tzur, an attorney, one-time chairman of Zim Lines, and a past director-general of Israel's Ministry of Commerce and Industry. The stage was set for Israel's biggest financial scandal.

Rosenbaum and Tzur entered into a series of self-serving schemes that involved all the elements of white-collar crime: bribery, fraud, larceny, and illegal currency transactions. In essence, Tzur took funds from the Israel Corporation and some of its portfolio companies and placed them on deposit in Rosenbaum's bank without the knowledge of the companies or individuals involved. The total swindle involved $20 million, with the actual losses close to half that figure. Rosenbaum, in turn, placed the funds in Liechtenstein trusts, which are perhaps more legally impregnable than Swiss ones, and used the money in some of his investment schemes. Tzur promised investors a reasonably high rate of return — 6.5 percent — while he was actually receiving 8 percent, skimming the difference. Other monies from large-scale investors, mostly German, were headed for Israel but were stopped short in Switzerland.

The scam might have continued longer, but the long arm of the Rothschilds caught up with Rosenbaum and Tzur. Famous for his access to financial intelligence, the Baron was informed by a German Banker that there were rumors circulating that International Credit Bank was in trouble and that the $20 million Israel Corporation deposits were in danger. He found that the Israeli government and the deputy director of the Israel Corporation knew nothing of the enormous investment. Rothschild pressed for a thorough investigation, promising to curtail his philanthropic activities in Israel if a full and thorough examination wasn't made. Tzur, who was indicted on fourteen charges, pleaded guilty, and was sentenced to fifteen years in jail out of a possible 210. The judges found that his actions had "damaged the credibility of Israeli companies abroad and shaken the confidence of potential investors . . . the hand of the law will reach such swindlers and mete out the justice they deserve." In the meantime, Rothschild was reaching out to Geneva, where he pressed criminal charges against Rosenbaum, who was forced to close his bank after depositors caused a run on it. The Swiss imprisoned him, but he was freed on $2 million bail, the highest in Swiss history. It is not known whether Cornfeld returned the favor and helped with the bail money.

The last Jewish bank to go down in a maze of international intrigue was the American Bank and Trust Company of New York City. Hardly a major bank — it was capitalized at $25 million with deposits of $229 million — but one with an unusual set of connections in the New York political scene and among the Mexican- and American-Jewish establishments. Its failure constituted the fourth largest bankruptcy in American banking history.

The history of American Bank and Trust is riddled with curious connections, both in Mexico and in the Middle East. Originally established by a Mexican bank in 1929, it changed both its name (to American Trust) and its management in 1949 at the urging of the New York State Banking Department. The state of Israel subsequently started a bank in Switzerland, the Swiss-Israeli Trade Bank, and through it, eventually took control of American Trust in 1963, changing its name to American Bank and Trust Company. Israelis, including the Minister of Finance, encouraged prominent American Jews and businessmen to use the bank. Some of the more noteworthy men to subsequently become associated with the bank were Abraham Feinberg, a New York businessman active in Democratic party politics and an important fundraiser for Israeli causes; Philip Klutznick, a wealthy Chicagoan (and later Secretary of Commerce in the Carter Administration), another powerful Israeli fundraiser, and honorary president of B'nai Brith; the late Vincent Albano, Republican party leader in New York City and close associate of Nelson Rockefeller; Howard Samuels, New York State businessman and Off Track Betting Commissioner; Arthur G. Cohen, head of Arlen Realty and Development; Mead Esposito and Patrick Cunningham, the respective chiefs of the Brooklyn and Bronx Democratic Parties; and finally, Mayor Abraham Beame, between terms as City Controller, who was chairman of the bank's finance committee and a director. This reliance on political clout paid off, for *protectzia* works just as well on this side of the world: at one point, ten percent of the bank's deposits came from city and state agencies — remarkable for a small bank.

In the late sixties, Israel sold her interest in the Swiss bank to Jose Klein. Reputedly one of the richest men in Chile, with holdings in transportation, shipping, and minerals, Klein became the largest owner of American Bank and Trust. For the next half-dozen years, the bank's assets were placed in high-risk, poorly collateralized loans, dubious investments, and speculative acquisitions. Not only were loans made in excess of their legal limit, but they were made to companies in which the bank's officers had personal equity investments. New York State banking authorities and the Federal Deposit Insurance Corporation, which had the bank under observation for many years should have moved to close the bank, but were perhaps thwarted because of political considerations. Meanwhile, the bank maintained its original Mexican connection — Mexican Jews were solicited for funds by an Israeli, who had also been a major salesman of Israeli government bonds for many years.

It is not hard to convince Jews that some of their assets should reside in another country. They are aware of their personal and financial security — in fact it may be no exaggeration to say that their history has created in them a hypersensitivity to insecurity, economic change, and political uncertainty. Presumably, any people who are harassed and persecuted for a couple of thousand years will develop this mentality, but there is little question that Jews have developed it as a survival technique, almost a law of natural selection. If this awareness is not quite Darwinian, it is surely what the French call a *deformation professionelle*. The profession, of course, is Judaism.

In practice, this heightened sensitivity is a double-edged sword, for it brings about gullibility and greed simultaneously. Again, gullibility and greed are not solely Jewish characteristics, but all too often they are evoked by friends and associates who prey on Jewish insecurity. Such was the case in the Klein affair. It was not so much a question of escaping domestic taxation or inflation, the appeal of a profitable foreign investment, or shrewd money management abroad — it was that visceral fear that "It" might happen here. Of course, the "It" is a wave of anti-Semitism, which would make the tenure of Jews precarious regardless of how old their ties are to their native land. It was the kind of fear that enabled Rosenbaum to successfully solicit funds in France among Jews for his Swiss International Credit Bank and for American Bank and Trust to tap the Jewish communities in Latin America. Naturally, the anti-Zionist vote by Mexico in the United Nations in the fall of 1975 was precisely the type of move to send Jews scurrying to find foreign financial havens. Perhaps as much as $20 million was placed in American Bank and Trust and maybe an equal amount from other South American countries.

About this time, Jose Klein sold his interest in American Bank and Trust to a fellow South American and another mysterious Jewish financier, David Graiver, for $14 million. David Graiver was the son of an Argentine Jewish family that had originally migrated from Poland. During the first Perón regime, Juan Graiver amassed a fortune of $40 million to $50 million in real estate, ranching, and banking. His son, David, played a role in the resurrection of Perón the second time around and was later purportedly involved in washing funds for the late dictator's wife through one of his banks. With Argentina politically unstable and the economy failing, the Graivers sought to place some of their assets overseas.

They established a small bank in Brussels, bought a small bank in New York, and Klein's interest in American Bank and Trust. From a Fifth Avenue apartment, Graiver made the rounds to politically potent New Yorkers, hoping that with their assistance he would pass muster with the State Banking Department. Introduced about town by Theodore Kheel, the attorney and labor mediator, Graiver eventually was able to get letters vouchsafing his banking credentials and character from one ex-Secretary of State, William P. Rogers, one exchairman of Citibank, George Moore, and other New Yorkers. Some of these letter-writers consequently became involved with Graiver, much to their dismay.

Once in control of American Bank and Trust, he moved its headquarters to the regal Olympic Towers and entered into a series of self-serving deals: loans to his private corporations; the purchase of certificates of deposit from his family banks in Argentina, Brussels, and Tel Aviv; deposits to dummy accounts; and kited checks. By carefully timing deposits and withdrawals to obfuscate or circumvent the regulatory agencies, he manged to relieve American Bank and Trust of millions of dollars of deposits. The swindle came unglued when a bank employee, who was a former bank examiner, realized that the underlying collateral in Graiver's other banks was insubstantial, too often worthless commercial paper in one of the family's phony companies. Graiver's deals were all devices for looting the bank, but he was obliged to pay off Klein on the sale of the controlling interest in American Bank and Trust.

With the pressure mounting, David Graiver chartered a jet to fly him to Acapulco for a weekend in August, 1976. It was a common enough trip for him, but that weekend, he never arrived. His plane was found on the side of a Mexican mountain thoroughly destroyed, and the three occupants incinerated. The crash and supposed death of Graiver remains shrouded in mystery. Everything from the ownership of the plane — apparently leased from a tax-shelter group of which the Cohen brothers of Arlen Realty were a part (the Cohen brothers were also involved both in managing the bank and borrowing from it) — to the nature of the accident (the plane might have exploded in mid-air from a bomb) elicits questions.

Shortly after Graiver's death or disappearance, American Bank and Trust was closed on the grounds that it was "unsafe and unsound." The move was precipitated by the prior failure of the Belgian bank. The New York State Banking Department closed the bank and the Federal Deposit Insurance Corporation immediately auctioned the assets to the highest bidder. Perhaps it was no surprise, but the bank ended up back in Israeli hands — the winning bid of $12.6 million came from Israel's Bank Leumi. In fact, Bank Leumi paid twice as much as the nearest bidder even though it had a branch within shouting distance, because it had "our type of customers." American Bank and Trust had been bilked of nearly $50 million by the Graivers, and the Brussels bank lost $40 million. While the depositors were covered by the Federal Deposit Insurance Corporation, the failure had hurt a number of Jewish communities in Mexico and Latin America. The bank had aggressively sold its commercial paper and certificates of deposit to unwary Jews, who were forced to absorb large losses as these investments were not covered by the federal insurance.

# 7. Crime: Unzer Shtik (Our Thing)

A Jewish gun is a ballpoint pen.
— Anon.

We should notice how easily men are corrupted and become wicked, although originally good and well-educated.
— Nicolo Machiavelli, *The Discourses*

## La Kosher Nostra

At the turn of the century, a middle-aged, bearded Jew stepped off the ferry at Ellis Island without a job, a talent, or a vocation. He had made his way in this world by his wits, a trait that stood him in good company with a number of immigrants. He was not the first *Luftmensh,* someone who makes something out of nothing, nor was he destined to be the last. After settling in with relatives on the Lower East Side, he started to pursue his livelihood. Tuning in on the miseries of the ghetto, he would visit the tenements of neighbors with illnesses. But before ringing, he would take apart the *mezuzah* (a case which houses scrolls with verses from Deuteronomy), which was tightly affixed to the door jamb. With a pin or a nail, he would repeatedly pierce the parchment and then reassemble the housing. He would then call upon the household and commiserate with it over the sickness. During the conversation, he would offhandedly inquire if they had recently checked their mezuzah, implying the scrolls' condition might have something to do with the disease. Of course they had not. In the general confusion upon finding the damage, he would volunteer that he represented a religious organization that just happened to have a selection of door scrolls. With the sale consummated, he was off to another diphtheria-ridden household. Not a terribly sophisticated scam, but they were not terribly sophisticated times.

Of all the areas of Jewish enterprise, none has been so overlooked as the field of crime. And it isn't because of a lack of Jewish criminality. For an introspective people, this oversight is significant. It is as if Jewish crime did not exist, an unsavory skeleton best left in the family closet. Naturally, it goes against the grain to think that among all the other Jewish-American prototypes — doctor, lawyer, businessman, financier, artist, musician, scientist, and academician — there is also a Jewish gangster. Recent circumstances have forced this unpleasant recognition, for Jewish criminals are again in the limelight.

It might be expected that any group in the vanguard of other human endeavors would lead in the activities of the underworld as well. But the sociopathology of Jews is not an acceptable notion since it runs counter to both religious precepts and preconceived ideas that Jews have of themselves.

The standard images run something like this: first, Jewish tradition stressed the study of Written and Oral Law. An important tenet of Judaism is respect and obedience for the law, whether religious or temporal. The mezuzah is on the door post to remind Jews to obey the Laws, both in and out of the house.

Second, the Jewish reverence for learning lavished prestige on the rabbi — the teacher, and the wise man. In America, this prestige was transferred to secular learning, where schooling was expected, intellectuality praised, and degrees and advanced degrees sought. The result was a disproportionate number of professionals. In a society that correlates education with job status and degrees with earning power, the Jews had it made.

Third, since Jewish values account for their economic achievements, it would seem that crime would be an unlikely pursuit. In the words of one sociologist, "They respond psychologically to extrinsic and intrinsic work rewards." Hence, there is no need to steal or rob since normal Jewish upbringing establishes the belief that whatever is desired will eventually be provided.

Fourth, for Jews, crime was always someone else's doing — especially the Irish, Italians, blacks, Hispanics, the poor, or the unemployed.

The attitude toward education, achievement, and social adaptability differs considerably from ethnic group to ethnic group, especially in first- or second-generation Americans. The Italians, for example, whose crime rate from the 1930s to the 1950s was higher than American norms, had a far different tradition, especially if they were from Sicily or other depressed areas of Italy. Children were looked upon almost in feudal terms, as assets to help with farm work. Education was thought to be a deprivation of manpower, since the subjects taught — whether classical Italian, geometry, or geography — had little to do with everyday life. Education was thought to be a ploy by the government to subvert family power, perhaps even to get the families off the land.

Consequently, Italian immigrants distrusted the American school system. It took them a while to realize that education was the key to success in America. Before they understood, parents saw little reason to encourage schooling and the results were predictable: high truancy, early dropout, poor grades, and high delinquency and crime rates. By 1930, Italian youth in New York City had delinquency rates almost twice as high as other white youths. The crime rate among Jews, in contrast, was roughly half of what might have been expected.

Thus the unquestioned wisdom has held that good, well-raised, religiously indoctrinated Jews do not become criminals. It's not the kind of life for a "nice Jewish boy." Since the legitimate lines of advancement in America are open, Jewish ambition has been channeled into socially acceptable behavior. In the last analysis, Jews earnestly believe that "American society can learn from its Jewish subculture that placing a high valuation upon intellectual achievement is an indirect approach to crime prevention."

Or is it? To some, it becomes apparent that ambition in the form of intellectual achievement and crookedness are not antithetical, that a good middle class upbringing does not guarantee that one will be law-abiding. Increasingly, in the crimes in which money really counts, the criminals are well born and well educated, hardly suffering from "status frustration," and, often, not even suffering from a lack of money. And increasingly, Jews are constituting a significant portion of the underworld.

While contemporary Jews believe that crime is someone else's problem, Jewish criminality is well established. Perhaps the refusal of the Jewish establishment to examine dispassionately the record of Jewish-American crime "reveals a fundamental lack of security and self-respect." Jewish criminals, however, cut out a niche for themselves quite a while ago, whether or not other Jews wish to recognize their achievements. The list of prominent villains is long and the aliases are intriguing: Louis "Lepke" Buchalter, Mickey Cohen, "Tootsie" Feinstein, Solly Gross, Jake Guzik, Phil "The Stick" Kovolick, Abe "Kid Twist" Relis, Arnold "The Brain" Rothstein, Benjamin "Bugsy" Siegel, and Maier Suchowljansky, a.k.a. Meyer Lansky.

For the most part, Jewish crime has followed the tradition of the Jewish people: it is verbal, intellectual, quasilegal, and nonviolent. From the beginning, Jewish criminal activity has mirrored the activities of legitimate business. While some Jews were involved in the seamy, violent forms of crime, especially the gang warfare of the Prohibition era, more Jews drifted to white-collar crime and to the economic organization of crime. They left the more vigorous bully work to the Italians, with whom they allied in their joint effort to make a name for themselves. In the 1920s, rum-running and manufacturing illegal liquor were the major underworld activities. However, smuggling drugs and diamonds, loan-sharking, betting, numbers, stock swindles, and securities fraud were also rackets.

Perhaps the most notorious Jewish criminal of that period was Arnold Rothstein. After fixing the 1919 World Series, Rothstein turned to smuggling whiskey across the Atlantic, but not before bribing the Long Island police and the Coast Guard commanders in the area. Rothstein retired before he was caught, and provided the financial backing and the political protection for his one-time bodyguard, Legs Diamond. Rothstein was murdered, but his two spiritual heirs, Dutch Schultz (nee Arthur Flegenheimer) and

Waxey Gordon (nee Irving Wexler), took over. Also around that time, Meyer Lansky and "Bugsy" Siegel were busy making their reputations as killers and hijackers.

In 1934, the criminals got together in an ecumenical congress, a clandestine gathering that became the National Crime Syndicate. It was Rothstein's vision to organize lawlessness on a regular, paying basis, and reduce intergang homicides. Organized by men of ethnic backgrounds, the syndicate was led by Luciano, Lepke, Lansky, and Siegel. Lansky, the chairman of the board, set up an organization to settle jurisdictional disputes.

Under Lanksy, crime was no longer a cottage industry of small, warring groups disposed to petty rackets and grand violence, but an elaborate corporation with subsidiaries and affiliates in gambling, prostitution, narcotics, industrial racketeering, bribery, and political corruption. Muscle was still used, and Lansky, the "little enforcer," knew when to apply it. But the wholesale slaughter that existed earlier was largely a thing of the past. Some observers mark the Lansky chairmanship as a maturation of American crime, a watershed. A contemporary, Al Capone, was a product of the era of guts, while Lansky was a forerunner of the era of brains. Capone didn't have a bank account; Lansky left a trail of paper. The former died from syphilis in jail; the latter retired with an officially reported net work of $300 million.

Lansky has been remarkably silent about his activities except in one or two interviews when it served his purposes. Isaac Babel's character, Benya Krik — The King — the head gangster in Odessa, was also a man of few words. "Benya says little, but what he says is tasty. He says little, and one would like him to say more."

Thus, what is known of Lansky is from other, not wholly disinterested sources — usually government intelligence agencies. As with Benya, Lansky was born in Russia on July 4th, 1902. Though small in stature — 5′ 4½ inches and 140 pounds — he started his career by stealing and customizing cars for thieves and then moved on to contract killing. He claims that he was not the head of the syndicate, that his only involvement was with gambling in Las Vegas, Miami, and Havana. Indeed, the only time Lansky was jailed was in 1953 for a few months on a gambling charge. During the 1930s he reputedly organized Jews to knock heads in the "Reich Valley," Manhattan's bund-dominated Yorkville. And during Israel's war of liberation he killed an arms exporter who was selling to the Arab countries. Lansky has contributed substantial funds from his gambling fortunes to Jewish causes, particularly the United Jewish Appeal. So while he has acknowledged knowing some underworld characters ("Who do you think comes to gambling casinos, Yeshiva students and rabbis?" he retorted), his connection with the syndicate is shadowy.

Lansky thought that the Mafia, though part of the syndicate, was quaint, with its blood oaths, violence, archaic honors, and parochial organization. However, the Mafia tolerated him because of the profits brought in by his National Crime Syndicate. Two German sociologists, Weber and Sombart, saw the Jews applying rational business principles in crime, making it more efficient. Lansky's management stressed accounting procedures, dummy organizations for tax evasion, and skimming of gambling revenues in otherwise legitimate organizations. He made crime systematic and efficient, a fact that did not escape notice of the Mafia. But not all branches of The Family were happy about it. One dissident, Albert Anastasia, voiced his disapproval when he wanted to muscle in on Lansky's Cuban casino. "You bastards have sold yourselves to the Jews. The traditions of the Honored Society have been forgotten. The old days were bad, maybe, but at least we could hold up our heads in pride. We had respect then; now we're a bunch of fucking businessmen." Anastasia, not a Harvard Business School graduate, missed the point of rational management, a fatal mistake for the old High Executioner of Murder Incorporated. He was killed in the Park Sheraton Hotel, the same hotel in which Arnold Rothstein retired from service a generation earlier.

Lansky's contribution during World War II apparently earned him the gratitude of the Justice Department. Operation Underworld kept the East Coast ports quiet, giving the authorities the chance to fight the war rather than domestic scoundrels. Again Babel caught the timbre of that symbiotic relationship: "Where do the police begin and where does Benya end?" "The police end where Benya begins," replied sensible folk.

Up to 1970, according to one crime reporter, Lansky had been "strangely immune to prosecution on the federal level." Though twice, federal agencies wanted to prosecute, both times the Justice Department declined.

In 1970 Lansky's fortune changed and the federal government indicted him for skimming revenues in Las Vegas. He was in Israel when the nonextraditable indictment was handed down. Immediately, the government canceled his passport. Israel denied an extension of his visa. Lansky then applied for Israeli citizenship under the Law of Return, a statute that is a cornerstone of the state. But Israel's Supreme Court ruled in 1972 that he "had operated within the framework of organized crime in the United States and had been closely connected with it." Lansky was ordered to leave: a psychological blow to a man who had, in his own eyes, done so much for Israel.

Lansky brought reason and order to crime, brought it to a point at which it paralleled American business in structure. He imitated free enterprise, delegated responsibility, and divided and administered markets. Perhaps it wasn't quite a mirror image, but it was an alternate life-style that was recognizable, understandable, and one that elicited some empathy. But most of all, equating big money with big crime was seductive to first- and second-generation Jews. They knew that there was money in crime.

Whether criminality is anomalous to a Jewish background is a debatable point. There are certainly criminals in Israel, a predominantly Jewish society. One Israeli criminologist estimates that perhaps as many as several hundred Israelis make their livings from robbery, burglary, prostitution, narcotics, gambling, smuggling, and protection. Indeed, the overall Israeli crime rate climbs nearly ten percent annually.

If Lansky started on the low road, some Jews started on the high road, managing to lose their ethical compasses as they went along. Two modern businessmen in particular reflected that ambivalence in the American business ethos — the striving for commercial success while skirting the edge of the acceptable and moral. Both considered themselves astute, shrewd, well connected, and influential, and were so considered by their peers. Both transgressed legal boundaries, however fractionally, and both crossed the line of acceptable behavior. Both considered themselves exemplary Jews — indeed, one was a rabbi and active in Jewish affairs, and the other involved with, and sought after, by the Jewish establishment. Both were substantial providers, good family men, and loyal if somewhat uncritical employers. Generally respected in the business and financial world, they were lone wolves and corporate raiders par excellence. Whether it was hubris or chutzpah, overreaching ended both men's careers at their apogees: one in jail, the other in suicide.

Louis E. Wolfson and Eli Black represent no one but themselves, yet they are typical of the first-generation Jew in the economic pressure-cooker. Perhaps it was more than coincidence, but both Wolfson and Black were brought low by transgressions that were either commonplace or accepted business practice.

## The Benign Deceit

Wolfson, the son of an immigrant junk dealer, was one of the financial whiz kids in the 1950s and 1960s. His wheeling and dealing had started earlier, though, when he was an undergraduate. A star member of the University of Georgia football team during the Depression, he demanded and received spending money of $100 a month to play when all the other players had to make do with $5.

Borrowing $10,000, Wolfson built a scrap iron yard into a highly profitable business. By the time he was twenty-eight, Wolfson had made his first million. In 1949 he took over the Capital Transit Company, a surface transportation system in Washington, D.C., for $2.1 million. Not long afterwards, he declared an increase in the dividend, a common enough practice, except in this case the dividends exceeded the company's earnings. In other words, he was raiding the corporate treasury. Congress was incensed at this particular form of free enterprise and chose not to renew the company's franchise. Wolfson sold his interest for nearly seven times what he originally paid — not exactly a case of *sic gloria transit mundi.*

Then Wolfson decided to try for a really big company —

Montgomery Ward & Company. Under the leadership of Sewell Avery, Montgomery Ward was sitting on almost $300 million in idle assets. Wolfson tried to acquire the company, but Avery was stubborn and Wolfson lost the proxy fight.

As Wolfson acquired interests in other companies (at one time he was the largest stockholder in American Motors), his main energies went into building Merritt-Chapman & Scott Corporation. Merritt-Chapman was considered by some financial observers to be the first of a new hybrid — the conglomerate — and Wolfson was its father. Eventually, the company was involved in shipbuilding, construction, chemicals, and moneylending. Though sales were in the neighborhood of half a billion dollars, the disparate elements never hung together and the company had an erratic track record. At the height of Merritt-Chapman's success, Wolfson was one of the highest paid executives in the United States, grossing over half a million dollars annually.

In all his acquisitions and trading, Wolfson had frequent brushes with the Securities and Exchange Commission (SEC), which went to court and obtained an injunction against false and misleading statements he had made in conjunction with the sale of his American Motors stock. Again the SEC went to court on similar grounds in relation to his trading in Merritt-Chapman's stock, and Wolfson was convicted of perjury and conspiracy to obstruct justice.

Wolfson's dealings were under continuous examination by one agency or another. At one point he complained that "no industrialist in America has been investigated by as many investigative committees as I have."

Finally, an indiscretion in trading the unregistered stock of Continental Enterprises Inc., a company that he controlled, landed him in a major confrontation with the SEC. The agency, faced with the growing volume of white-collar financial crime, was looking to set a precedent for the punishment of wayward financiers. Wolfson was a likely candidate: well known, respected, and a financial power with a high exposure.

In an unusual criminal indictment (it was perhaps the first time such an action had been placed in the criminal category), the

SEC charged that Wolfson was selling unregistered shares while Continental was issuing favorable press releases on an aerosol valve, Propel-Pak, that the company was licensing. In other words, he was producing bullish news and simultaneously profiting by it. Wolfson countered that the government was making a mountain out of a molehill, that it was a mere technical violation. Moreover, he was innocent since he was only acting on advice of his staff and consultants.

The case was pursued by United States Attorney Robert Morgenthau. Wolfson's defense, that he had consummated the sales openly and above board, that he had acted in his own name rather than through a foreign nominee account, that he had even reported the sale to the SEC, was rejected. He was found guilty and sentenced to a year in jail.

By then Merritt-Chapman & Scott was in liquidation, and other parts of his business empire were coming unglued. Ten years of stockholder suits and litigation with the government had cost him a few million dollars, his health, and finally his freedom. The story of Louis Wolfson might have ended there, one spring day in 1969 when he entered jail for the financial equivalent of spitting on the sidewalk.

However, that was not the end of the story, for in his fall he took with him the "Jewish seat" on the United States Supreme Court.

Wolfson had, of course, made many powerful friends in his successful years: two in particular — Lyndon Johnson and Abe Fortas. Indeed, shortly before entering prison, Wolfson boasted that he could have obtained a Presidential pardon from Johnson, but declined to accept it. It was offered by "someone who is as close as anybody could be" to President Johnson.

One person close to Johnson and Wolfson was the late Abe Fortas, one-time partner of the most potent Washington law firm of Arnold, Fortas, and Porter. Fortas had been appointed to the Supreme Court by Johnson. When Chief Justice Warren resigned, Johnson nominated Fortas to succeed him, but the nomination ran into trouble immediately. Fortas was considered too liberal, and the charge of "cronyism" was also raised due to

Fortas' extrajudicial role as presidential confidant. In the face of such opposition, Fortas withdrew his name. Shortly thereafter, he was charged with accepting a check of $20,000 three years earlier from Louis Wolfson. Wolfson's family foundation had retained Fortas for studies and advice on religious and racial relations after he was already seated on the Supreme Court. Subsequently, they had met a few times to discuss such matters. After nearly a year, and following Wolfson's indictment for the sale of unregistered stock, Fortas returned the money. Whether the retainer had been tendered to smooth, alleviate, or simply fix Wolfson's deepening imbroglio with government agencies and the courts can only be surmised.

Fortas denied any wrongdoing and wrote that he had no reason to believe that the fee "would induce me to intervene or make representations on Wolfson's behalf." No evidence ever emerged to contradict his assertions. When Wolfson's case did come before the high court, Fortas abstained from the review.

But the damage had already been done. Fortas resigned from the Supreme Court, the first Justice to quit under pressure for allegations of personal impropriety. Thus the fifth Jew to have served on the high court resigned, a victim of his own moral myopia.

Perhaps it is the nature of American capitalism, its organizational structure and bias, that stresses the financial side of business and lets it play the dominant role. And that is the side that is most highly rewarded. In larger corporations, there is greater likelihood of a chairman or chief executive officer either ascending from the accounting-legal-finance staff or being brought in from the outside to represent the controlling or dominant shareholders. The financial interests, rightly or wrongly, feel most secure when the new chief comes from their own ranks. It is only after companies begin to flounder and perform poorly that the nuts-and-bolts managers are rounded up and pressed into service. Nevertheless, the myth prevails that anyone clever and cunning enough to acquire a company, especially a multimillion dollar property, must have the wherewithal to run it profitably. It is a costly fantasy, but one cherished in modern America.

Eli Black, like Wolfson, was shrewd at appraising value. Opponents had another term for his talents — they said he was a corporate raider or pirate. Black was one of the more interesting businessmen in the sixties and seventies — a man with dimension and depth. But he was a man, in the last analysis, who succumbed to the problematic morality of the times.

It is ironic that this was the case, for Eli Black's background was rooted firmly in an orthodox tradition. An ordained rabbi and a graduate of Yeshiva University, Black came from a long line of rabbis. His parents emigrated from Lublin, Poland when he was very young. After three years as an Orthodox rabbi in a Long Island congregation, Black changed his name from Blachowitz. Observing to a friend that "sermons didn't do anything," he left the practicing rabbinate for the Columbia Business School. After a stint at Lehman Brothers, managing the money of the Rosenwald family, Sears, Roebuck heirs, he took over one of the sick companies in their portfolio, American Seal-Kap, a bottletop maker. It was, Black later said, "a tiny company with huge problems." After turning the company around and changing its name to AMK corporation, Black embarked on the acquisition trail. Before long, his $40 million cap company went after another problem company twenty times its size, John Morrell & Company, a meat packer. It was a classic case of the mouse taking liberties with the lion.

Black tucked Morrell into his bag, problems and all, and went after a venerable Boston-based banana growing and transportation company, United Fruit. With its Great White Fleet ("Every Banana a Guest, Every Passenger a Pest") and hundreds of thousands of acres of plantations in Central America, company sales were an enviable half billion dollars. Though the company had more than its share of ups and downs — Castro had seized its sizable holdings in Cuba — it was performing better than its shares indicated on the New York Stock Exchange. It was considered a weak defensive stock — not exactly the kind of holding sought in an aggressive bull market of electronic, aerospace, and high-technology issues. However, it had a couple of obscure selling points: it was debt-free and it had a $100 million in cash and liquid assets.

Alerted to the situation by a brokerage house, which had recommended the stock to clients a couple of years before at higher prices and was now looking for a bail-out, Black moved quickly. The brokers had close to ten percent of United Fruit in customers' portfolios, thus assuring a foot up in any proxy fight. Black borrowed $35 million from a group of banks headed by Morgan Guaranty Trust and bought 733,200 shares at $56, or four dollars above the market price. The transaction was the third largest block purchase in the history of the Exchange.

Black preferred an amicable takeover of United Fruit but was prepared for a battle. Other sharp-eyed predators had also cast an eye toward Chiquita Banana, seeing enticements in her balance sheet. The chiefs running United Fruit were operational people, successful in running the old company, but seemingly at a loss in utilizing the idle assets. Only when the takeover strategy became obvious did they adopt a defensive strategy and look for a friendly merger. All the interest shown in United Fruit was flattering — three tender offers had moved the price from $56 to $88 per share in the course of a few months. That year, 1968, was the height of the merger mania in the sixties bull market, and Black's package of convertible debentures and warrants worth between $86 and $100 was exceedingly sweet. When the smoke cleared, AMK was the winner, having acquired 360,000 more shares through Goldman, Sachs' Gus Levy.

Indulging in his penchant for name-changing, Black called his conglomerate United Brands. Though it was a formidable food processing complex, the spirit of synergy evaporated with the 1969 market debacle and Nixon's first recession. In the new decade, losses started to grow inexorably — $2 million, then $24 million. Dividends were then dropped completely and a marginal recovery in 1972 and 1973 took place. By 1974 the company's revenues had reached $2 billion, but in that year, the losses (after extraordinary items) grew to $43.6 million. The company was running afoul of Mother Nature: hurricanes had destroyed much of the Central American fruit crop; droughts and poor harvests caused a worldwide grain shortage and a consequent jump in the price of cattle feed. In its two principal markets, United Brands was taking a severe beating.

Under Black's leadership, United Brands was losing twice as much money as it was making. One close participant who watched the action wrote that it was not a case of Black's not knowing anything about growing and marketing bananas, operating 37 refrigeration ships, or the niceties of banana republic politics, but that he thought he knew.

If the company did not exactly prosper under Black's leadership, its image improved. In the old days, United Fruit dominated the economic and political life of Central America. It ran its operations with an autocratic indifference to its farmers and workers, it traded in governments when they no longer served its purposes. United Fruit ran some countries the way some coal mine companies have run towns. Its sobriquet, "el pulpo" — the octopus — was probably well deserved. Though the company had instituted reforms before Black arrived, it still had a long way to go before it could erase its image of Yankee exploiter. Black raised wages, supplied company houses, built homes for sale to its employees below cost, and recognized farm workers' unions before other major agribusinesses. Black was much preoccupied by social and humanitarian issues, devoting his extracurricular energies to philanthropic causes and cultural publications. When he signed a contract with United Farm Workers Union, he invited Caesar Chavez, its leader, to Rosh Hashanah services — the company that prayed together stayed together. It was, the *Boston Globe* wrote, "the most socially conscious American company in the hemisphere."

But an improved image was inadequate. The internal problems of the separate divisions, the internecine warfare and jockeying for power, the coups, and board meetings that almost ended in fist-fights were all beginning to take their toll on the quiet, non-violent Black. Perhaps the final pressure, outside of the acts of God that seemed to plague the company through 1973 and 1974, was the decision of seven South and Central American nations to imitate the Organization of Petroleum Exporting Countries (OPEC).

If the oil cartel was successful, why not a banana cartel? The Union of Banana Exporting Countries would push for higher prices to offset their energy costs by passing an export tax of fifty cents or a dollar per forty-pound box. Only three countries actually passed the tax and Honduras was one of them. Honduras placed a levy of fifty cents per box. This was very expensive for United Brands since thirty-five percent of its bananas came from that nation. But unlike the oil situation, there was at that time, a glut of the fruit on the market and prices were depressed. More important, Equador, the Saudi Arabia of bananas, did not participate in the tax scheme.

Honduran government sources, however, made it known that for a "consideration," the tax could be partially rolled back. For a mere $5 million, the Honduran president would impose a twenty-five-cents-a-box tax, a saving of $7.5 million. The company negotiated, apparently with Eli Black's knowledge, agreeing to a $2.5 million payoff. Through its European offices, $1.25 million was deposited in a Swiss account with the promise of more to come. This situation was not new for United Brands, for subsequent investigations turned up questionable payments of $200,000 to Italian officials.

Heretofore Black had preferred social contributions to outright bribery, something that was of value to the people rather than something that lined the pockets of the crooked officals. Thus he sent a variety of relief materials to the Hondurans after devastating Hurricane Fifi. He built a medical center in Guatemala and sponsored a polio prevention campaign in Costa Rica. Whatever the reason, he believed that there was more to running a company that was intimately involved with the affairs of foreign countries than simply taking el presidente to lunch.

Undoubtedly the pressure on Black to acquiesce to the payoffs was very great. The second portion of the bribe was never delivered, for the hurricane had made the question of taxes irrelevant: it had destroyed seventy percent of the Honduran crop and cost the company $19.5 million in damages.

In late 1974 it became apparent that United Brands was in for a disastrous year, with losses of $40-odd million, possibly double that when all the debits were counted. The devastation from storms, high interest charges, high foreign export taxes, and soaring cattle-feed costs, forced Black to quickly sell one of his more profitable subsidiaries, Foster Grant, after selling Baskin-Robbins and Revere Sugar the previous year. Meanwhile, the backbiting in the front offices grew more fierce, the nagging of the bankers more insistent, and the price of United Brands stock had fallen to $4 per share. The investing public was evaluating a company with over $2 billion of revenues for little more than $40 million. It was as if the company was going out of business rather than just experiencing some severe problems.

Black's own reactions were not that different from the investing public — he was seemingly unable to turn the situation around, regardless of his earnest commitment and exhaustingly long hours. In reality, the Foster Grant sale had given the company some breathing space and many of the year's disasters were one-time happenings. But Black, for all his diverse interests — from the publication committee of *Commentary* to devising new forms of Jewish rituals — was a sober, intense man who believed in being totally in charge. In fact, he retained the top three titles in the company: chairman, president, and chief executive officer. Consequently, the rise and fall of the company's fortunes were his sole responsibility, a judgment on his abilities. So while the worst might be over, and conceivably the cyclical nature of business was beginning to swing positively, the gap between his original ideals for the company and the reduced image of himself as a ubiquitous, all-powerful businessman had grown dangerously wide.

On February 3, 1975 his chauffeur drove him to the Manhattan offices of United Brands, a suite high up in the Pan Am building. A few minutes later, Black smashed a plate-glass window on the forty-fourth story and leapt to his death. Suicide, though prohibited in Judaism, was the only way out of overreaching and underachievement. Of course one will never know precisely why Black committed suicide — he left no explanation. His involvement in the Honduran bribery may well have been the last straw. For though he did nothing significantly illegal under American law, he did raise foreign payoffs to a new level.

American corporations in international trade have always had to contend with the "B" element, the baksheesh factor. Whether in outright bribes, kickbacks, or tax evasion schemes, many American companies have been involved in the illegal activities. But in the post-Watergate years, the Securities and Exchange Commission has made an issue of foreign bribes. United Brands was one of the first major corporations to be chastised, not because it did anything terribly wrong other than set a poor example, but because it refused to disclose the nature of the overseas payments in its statements of earnings to the public. Since then, the public has been treated to an unending series of first-class American names involved in payoffs. For a sensitive and ethical man like Black, the public notoriety must have been a discomforting prospect. Perhaps in suicide Black had found, in the words of his nephew, "the one way to hurt everybody."

Still another explanation for his suicide emerged from the pages of the *Harvard Business Review*. Harry Levinson, a psychologist of that school, wrote of executive suicides as a "way out to a dynamic individual." He elaborated:

> Executives are men and women of high aspiration. As a rule, they are very ambitious, seeking power, prestige, and money, and nearly always they are competing intensely against other executives. In psychological jargon, they have extremely high ego ideals that revolve around power. They have deepseated, unconscious pressures for attainment; their conscious goals are merely the tip of the iceberg. People who have such high levels of aspiration are frequently nagged by the feeling of being a long way from achieving their goals. No matter what their achievement, it never seems to be enough. As a result, they always view themselves as inadequate. . . . Regardless of any achievements, such persons always see themselves as deficient and, according to their logic, deserving of self-punishment.

The same qualities that made Black one of the more sympathetic and interesting businessmen — his concerns, his conscience, his seriousness — were also his undoing. He had never learned to laugh at himself or the world. His teacher, president of Yeshiva University, Samuel Belkin, remarked at his funeral that Black was "a boy who always smiled but never laughed."

## The Nursing-Home Czar

> I do not pretend — to you, sir, to be in this business as a charitable enterprise.
>
> — Bernard Bergman, before the United States Sen-- ate Committee on the Aging

It was the general consensus of Jews watching the various legislative hearings starring Bernard Bergman, the nursing-home king, that "he set Jews back a thousand years." Bathed in the merciless television lights of Congressional hearings, the witnesses exposed to a national audience the morbid, pathetic, and sordid conditions of senior citizens in nursing and old-age homes. It was as if they had found that a Jew was in charge of a concentration camp. The whole proceedings were a *schanda* (shame) of the first order, for the scandal not only uncovered the seamy, immoral, and illegal practices of a rabbi and other prominent Jews on a captive population unable to protect itself, it also illuminated a world in which children forget parents, society neglects the aged, and the state ignores massive improprieties in a licensed industry.

Warehousing old people — the average age in nursing homes is eighty-two — is a lucrative if unsentimental business for the owners and operators. The unscrupulous ones have maximized profits by minimizing care. Public inquiries into the condition of private homes revealed neglect, indifference, and sadism. Elderly patients admitted to hospitals from nursing homes — dehydrated, ulcerated, grossly infected, and in shock — received little medical attention. The chief medical resident of one hospital observed that "some of these patients are so dry that they can no longer salivate or form sweat or tears. Occasionally we find dried food and unswallowed pills in their mouths." The nursing home inhabitant became a victim of a medical syndrome. The old people were often unwashed — stinking from unchanged clothes and soiled linens — and unfed. Famished patients from one private home took to ringing neighborhood doorbells begging for food.

Bergman was more than a symbolic figure of evil in the nursing-home industry — he was the industry. At the hearings of the

New York Temporary State Commission on Living Costs led by Andrew Stein, a subcommittee of the Special Senate Committee on Aging under the chairmanship of Senator Frank Moss of Utah, the Moreland Act Commission on Nursing Homes and Residential Facilities headed by Morris Abram, and the investigations of special prosecutors for the state and federal governments, it became clear that Bergman had almost oligopolic powers, with interests in close to a hundred different homes across the nation. It also became clear that, perhaps more than in any other industry or service area, Jews dominated the field, that many of the major operators were Jewish, including Bergman, Eugene Hollander, and Albert Schwartzberg. It would have been comforting to the Jewish community had the nursing-home industry been operated with pride, with sympathy, with care and concern — in short, with *rachmones*, (that heightened sensitivity or humaneness that is at the core of Jewish tradition). Instead, insensitivity, greed, and human degradation were the hallmark of a majority of the private facilities. And that the chief perpetrators of this terminal inhumanity should be an Orthodox rabbi and a prominent Zionist was a mind-boggling reversal of values.

Central casting could not have found a more perfect image of orthodoxy and self-righteousness — that mixture of piousness and studied indifference to modernity — than Bernard Bergman. He was born in Hungary but in 1929, immigrated to the United States, where he was ordained in 1934 at Yeshiva University. After a brief visit to Jerusalem, he returned to New York City. At about the same time, his stepfather was arrested in Paris, passing himself off as the "grand rabbi of Brooklyn," trying to smuggle seventeen pounds of heroin among his religious books. Bergman's mother pleaded guilty as an accomplice.

Bergman's first association with a nursing home was as a rabbi at a Lower East Side establishment. After the war, he gave up the active rabbinate and moved into nursing homes and real estate as businesses. His first partner was sued by the state for bilking Jews out of $2.3 million in a cemetery swindle. Bergman attracted characters of dubious ethics.

While Bergman was busy wheeling and dealing, he maintained an active role in Zionist activities and Jewish philanthropic work.

From the time he gave the invocation before the United States House of Representatives, he cultivated politicians the way some people cultivate roses. He understood the relationship between money and power. "I met them at many dinners and affairs, and naturally they sought my help in their campaigns. I did help them by contacting many of my friends. There might have been occasions when I came to them for help. That is only natural when one needs help, one goes to the elected officials," Bergman testified.

As his holdings grew, he had few qualms about using his contacts to expedite permits, quash unfavorable reports, and promote rate increases. From an inheritance of $30,000, left to him by the founders of the first nursing home he worked in, Bergman's net worth grew to exceed $10 million by 1960.

By that time, his nursing homes earned big money and had attracted the attention of city authorities. Some of the practices of the nursing facilities were fraudulent. The Commissioner of Investigation, Louis Kaplan, found that the private nursing homes were overbilling the city for the care of welfare patients — giving them minimal care but charging maximum rates. Kaplan found the records so badly kept that his accountants had to extrapolate a formula for the erroneous billing. He concluded that the city had been overcharged $3.7 million in a two year period in the late fifties, much of it due to simple fraud. One Bergman home was responsible for $213,000 in overcharges, and the president of the trade association, Eugene Hollander, had overbilled by $237,000. The case was forwarded to the District Attorney for legal action while the corporation counsel recovered $650,000 for "unjust enrichment," an out-of-court settlement in which the city collected seventeen cents on a dollar. If the recovery was incomplete, due to the difficulties in proving the case in court, the criminal acts of the defendants were mysteriously forgotten. Forty out of 119 houses were closed after Kaplan's report. However, the nursing home operators filed for and received rate increases of thirty percent.

By then Bergman had interests in eighteen private homes, but was the moving force in varying degrees in eighty-eight other homes that served welfare cases. Indeed, Kaplan spoke of a "cartel" headed by a promoter "who never held a license in any of the homes." Even Bergman later admitted that he knew little about nursing care.

As a consequence of the Kaplan report, Bergman was notified by the New Jersey authorities that he was "persona non grata." Undeterred, Bergman moved into that state through front organizations nominally owned by members of his family.

In the sixties nursing homes were so lucrative that shares of them were sold by the bed. A shortage of space assured the owners of full capacity. Moreover, with the advent of Medicaid and Medicare in the mid-sixties, the government picked up at least eighty percent of the billing. Bergman went to Wall Street and floated a stock issue for Medic-Home Enterprises, Inc., a string of thirty-six nursing homes on the East Coast. The company went public at $10 per share, eventually rising to $40 a share before sinking under Securities and Exchange Commission charges of violation of the antifraud, reporting, proxy solicitation, and tender offer provisions of federal securities laws. Some company officers indulged in substantial insider trading, diversion, and siphoning off of funds — the usual hanky-panky of financial crime.

Bergman's "success" in the nursing home business can be attributed to a number of things: his presence in the right field at the right time; the indulgence of government agencies, which seemed more concerned with custodial space than care for the elderly; but probably most of all, to chutzpah, plain gall. One illustration is perhaps typical of Bergman's operations, his persistence, his political connections, and his unabashed use of his "Jewishness" that he paraded as if he were its victim. The Danube Nursing Home in Staten Island was in trouble even before it got off the drawing boards. It was built by Bergman's own construction company, after the original owners had entered into a purchase and leaseback arrangement with another of Bergman's companies.

The owners had applied, in 1965, to establish the facility under the New York City Department of Hospitals and were given preliminary approval, but the actual construction did not follow the original plans. Further authorization was needed by the New York State Public Health Council and the New York State Department of Health. In 1971 construction was underway without the prerequisite approvals. The City Department of Health notified the State Department of Health and that department turned to Attorney General Louis Lefkowitz for an injunction. A new application was filed in 1972 under a new law, and the Attorney General ceased to pursue the matter. Meanwhile Bergman, the landlord of the building, looked for relief by enlisting Samuel Hausman, a friend and fundraiser for Governor Rockefeller, to expedite the application. Hausman had intervened previously for another of Bergman's homes and was an old friend. This started a whole sequence of efforts by state executives and legislators to pressure the bureaucracy to do what it thought best not to do.

Hausman, a successful businessman, was considered by Rockefeller as his informal "eyes and ears to the Jewish community" and was a linchpin to important Democratic Jewish voters. Hausman "reveled" in his role as go-between and expediter, happily paying homage to Bergman as a leading force in Orthodox Judaism. To solidify this relationship, Bergman threw some business to one of Hausman's relatives.

Hausman's principal political friend was T. Norman Hurd, Secretary to Governor Rockefeller and subsequently, to Governor Wilson when Rockefeller resigned. Bergman used other politicians or well-connected attorneys as well: at one time or another in his efforts to certify the Danube, he called upon Governors Rockefeller and Wilson; New York Mayor Beame; Speaker of the New York State Assembly Stanley Steingut; Steingut's counsel, C. Daniel Chill; Albert Blumenthal, Assembly Majority Leader; State Senator John Marchi; Stanley Lowell, one-time Deputy Mayor of New York City and Chairman of the Human Rights Commission; and Dr. Andrew Fleck, Jr., First Deputy Commissioner of the New York State Health Department.

Hausman elicited Hurd's sympathy, if that were needed, by complaining that an important personal friend, Bergman, was the victim of discrimination at the Health Department. Regardless of the truth of the matter — and the subsequent investigation found the allegation to be false — the hypocritical Bergman was using the lethal and explosive charge of anti-Semitism as a foil for his commercial maneuvers. Hausman, in the political argot, was "sure a call to Commissioner Fleck is all that is needed." But the first review of Bergman's corporate application found that the earlier financing was not fully disclosed and that the applicant had "demonstrated a willingness to deceive the [Health] Department and the Public Health Council." The sale and leaseback arrangement, among other things, included a special fee of nearly a quarter of a million dollars to Bergman, a fact that might "jeopardize the adequacy of their source of future revenue." In addition, "their involved financial transactions could affect the real property value which in turn affect Medicaid claims for reimbursement." Moreover, there were already too many "public need nursing home beds" on Staten Island. Finally, the review revealed that Bergman had failed to satisfy the Public Health Council as to his character, competence, and standing in the community.

In the course of Bergman's lobbying efforts for the Danube Facility, he revealed his usual modus operandi by hiring Rockefeller's recently departed Secretary, Robert Douglass, as counsel on the matter. But Douglass withdrew from the case when he became aware that Bergman was supplying misinformation. Bergman then hired Senator John Marchi as counsel. It is legal in New York State, as in many others, to hire a member of the state legislature to pursue a problem with a state agency. The conflict of interests, both real and potential, has not dawned on the majority of the state's legislators, though over the years there have been proposed laws to curb the abuse but they invariably meet defeat. Senator Marchi was, of course, particularly apropos since Staten Island was his home district. Still, the inconsistencies in Bergman's application could not be overlooked.

Frustrated with the Danube as a nursing home, Bergman decided to turn it into a school for mentally retarded children, another relatively docile, captive group. The Danube was turned into the Victory Residential School: it would take children discharged from Willowbrook, a nearby mental hospital. This time Bergman lined up a different front organization. He convinced Rabbi Schulem Rubin and his Lanzuter Congregation Beth David to sponsor the school, though all the necessary money was put up by a Bergman associate. Bergman enlisted State Senator John Calandro and even had United States Congressman John Murphy of Staten Island ask the city agencies about the status of the school's application. The city agencies found the proposed program and funding inadequate. It was the Danube story all over again: more petitions from Bergman's son-in-law, Amram Kass (who was an attorney and principal in some of Bergman's corporations) to Hausman and Hurd. But all the political pressure failed again and the State Board of Social Welfare rejected the proposal.

But one doesn't become wealthy without persistence, and Bergman was nothing if not persistent. Another metamorphosis and the Victory Residential School was changed into the Richmond Habilitation Center, a residential facility for retarded adults discharged from Willowbrook. This time an associate of Bergman's, Robert Lipkin, formed a partnership with the law partners of C. Daniel Chill, Steingut's counsel. It was understood that Chill's law firm would share in the profits for expediting things "through the good offices of Governor Rockefeller." There was no question that Willowbrook needed the facility, since it had a horrible history of overcrowding and understaffing. This time the New York City Department of Mental Hygiene and the Staten Island Mental Retardation Regional Council found the proposed center faulty for half a dozen reasons: the rent paid to the landlord, Bergman, was so large a percentage of the project that it jeopardized the program; the space, far too large when modern treatment theory called for small, homelike residences; Staten Island was already overtaxed with such facilities; and the sponsors failed to work with the community. Hausman, Bergman, and Kass met with Governor Wilson, asking him to intercede on their behalf, but the Department of Mental Hygiene issued its final rejection.

One final time, Bergman tried to pass the empty building off as an intermediate care facility, the Island View Care Center. Though not strictly analogous to state law institutions, this federally designated facility would be eligible for Medicaid funds. It would not be licensed by the Department of Mental Hygiene, only authorized, after an inspection, to receive government monies. This approach solved a number of problems: it would have circumvented some of the regulatory agencies that had been critical of Bergman's operations, but at the same time, it would have brought nursing-home space into the state while the costs were shifted to another level of government. And, of course, the solution would have paid some political debts.

Thus there was a secret agreement between the Department of Mental Hygiene, Willowbrook, and Bergman. When it became public knowledge on Staten Island, community opposition quickly developed. But Bergman was ready to bully the project through. He even used Hausman's brother, Leo, president of the United Cerebral Palsy, Inc. (UCP), to bring pressure on Sonia Braniff, then president of the Staten Island Mental Retardation Council, a quasi-public body that was against the center, to change her position. Leo Hausman called her several times. A mother of a cerebral palsy child herself, she felt "intimidated" and fearful that she might receive no further aid from UCP. Regardless of the "strong pressure, political and private . . . exerted to have the Council approve the proposal," Bergman's Island View Care Center was rejected.

In a final attempt, Steingut set up a meeting for Bergman with New York City's Mayor Beame, claiming that community opposition had dwindled. Beame found that this was not the case. Moreover, if the scheme went through, support for Willowbrook patients would be shifted from the state to the city budget, a burden that near-bankrupt New York could not afford.

Late in the summer of 1974, a number of investigating bodies were hot on Bergman's heels. His Danube home on Staten Island would never open. It was undoubtedly a blessing, saving untold numbers of clients incalculable misery.

Bergman's single-minded profiteering was his undoing. He milked Medicaid, taking advantage of the latest government-sponsored program to aid the aged and indigent. What was heinous about Bergman's activities was not the theft of government funds — in those terms he was no different than the wanted men on post office bulletin boards — but that he was preying on people who were unable to defend themselves. It can, of course, be argued that Bergman was no different from any other fast-buck artist. He was just dealing in volume. But perhaps he should have been different — as a man of the cloth, he should be devoted and held to higher standards of morality.

The heart of Bergman's swindle was the manipulation of nursing-home financing to inflate his Medicaid billings. Each state selects which method it will use to reimburse health-care dispensers for providing services under Medicaid. Basically there are two systems: cost-based or flat-rate. Some states designate a fixed fee on how much they will pay for specific services. Most states, including New York, use cost-based reimbursement, relying on a previous year's expenditures to determine current payments, plus an inflationary increment. During the height of Bergman's empire, New York was operating under a cost-plus system, where the facilities were reimbursed for all their expenses in addition to a fixed percentage for profit.

"It was the kind of system," Senator Moss said, that was "enough to make defense contractors drool." The more you spend, the greater the profits.

Both systems are subject to abuse. In the cost-based system, the expenses can be inflated by any number of devices: kickbacks; phony bills; the lack of arms' length transactions with purveyors; real estate wash sales and construction padding. In fact, the Temporary State Commission on Living Costs totaled up sixteen ways crooked proprietors had bilked the state of $400 million since the inception of Medicaid.

Dr. Fleck, the first Deputy Commissioner of the Department of Health summarized Bergman's activities:

> A long history of repetitive arrangements . . . which follow a consistent pattern under which the parties fulfill, on an alternating basis, roles as buyers and sellers, lessors and lessees of real estate devoted to nursing home purposes. The only standardized and consistent relationship in these arrangements is continued inflation of paper real estate values. . . . Dr. Bergman wishes to choose among the various options available to him under our current laws and regulations in order to maximize the profits he can obtain by an eventual sale of real estate. Apparently, the quality of the nursing home operation and the service to be provided to the public is not an important consideration influencing Dr. Bergman's choices. . . . The Public Health Council is concerned about the inflation of costs as a result of this type of decision-making which is characterized by them as

"trafficking in nursing home real estate values" with regard to its effect on patient welfare.

Bergman had simply refined the system of political influence peddling. The nursing home scandals revealed no great graft or payoffs; no high offices were sold; the most blatant forms of political pressure were absent. But on another, perhaps more insidious level, the scandals exposed the assumption that legislators and regulators can serve two masters, their public constituencies and their private clients, without an inherent conflict of interests. To pursue a case before a regulatory agency, one should get the advice of a well-connected politician-lawyer, who has preferably just left the regulatory agency. In New York State, the permissive attitude of the legislators toward this dual practice encourages such abuse.

Moreover, the Rockefeller administration was terribly lax in expanding and enforcing the regulations governing nursing homes. Critical reports were turned into "love letters," inspectors were told to accent the "positive," and operators could evade and manipulate. Rockefeller's steadfast refusal to appoint more auditors, even though their audits would have paid for the added expense many times over, defies explanation. As a result, when Bergman and his friends stole, they were unlikely to be audited. And if audited, they faced no penalty.

The Moreland Commission concluded that the private nursing homes "enjoyed almost total freedom from effective regulation. Massive paper pushing by the New York State Department of Health disguised its negligible enforcement of adequate standard of care and fiscal inadequacies went uncorrected as the department's direct and repeated warnings to Governor Rockefeller, and later to Governor Wilson, about the need for more auditing went unheeded."

Perhaps the key to the scandals was not Bergman's avarice but Rockefeller's obtuseness. Year after year during his administration, "ten to twenty percent of the state's nursing homes had significant operating deficiencies." In 1973 two-thirds of the city's homes had such deficiencies. While these defects made the homes a living hell for their inmates, Rockefeller had the poor taste to ask the Moreland Commission, when he appeared before it, just what the Commission meant by "bad care" — as if the public documentation of insufficient food, lack of heat, excessive use of chemical tranquilizers, physical restraints, gang visits by physicians, theft of personal spending monies by the managements, and other patient abuse did not constitute "bad care."

To turn $30,000 into $24 million — according to his accountant his net worth before his fall — Bergman used old and new techniques.

Jews have learned firsthand about corruption and influence peddling in hostile surroundings, where the established power structure was either outwardly anti-Semitic or subtly prejudiced against Jews. In that sense, Bergman's cultivation and use of his connections was atavistic. The cry of anti-Semitism was the reverse side of this coin, even though there was no proof that the regulatory authorities were anti-Semitic in any fashion. He used his "orthodoxy" in a hypocritical manner and the Rockefeller administration did Jews a disservice by never investigating such a charge from a seemingly eminent source. If Bergman and Hausman were credible, why didn't the governor's office or the attorney general look into their charges? Or did Rockefeller's staff simply assume that their complaint was an excuse, however flimsy, for exerting political influence? And any excuse would do to help "friends of the Administration."

In that light, Bergman's betrayal of his tradition is even more ironic for, under the cloak of Judaism, he was busy ripping off elderly Jews. Again a reversal of values. Judaism honors age and longevity ("May you live to be a hundred and twenty," is an old greeting), but Bergman's pursuit of wealth blatantly denied the aged the modicum of comfort and respect they might have expected. Bergman had adapted to some of the less positive American mores all too well, denigrating the aged confident that he could get away with it since society didn't care what happened to its elderly.

When the courts caught him, Bergman was sentenced in federal court to four months for Medicaid and tax fraud and in state court to one year for bribery of a state legislator. He signed over his assets to satisfy a government claim of $2.5 million as the judge termed him "an unscrupulous and corrupt individual" with "little or no remorse." Bergman then left for a minimum security prison with minimum fences "not designed to keep people in or out, they're just designed to let us know where our property ends," said the superintendent. Fences are probably a good idea; otherwise Bergman might have tried to subdivide the property and build a nursing home after he arranged a sale-and-leaseback dodge with the warden. Bergman served ten weeks for his federal offenses.

# 8. The Art World

The arts, you know — they're Jews, they're left-wing — in other words, stay away.
— Richard Nixon, advice to his daughters, 1972

Art, like morality, consists in drawing a line somewhere.
— Sidney Janis

*I Never Knew He Was Jewish*

Is there Jewish art? In recent years the question has been asked with increasing perplexity. Perhaps no field of human activity is as debatable as art — unless it is religion. Commentaries and aesthetic criticism, as the late Barnett Newman pointed out, bear as much relation to art as ornithology does to birds. When you mix aesthetics and theology, confusion is bound to result. But Jewish art? Not long ago, the phrase would have been a contradiction in terms. In 99.9 percent of the Jewish experience there was no high art. Folk art yes, decorative and ornamental, but serious work in the Western sense, no. Today, the picture is completely changed, and Jews enjoy every phase of the art world: as artists, dealers, collectors, critics, curators, consultants, and patrons. In fact, the contemporary art scene has a strong Jewish flavor. In some circles, the wheelers and dealers are referred to as the Jewish mafia since they command power, prestige, and most of all, money. And, as with the family *capo,* influence is dispensed adroitly: artists who lived through years of neglect are turned into overnight successes; successes are guillotined so swiftly that they may not know they've been decapitated.

The reasons that Jews are drawn to the art world are many,

complex, and curious. The affinity may tell more about Jews than it does about art, but the first thing to note is that there exists a strong and unmistakable sympathy between artists and Jews. Both are outside the mainstream. Thus, an empathy arises — one common to *auslanders* in strange countries or tourists abroad. The world doesn't understand them, so they withdraw from the world: the Jews into Judaism, the artists into Bohemia. To be sure, the two societies are markedly different. The orthodox live a highly structured existence, following with precision the 613 rules (248 positive and 365 negative) of a pious life. The artists live in an open society, bound by few rules and forever willing to experiment. In their own ways they are totally different, joined only by their separateness.

In the last generation or so, the ground rules have changed; the sympathy remains. However, the mainstream has engulfed Jews and artists alike, and both groups are now considered respectable in many parts of the country. And for the first time in Jewish history, Jews are turning to art in droves.

Jewish craftsmen had gained substantial reputations throughout history as glassmakers, weavers, silversmiths, minters of money, woodcarvers, and cabinetmakers — they exercised their talents on everything from belt-buckles to bookstands. Much of their work was for pedestrian activities, but some of the finest craftsmanship was reserved for ritual and religious adornment: the woodwork on the holy ark, the elaborate silverwork on the breastplates of the Torah, the calligraphy of the scrolls, and the traditional marriage ring. So while the craftsmanship was of the first order, Jews did not paint or sculpt anything representing the human form. The body was respected, but not venerated in the Greco-Roman tradition.

Furthermore, Jews as a group were not considered visually oriented. The great Jewish philosopher of the twentieth century, Martin Buber, observed that the early Jew "was more of an aural than a visual man . . . the most vivid descriptions in Jewish writings are acoustic in nature, the texts espouse sound and music, are temporal and dynamic, not concerned with color and form. The Jew seems not to see the things he looks at, but to think them."

Another observer has remarked that Jews and Arabs share a

"Semitic lack of talent for the figural arts." Pragmatically, Jews needed art less than Christians did. Judaism taught its traditions and told its history solely through the written word, while the Christians used illuminations, stained-glass windows, reliefs, and statues to tell the Christ story to an illiterate peasantry. Thus, Christian art portrayed a highly personified flesh and blood God. This was totally at odds with the Jewish idea of God. Jews viewed representational art with suspicion, as a handmaiden of heresy.

The Bible forbade the representation of human images. In Exodus (20:4), the second of the Ten Commandments ordered: "Thou shalt not make unto thee a graven image, nor any manner of likeness, of anything that is in heaven above, or that is in the earth beneath, or that is in the water under the earth." This injunction was relayed to the Israelites by Moses when he descended from Mount Sinai, and is a cardinal tenet of Judaism. It was not to be trifled with in the fight against polytheism. Painting the body and sculpting the human form ("And if thou make Me an altar of stone, thou shalt not build it of hewn stones; for if thou lift up thy tool upon it, thou has profaned it") was thus forbidden lest the children of Israel slip back to paganism.

It was thought until very recently that Jews lived by those injunctions with implicit faith. However, an archaeological dig uncovered a third-century synagogue in Syria — Dura Europos — covered by representational figures, biblical events, and dream sequences. This was a major find, though others followed, that has placed Jewish art in perspective. Little by little, Jewish artists evaded the biblical laws. By the fourteenth century, when Renaissance art was sweeping Europe and the Church was a major patron, a few Jewish artists went so far as to draw nudes and half-draped ladies. The admonition that "thy nakedness be not uncovered" was slowly losing its relevance. The introduction of the printing press seems to have accelerated the move to representational art. Nevertheless, the Jewish establishment maintained its ancient views that art was a "symptom of debilitating luxury." More than that, it was somehow insidious and subversive, a distraction from the worship of God. There was a danger that if you produce graven images "thou [will] be drawn away and worship them, and serve them." Jewish artistic energies remained centered on the ornamentation of synagogues and ritual items. Heroic or monumental works, common for painters and sculptors, were not part of the Jewish tradition.

All that changed in the twentieth century. Jews entered the world of art with a passion derived from thousands of years of suppression by ritualistic taboo. The Enlightenment and subsequent emancipation of Jews were responsible for the new-found freedom. Emancipation was also responsible for the breakdown of the tight Jewish communal structure and the dissolution of European ghettos. This movement was productive for the art world, but counterproductive to the Jewish world. For the first time in the modern period, Jews started to produce paintings with Jewish imagery. One art critic remarked that "as long as a vital Jewish religious life existed it was never accompanied by art; therefore, the moment 'religious' pictures come to be painted, they already signalled the break up of the ghetto and the end of religious life." The development of modern Jewish artists was the consequence of the dissolution of Jewish ideological power.

Starting at the turn of the century, Jews quickly entered the international art scene. Paris was the home of Jewish-European painters between 1920 and 1940 — they were almost a school unto themselves. Their leader was Chaim Soutine, with other luminaries such as Jules Pascin and Marc Chagall. Soutine had a great impact on the modern art scene, but there was nothing Jewish about his painting, and he became furious when he was so categorized. Chagall's work was more evocative of Jewish themes, the shtetl nostalgia, the peddler's existence, and the Russian antecedents. But he, too, adamantly refused to be called a Jewish painter: "I am a painter. That's all!"

What has clearly emerged is one of those wonderful paradoxes. After a millennium of bowing to religious law and producing no great plastic art, Jewish artists are now free to produce great art, but it is no longer especially Jewish. The paradox is nowhere better seen than in America as it became the center of the art world. The first significant appearance of Jewish artists took place in the twenties and thirties with the art of social realism and political protest. Many of the participants were Jews: Chaim Gross, Jack Levine, Morris Kantor, Ben Shahn, Raphael and Moses Soyer,

Saul Steinberg, Abraham Walkowitz, and Max Weber. Many others of those movements were not: Hopper, Marsh, and Sloan. While there was nothing inherently Jewish in the style of realism, Jews could and did use folkloric figures and symbols — beaver hats, *payess,* lower East Side streets, ceremonial affairs, menorahs, Hebrew letters, and the Star of David. For a moment in time, the collective Jewish experience was represented in art, though the overall tenor of social realism was more generally concerned with a European style in an American environment.

World War II marked a turning point in art — impressionism and realism were in a sense relegated to the nineteenth century. The previous work had joined figural style and Jewish symbolism into a pungent sentimentality. Perhaps it was not only immigrant art, but first-generation art of newly freed artists. When abstract expressionism was invented in the forties and fifties, the symbolism was gone. One of the more perceptive art critics, the late Harold Rosenberg, wrote that "since the Second World War Jewish references in a painting increased the odds against its being a good painting."

Jewish artists either could not or would not deal with some of the most tragic experiences of Jews since the Inquisition or the fall of the Temple: the Holocaust, the liberation, or the founding of the State of Israel. In the words of one curator, "these experiences find little direct expression in the visual arts." The Jewish artists who flourished after the war turned their backs on representational work to take up abstract expressionism, pop, optical, kinetic, minimal, color-field, and conceptual art. The old Jewish archetypes and symbols no longer held relevance since American Jews, outside the ultraorthodox, had created new images in surroundings strikingly different from their fathers or grandfathers. The old images were reduced to "vestigial details in the aesthetics of seminary graduates, caterers, florists and funeral directors," in the words of Rosenberg. Nor does it seem that the "campaigns of the United Jewish Appeal, or family celebrations at the Palace Manor [are] likely to inspire new art."

The new art movements produced a prodigious number of Jewish artists: Milton Avery, Leonard Baskin, Eugene Berman, Leonid Berman, Hyman Bloom, Jim Dine, Louis Eilshemius,

Sam Francis, Helen Frankenthaler, Adolph Gottlieb, Philip Gus-
ton, Hans Hofmann, Jacques Lipschitz, Morris Louis, Louise
Nevelson, Barnett Newman, Jules Olitski, Philip Pearlstein, Larry
Rivers, Mark Rothko, George Segal, plus a host of others perhaps
less well-known. Some had made the stylistic transition from realism; some had not, and receded into the shadows.

With representational art no longer in vogue, what is Jewish
about contemporary Jewish artists? If there are no Jewish subjects
or symbols, then their work can be called Jewish only through
metaphysical conjuring — an exercise in shoveling smoke. Some
critics have suggested that the whole field of modern abstract art
is especially Jewish, falling back on the Second Commandment.
However, abstractionists provide singular and unique images —
images that have nothing to do with group experience, Jewish or
otherwise. Just as Rembrandt painted rabbis, a fact that does not
make the Dutchman a Jewish painter, so it makes little sense to
wrap abstract painters in the tallith of Judaism. There are collective creative movements that can truly be isolated, defined, and
identified — French impressionism, cubism, baroque, and primitive art, but not Jewish art. Up to this point, no Jewish school
exists — no special technique or common themes tie modern Jewish artists together. And most modern artists who happen to be
Jewish understand the dilemma: if the artist wished to be universally accepted, he cannot perform in the constraints of an ancient
creed, a sentimental nostalgia, or a juxtaposing of quasireligious
titles. He must use the symbols, images, people, and ideas as he
sees fit, apropros of his vision, rather than conform his vision to
the traditional values of his background. Thus Larry Rivers' *Bar
Mitzvah Portrait,* with its stenciled "rejected," is as valid a statement as Chagall's *White Crucifixion* or *Green Violinist.*

Perhaps Martin Buber was right when he said that "it is not
possible for a fully realized Jewish art to develop in a physical or
psychological Diaspora. Such a national art requires a common
origin and experience for its artists, and as such can exist only on
Jewish soil and within a wholly Jewish culture." Whether Israel
will provide such an art remains to be seen.

Whether or not there is "Jewish art," the number of Jewish artists and Jews in the art world is great. Jews have come full circle,

from total rejection of the arts to total commitment to the arts. Until very recently, the prevailing attitude was characterized by Nathan Rothschild, the founder of the London branch of the banking house, when he was offered a work: "Can't throw away money on paintings," he said. Only when the Chief Rabbi of London sent a dealer did he consent — and then reluctantly: "Alright, give me a £30 picture. I don't care which one. Goodbye." Presumably, the bank's walls were as barren as his cultural sensitivity.

But the attitude continued. At the beginning of this century, Lesser Uri, a painter, remarked that "a Jewish artist receives more encouragement from Christians than from Jews. The rich Jew shrinks from any documentation of his heritage." Chagall, when a refugee in New York during the Second World War, also complained of a lack of Jewish interest in his work. He received most of his support from Catholic collectors.

Chagall is now classified as the quintessential Jewish artist — his works grace Lincoln Center in New York and the Israeli Parliament in Jerusalem — and Jews are now leaders in supporting the arts. Jews may or may not have become more culture conscious, but they certainly were among the first to realize that modern art is not a bad investment. Nevertheless, some rich Jews still view the arts circumspectly and attitudes like Nathan Rothschild's have not disappeared. For example, Leonard Stern, head of Hartz Mountain Corporation, had the foresight to take public the family business (founded by his immigrant father with an inventory of twenty-one hundred canaries) in the 1960s and became one of the wealthiest Jews in America. Overnight, the pet food business made him a multimillionaire, with ten million shares of the company, at one point worth more than $500 million. But flea-collars are folding money: art is something else.

"I can't understand the value of art. I can't see all that money hanging on the wall without earning interest," Stern has said.

A number of successful Jews naturally disagreed, seeing in modern art one of the most lucrative ways to duplicate money since the invention of compound interest. The most colorful ones — the late Joe Hirshhorn, the uranium king, and Robert Scull, the taxi-fleet operator — made substantial sums as their collections appreciated. And so did Nathan Cummings of Consolidated Foods and David Krieger of Geico Insurance, both with modern but relatively unpublicized collections.

What has changed in the last generation is not the value of the artist, but the value of his work. Jack Levine's parents did not want their son to be an artist, for in their minds, it was a guarantee of poverty. They called it "a poor man's trade," and rightly so. Art was only valuable after the artist was dead, if then. But after World War II, a number of converging factors altered the old scene where Joseph Duveen, that extraordinary impresario, had played Chinese checkers with old masters and new millionaires. Popular demand for all styles grew, but particularly for modern and abstract works. And a new element was added in collecting: investment value. Jews were perhaps the first to appreciate the new art and the new ingredient. Sidney Janis was among the first to sense the trend in the United States.

## Gallery Patriarch

The art dealer's mantle is something of a Joseph's coat of many colors. A splendid raiment, spun with gold, glitter, and glory, it affords easy entree into all sorts of worlds — social, scholarly, and humanistic. It is a passport to the land of the Midases and to the hairy world of art. It can be worn in the rarefied air of the museum or it can be a useful garment to hide the huckster, shield the scholar, or clothe the impresario. Art dealers, successful ones at least, play some or all of these roles, simultaneously or in sequence at times during their careers.

An art dealer does not run a museum, nor is he established solely to uplift the public's taste. This might well be his inclination. But to survive and thrive in a high rent district, he must deal in expensive masterpieces. Some dealers are commodity brokers, not selling pork bellies or soy bean futures, but works by recognized artists, mostly dead. They buy and sell their works as they would any other product. They do it with more refinement, discernment, knowledge, and flair, and fewer gesticulations than the floor broker of the Chicago Board of Trade. Yet they are basically brother traders. Others have a touch of the educator in them.

Most avant-garde art dealers are aesthetic evangelists, crusaders bent on conquest, paladins with a cause. They set out to break down the doors, storm the academy, *epater le bourgeois,* convert the heathens, and sell the public their artistic vision. In short, with aesthetic brickbats in hand, they champion a particular cause. A mere two, five, or ten years may elapse before a new frame of reference is formulated and a new "aesthetic" appears on the scene. More confusing still, several trends may be spawned simultaneously. Rarely does a dealer span several modes and several successive uprisings.

One that has is Sidney Janis, a gray-haired septuagenarian who has managed to span quite a few artistic generations. In this respect, he is unique on the New York art scene. As head of the Janis Gallery, he has been a pacesetter and trend-maker for four decades, showing such artists as Leger, Mondrian, Delaunay, Albers, the Fauves, De Stijl, the Dadaists and the futurists in the late forties and early fifties. When the abstract expressionists came into their own, he showed Pollock, de Kooning, Gorky, Rothko, and Kline. He then went on to put on the first international pop art show in 1962. It raised a storm of controversy and led to the mass walkout of the then reigning group, the abstract expressionists. Entitled the *New Realists,* the show overflowed Janis' gallery space. He rented a store on 57th Street and installed the rest of the show in this ground-floor gallery. Rothko, Motherwell, and Gottlieb left together as a protest.

Warring factions in the arts were nothing new to Janis. Almost a decade earlier, a De Kooning show on women called forth all sorts of invectives from fellow abstract expressionists. This time around, however, the uproar was louder and the break definitive.

"I pointed out to them that I had shown their work next to the best of the previous generation — the modern old masters, Picasso, Leger and others. I couldn't see that the abstract expressionists were competing with the younger pop artists. First off, these painters had established reputations, their works were selling for several thousand dollars, while pop artists' works could be bought for a few hundred dollars. There was no competition in this juxtaposition," Janis remarked.

Sidney Janis, private individual, one-time shirt manufacturer and art lover, had been collecting for some twenty years before he decided to open a gallery. With Mrs. Janis, who then had her own jazz recording company, Janis had built up a collection of the school of Paris. He had met Leger, Picasso, Matisse, and Klee on trips to Europe and later came to know Miro, Dali, and Ernst. He had been writing on art, knew a group of sizable collectors and enjoyed the pleasant notoriety of having the Museum of Modern Art show his collection in 1935. Requests from other museums to do likewise followed. Why not do professionally what he had been doing for pleasure since 1926? Why not open a gallery?

After Janis' third book was published, he decided to do just that. The year was 1948; Valentine Bundesing had closed the year before, deserting the rigors of New York for France. He had specialized in German expressionists and had had the best gallery in town. Janis wanted to fill the gap.

The New York art scene in the early fifties was dominated by Europeans. American artists had no audience. "In the early fifties who was prominent among Americans? Arshile Gorky, Stuart Davis, that was about it. I recall that after Gorky's death his paintings were selling for $450 each."

"Pollock did his first drip painting in 1946; I sold that painting in 1955 for $200. A musician bought it," Janis said, "and insisted on a money-back guarantee." He never did demand his money back. The painting came up at auction at Sotheby's in the sixties and fetched $14,500, a seventy-three-fold increase. The purchaser? Sidney Janis.

Janis met Lee Krasner, Pollock's wife, some time in 1942 while amassing material for a book. She took him to Pollock's studio where Janis found Thomas Hart Benton's prize pupil of a decade earlier working in a Mexican style of sorts. Pollock was still interested in plant and animal forms then, but two paintings tended toward complete abstraction. Janis asked if he could have a photographer come in, but found the results disappointing: "There was no telling value; the textures of the paint simply didn't come across in black and white." Pollock said absolutely nothing all afternoon, Janis recalled, but somehow managed to impress him nevertheless.

"I was the first writer to have visited Pollock's studio."

Does a dealer make his artists famous? "No, it's not the dealer; and the critics are usually way behind. New trends and movements are not a marketing proposition. They just click and make sense. Willem De Kooning's first show sold two pictures, and he was just as good then as he is now. It's just a matter of a lag in taste," Janis said.

"A curious thing happened with the market for the abstract expressionists," he continued. "It was right after Pollock's tragic death in the car crash, in August of 1956. You know that Pollock was picturesque, a bad boy, and his death got a lot of publicity. Collectors became interested and prices for Pollocks, Rothkos, De Koonings and all that group shot up."

It was bitter irony: traumatic death brought what life had not. Heavy drinking was part of the abstract expressionist scene, a return to the primitive state, a way of exorcising the goblins of middle-American life and its stuffy parlor inhibitions. An autopsy revealed that Pollock had so pickled his liver that death had been imminent. Yet, had he died of natural causes, the whole art market would have been affected quite differently.

Janis, like most dealers, keeps the number of current gallery artists at around a dozen. The work he handles spans styles from Giacometti's long, lean nudes, to George Segal's plaster casts from live people, frozen in gestures by the hardening gypsum. Albers' squares play visual tricks on the retina next to the pop personages.

Janis' artists have the best of worlds: for the most part, there is such demand for their work that collectors must line up and take numbers as they would in a crowded bakery. The limited supply of new works puts Janis in a conundrum: "You can only write to one person at a time. If you write to two, and you sell to the first, the second feels cheated. After all, you are dealing with a unique work." Moreover, by the time the letter braves the mails and the collector gets himself physically to the gallery, days have elapsed. A peripatetic museum curator may well have snatched up the work before the collector makes it to the 57th Street building.

To call is even more dangerous. "If I pick up the phone to Mr. One on the list and say I have a Giacometti, it may be sold before he gets here. If I say that I am reserving it for him, then he feels that I am twisting his arm." It is a delicate situation.

Dealing with European collectors, or the Japanese is an even more lengthy process. The usual role is a reversal of the don't-call-us routine. It's I-won't-call-you, you-call-and-come. For the most part, it's first come, first served.

The more mundane matters of money are settled according to the artist's tax status and wishes. For some, Janis arranges a monthly drawing of cash. For sculptors who may need large advances to defray fabrication costs, separate arrangements are available. If Janis has an exclusive on an artist's works, and the work is not selling, rather than take the work on consignment or have the gallery buy the works outright, he prefers to lend the artist money. He finds it leads to fewer hard feelings.

Prices for works are set jointly. "I often have a fight with the artists on price," Janis recalls, "but I always take the artist's feeling about the quality of the work into consideration. He might say to me, 'This is my best piece, so I think it should go for X.' Another piece might have sold for a much lesser amount." Some artists would apparently price themselves out of the market if the dealer were to let them. "I don't like to set prices without the artist. On the other hand, I must admit that I'm always fighting for a lower price," Janis acknowledged.

Fifty, a hundred, two hundred and fifty thousand dollars — who can meet such price tags? Janis sells most artwork to museums. He has a following of some fifteen active museums, plus a hundred or so active collectors. A peripheral group of buyers is made up of dealers, less avid collectors, and, rarely, people who walk in off the street. The general public is naturally welcome at the gallery and often colleges in New York City and surrounding areas will arrange gallery tours for groups. Art students have always come, and there are groups from finishing schools — proto-collectors who will later convince their husbands to collect art. Women are more perceptive, Janis feels, and he encourages these groups.

Who figures on the roster of collectors? For the "old masters of modern art" there is an international clientele as well as an international market. For American works, the collectors are mostly American, though the Germans, Swiss, and English are buying more. "The Germans were always adventuresome, not in making art, but in appreciating it. Whereas they will hesitate to spend a huge sum on one work, they will often spread it and purchase a number of works by younger Americans."

Most collectors have made money on their own generation. Old money, Janis feels, seldom gets into modern art with the exception of the Whitneys, Rockefellers, and Guggenheims. Collectors rarely buy art with the idea of giving the work away to a museum or other public institution as a tax deduction. "After several years, they may decide that their income is too big, and why not give something away. But they don't start out that way." Neither do they buy as an outright investment. "It is a cultural gain, and it accrues prestige; secondarily, collecting is a good investment."

Does Janis entertain his collectors a great deal? "Entertain? Not at all. The collectors are entertained by the works of art." Janis has a kind of staunch austerity that makes him an admirable patriarch of the arts.

## From Poverty to Patronage

Two foundations have made a significant contribution to the art world — one a Goliath, the other a David. The Ford Foundation is far larger, but the Kaplan fund may have a more immediate impact on American art. The fund is the stepchild of J. M. Kaplan, an energetic man of ninety. Kaplan has been assisting the arts for more than a couple of decades, from providing small grants for individual artists and neighborhood community groups to funding dance companies and civic efforts. Few people in America have contributed more to the welfare of the art world. It has, at times, been a thankless task, for artists are not the easiest people to deal with.

Kaplan made his money trading sugar and molasses in the twenties and thirties. At one point, he had an abundance of sugar, but demand was slack. Looking for an outlet, he decided to approach the Welch Grape Company, a major sugar consumer. Though interested in the product, they would not do business with him because he was a Jew. As a public corporation, they had crossed the wrong man. Kaplan, an inveterate stock market operator, started to corner the company's shares. When he had working control of the board, he fired the anti-Semitic managers. Eventually, Kaplan sold his interest in Welch and moved into real estate and portfolio investments.

"He has an uncanny knack of buying companies shortly before they become financially successful. I've looked at the balance sheets, the profit and loss statements and don't see anything unusual in them. But he buys them and they work out," said Lothar Stiefel, Kaplan's treasurer and accountant.

Kaplan's commitment to the arts is more than skin deep: one daughter is married to a prominent artist, while another, Joan Davidson, was the New York State Chairwoman of the Arts Council. One Fund project, its most unusual undertaking, tested Kaplan's fortitude and eventually got under his skin. Foundations, for the most part, sponsor the arts through grants to produce art works like sculpture, symphony and orchestra tours, or television documentaries. In the mid-sixties, the Kaplan Fund became involved in sponsoring a home for artists.

Roger Stevens, a theatre producer, was Chairman of the National Council on the Arts when William Zeckendorf, the real estate operator, brought to his attention the fact the AT&T's Bell Laboratories building was up for sale. The telephone company had moved its facilities to New Jersey, vacating "this great peculiar lump of a building" in Greenwich Village. Stevens was acutely aware of the shortage of decent artists' housing in the United States, and was also aware of the Kaplan Fund's interest in rehabilitating old structures for such purposes. Together, they moved to buy the Bell building by establishing the nonprofit Westbeth Corporation, each putting up $750,000 of seed money grants. The actual sale took place on July 12, 1967 for a price of $2.5 million.

The Bell Laboratories on West Street and Bethune Street (hence Westbeth) had had a remarkable history, one that was to continue in a slightly different guise under Kaplan's auspices. In the 1890s, the Western Electric Company bought the land for a modest $119,000 and erected a thirteen-story manufacturing shop in 1897. Electricity was a new phenomenon: Edison perfected the incandescent bulb eight years earlier, and the first generation of electrical equipment had started five years previously. Telephony was somewhat older — Alexander Graham Bell had invented his "harmonic telegraph" in 1876, but it did not begin to flourish until the 1880s. Thus, the workers in the West Street plant manufactured telephone equipment for the burgeoning utility. The research and development department was also under the same roof.

For the next half-century, a startling series of inventions came from Bell-on-the-Hudson. Scientists and engineers developed the first high-vacuum tube and amplifier, a necessary step before long-distance lines were to operate satisfactorily. Using the discovery of the amplifier in the condenser microphone — the "mike" — Bell produced a public address system, the phonograph record, radio broadcasting equipment, and developed the concepts for radio altimeters for airplanes and for radar.

Perhaps the most publicized development on West Street came in 1923. Edison had invented motion pictures. Could they be made to speak as well? Synchronizing the motion picture with sound was a major technical hurdle — one that took a decade to overcome. But in the spring of 1923, the first true "talkies" were developed. Three years later, Western Electric licensed the Vitaphone Corporation, partially owned by Warner Brothers, to produce sound movies. In 1926, they produced *Don Juan*, starring John Barrymore. A year later Al Jolson, in *The Jazz Singer*, was telling the public that they "ain't heard nothin' yet!" Bell engineers were demonstrating television and preparing the way for international radio service.

Other creative efforts from the prolific people of West Street included long-playing, high fidelity records; stereophonic transmission; coaxial cable; digital computers; and transistors. While on West Street, two Nobel prizes were awarded to the lab's scientists for their creative work. Thus the transition from science to art, though abrupt, was not necessarily inconsistent with what went before.

At first glance, there was much to recommend the conversion of the labs. While not in the most fashionable part of town, the complex was situated in the center city. Second, the buildings were massive — a total of 626,800 square feet. The space was ideal for artists: the ceilings ranged from twelve to fifteen feet in height; ample lighting was afforded by banks of windows; and the whole structure was fireproof. For its seventy years, the shell was in relatively good shape. Third, while a rehabilitation job is always more costly than anticipated — and Westbeth was no exception — it was still cheaper than starting from scratch.

The Kaplan Fund was not only sponsoring housing, but was attempting to incorporate working and living space under one roof. The renovation raised all sorts of artistic, social, economic, and bureaucratic problems. Many of them were solved by the architect for the conversion, Richard Meier, a one-time associate of Marcel Breuer. He came up with an imaginative solution to revamp the physical plant, transforming it from an industrial conglomerate to a residential community. His design called for creating 383 apartments ranging from studio efficiencies to three bedroom duplexes. In order to keep the apartments as spacious as possible, and to accommodate artists working on a large scale, the interiors were left without walls — except for kitchens and bathrooms. The *New York Times* commented on the "Olympian quarters" and the fact that the "ceilings are high and the plumbing works." The *San Juan Star,* in disbelief, ran an editorial entitled "Bohemians Have Running Water."

Obtaining government permission for this freeform housing was not easy. One of the fundamental axioms of zoning is to separate business and residential structures as much as possible. Westbeth was trying to combine the two. A zoning variance was passed after prolonged hearings. Other city regulations were changed.

The problem of securing mortgage money was compounded by red tape. A whole string of New York banks turned the project down, until Kaplan leaned on Bankers Trust Company, a bank that he had been doing business with for thirty years. They supplied the premortgage money for construction. Finally, the Federal Housing Administration approved a low-interest mortgage under its middle-income housing program (221-D3), replacing the Bankers Trust loan with a mortgage for $10.4 million at three percent interest. Though the whole project took three and a half years to complete, the renovation was a testament to the ability of overlapping jurisdictions to pick up their skirts and run when properly prodded. The Kaplan fund supplied the prod.

At first, artists werre reluctant to move to Westbeth. What kind of "asylum" would it be with hundreds of creative types under one roof? The very idea of a "project" was enough to turn off a number of potential applicants. But Joan Davidson, president of Westbeth Corporation and Kaplan's daughter, managed to persuade some better known artists to take up residence. And before the construction was finished, the apartments were filled and a waiting list formed. While Westbeth was designed primarily for painters and sculptors, it opened its doors to all the arts. At one time, there were thirty different artistic disciplines represented: actors, dancers, playwrights, photographers, cinematographers, poets, novelists, composers, musicians, writers, set designers, ceramicists — even a mask-maker.

Whether Westbeth will ever develop into the Corbusian *unite d'habitation,* a guiding idea of Richard Meier when he designed the building, remains to be seen. Westbeth remains a loosely knit community, receiving subsidies from federal and city governments, but supplying in return a certain leaven of creativity. The Kaplan Fund has slowly withdrawn from the noble experiment, somewhat disillusioned, for it seemed impossible to do enough for the resident artists.

"They seemed to think that we should support them forever," remarked one fund associate. After a rent strike (one banner read Kaplan Welch's On Rents), the fund turned control of the board of trustees to some prominent citizens active in the arts. But the value of the undertaking continues, for it set an example that a number of countries have imitated. Abandoned industrial buildings in inner city areas can be revitalized, artists can be supported by indirect government subsidies, and a city can benefit from their talent in a number of ways.

### Rothko v. Marlborough

In an earlier period the *Beth din* (a rabbinical court) might have settled the case: it was, after all, a commercial dispute among Jews involving questions of inheritance. The daughter and son of one of America's foremost painters were suing the executors of their father's estate and his gallery. But it moved so quickly from the complaints of disgruntled heirs to the most momentous civil case in a generation that it would have dwarfed the efforts of any voluntary religious court. Some even called it the art world's Watergate. Whether or not it was a Watergate, it was certainly a high-water mark. Never before in the annals of American art had so much money been contested, so many reputations laid on the line, the value of so much work questioned, and the machinations of art dealing so clearly exposed. And all over an artist barely dead. In brief, the case was a voyeur's delight that employed dozens upon dozens of attorneys.

In a sense, the case of Rothko v. Marlborough began long before the first papers were served in 1971. Perhaps it all started in Russia. Besides Chagall, a number of prominent Jewish artists were born there: Weber in Bialystock, Nevelson in Kiev, Shahn in Kuvno, the Soyers in Borisoglepsk, Gross in the Carpathian mountains. And a number of others — Gottlieb, Levine, Newman, and Rattner — were brought up in homes heavily influenced by Russian traditions. Mark Rothko was born in Dvinsk in 1903, but emigrated to America, where he was raised by his parents in Oregon. He studied at Yale and at the Art Students League in New York with Max Weber and Max Ernst. For most of his life, he was obliged to teach art, and for most of his life he earned, on average, $10,000 a year.

In the 1940s, he became one of the creators of a new art form — abstract expressionism. Along with Clyfford Still, Barnett Newman, Adolph Gottlieb, Willem de Kooning, Franz Kline, and Jackson Pollock, Rothko shaped the first truly American art style to have international influence. For twenty years, these action painters dominated the art scene. Rothko's work — large rectangles of scintillating, diaphanous color — were interpreted in various ways while the demand for them increased. To one, they were a reflection of open Oregon, to another, "a new type of votive picture . . . [with] its mythic religious space." For many observers, they evoked a strong sense of spirituality. A German critic found them "animated, stirring, concealing drapery" that could be interpreted as "ancient Jewish metaphors for the hidden God." The director of the Yale Art Gallery wrapped it all up: "There was in Rothko . . . a Zoroastrian sense of light and darkness as symbols of goodness and evil, growing out of an inheritance from a youth spent in virgin Oregon, merging with memories of his Old Testament ancestors and a deep recall of his origins in that great land of opposites, Russia."

Rothko rarely discussed his work, but in one interview he adamantly rejected the "abstractionist" category: "I'm interested only in expressing basic human emotions — tragedy, ecstasy, doom, and so on — and the fact that lots of people break down and cry when confronted with my pictures shows that I *communicate* those basic human emotions. . . . The people who weep before my pictures are having the same religious experience I had when I painted them. And if you . . . are moved only by their color relationships, then you miss the point!"

In the heyday of abstract expressionism, Rothko was represented by Sidney Janis. During those years the value of his work increased markedly as did his reputation. In the sixties he was courted by Frank Lloyd, the head of the Marlborough Galleries. Lloyd was something of a nabob on the American art scene, thought of as a parvenu by established dealers since he had only arrived in the United States in 1963. He was thought of as a businessman, not an aesthete, a description that Lloyd would be the first to agree with. Indeed, the newly formed Art Dealers Association considered excluding Marlborough because of the competition that would be fostered by that London behemoth.

Of the hundreds of galleries that make up the New York art scene perhaps only one hundred and fifty see themselves as taste-makers and conservators. They are the stabilizing force who withstand the gusts of this school or that, and, in a sense, hope to save art from itself — from its transitory fads and from novelty. They uphold Taste, Aesthetics, and Visual Sensibility — all in the name of Art. They have an eye on art history, if not immortality, and feel that they are promoting the discernment and taste that collectors will value. They are conservators of all the things that art used to stand for, leaving earthworks to farmers, process art to the theatre, and body art to dancers. They are involved with objects of beauty and value. And they must offer one other essential ingredient — reliability. But many of these galleries — some say a substantial majority — make no profit since they are either tax-loss operations, or exercises in aesthetic diletantism.

Lloyd was not out to undermine the art world or its values. He was interested in making money dealing in art. Though the art works are unique, the business practices and procedures associated with art need not be. A businessman could do a lot in the art world, an arena that vaguely held business in contempt. This gospel came not from a graduate of a business school, but from a Central-European Jew. Lloyd wanted to rationalize the art market in America, a job he had started earlier in London.

Frank Lloyd, nee Franz Kurt Levai, was born in Vienna in 1911. The family had dealt in antiques for two generations, but Lloyd had become financially successful through his ownership of a chain of Austrian service stations in the 1930s. He invested some of his profit in Picassos and Fauvists. When Hitler arrived Lloyd fled Vienna for Paris with ten dollars, a gold cigarette case, a passport, and an exit visa. Eventually he arrived in London, where he changed his name and met his partner-to-be, Harry Fischer, another Viennese refugee, in a British army unit. In 1948 they established the Marlborough Fine Art Gallery with some rare books of Fischer's, some paintings Lloyd had hidden in France during the war, and the money and connections of aristocrat David Somerset, later Duke of Beaufort. Introductions to old English families were particularly valuable since those postwar families, as Lloyd notes, had "an abundance of pictures and not much money." Marlborough sold the English Old Masters and Impressionists to European museums.

As the supply dwindled, Marlborough decided to deal in established modern artists. The London gallery was so successful that in 1963 it bought out the New York gallery of Otto Gerson. With only a small stable of artists, Lloyd started to wine and dine some of the leading artists. Before long he had negotiated contracts with Francis Bacon, Adolph Gottlieb, Jacques Lipschitz, Henry Moore, Robert Motherwell, Larry Rivers, Clyfford Still, David Smith, and the estate of Jackson Pollock. The gallery on 57th Street grew so rapidly that within a half dozen years it became the most successful outlet — in dollars — for modern art. Lloyd even opened a gallery on the Queen Elizabeth II for the trans-Atlantic trade. Marlborough clients came from all over the globe — Norton Simon, Clare Booth Luce, Picasso, Agnelli of Fiat, Mrs. Paul Mellon, and Otto Preminger (another Viennese who has remarked that his ancestors bought from Lloyd's ancestors). Perhaps his greatest coup was an audience with Pope Paul VI, where he interested the pontiff in collecting contemporary art.

The artists were kept happy by Marlborough's business-like dealings and professional conduct. For the most part, art work is taken on consignment, with the gallery receiving a commission on sales. The commission, negotiated by artist and dealer, runs between twenty-five percent and fifty percent of the price of the work. In turn, the gallery supplies exhibition space, publicity, promotion, catalogues, mailings, insurance, and transportation. No single aspect of the art world causes more controversy than the commission. And it was the problems of commissions that were to trouble Lloyd later on. Most artists were pleased with Marlborough and Lloyd, for their work commanded the highest price and, in time, appreciated in value under his aegis. Besides advantageous exposure, they could arrange for a guaranteed fixed monthly stipend, no small benefit in a feast-or-famine trade.

By now Marlborough was something of a colossus of the modern art scene, with galleries in Zurich, Montreal, Toronto, Rome, Tokyo, London, and a corporate headquarters in Liechtenstein. With more than a hundred employees, including six accountants, leased telex lines, tax-avoidance arrangements, payments in gold or most any currency, Lloyd and Fischer (who left in 1971 to start a new gallery in London) had developed the art world's multinational corporation.

Lloyd's primary interest in money earned him the enmity of aesthetes, poseurs, diletantes, some formidable art critics, and, of course, other art dealers. They've accused him of unfair business practices, raiding their stables of artists, discounting, and being too aggressive and slick. These are the accusations commonly heard when the markets of old businesses are challenged by newcomers. But in this instance there was, in addition, the unspoken assumption that Lloyd was a philistine because of his success.

Lloyd is unperturbed by the criticism. He sees Marlborough standing in the way of the alleged Jewish mafia, that small but highly influential group of critics, dealers, and curators that dominate the New York art scene. Membership in the mafia is select: Leo Castelli, a gallery owner; Clement Greenberg, an art critic; Henry Geldzahler, curator of the Metropolitan Museum of Art; Ben Heller, a dealer; Hilton Kramer, art critic of the *New York Times;* Larry Rubins of Knoedler Gallery; his brother William Rubins, a curator of the Museum of Modern Art; et al. This group is a formidable power in forming taste and promoting some schools of art to the exclusion of others. If the art establishment were dealing in securities, it would probably be out of business, but the doctrine of full disclosure has not reached the art world and aesthetic self-serving is not a problem that the SEC is mandated to deal with. Thus Lloyd squared off against the inbred art world.

"The only thing that blocks them [the art clique] from complete control of the art world is Marlborough. We're independent. We are the biggest handicap to that clique," Lloyd said.

But the Jewish mafia struck back, some suggested, in the Rothko v. Marlborough case. Business was going along swimmingly — gross sales at Marlborough were in excess of $25 million annually, probably between five percent and ten percent of the global art market. Impropriety occasionally surfaced in the art world, but for the most part, attracted little public attention. Major misconduct, of course, was another story. Shady business practices have a long and dishonorable tradition in American history and the art world has had its share. Most of the major scandals — forgeries, false attributions, and frauds — titillated and amused the public. Frequently it was a matter of one rich man taking from another. The Rothko case was different: it received national attention and the artist's children were subjects of sympathy. Though the executors were the defendants in the case, the real villain was Frank Lloyd of Marlborough.

The immediate case started with the suicide of Mark Rothko in February, 1970. Rothko was a man of intense feelings that changed rapidly and unaccountably. Perhaps he was somewhat paranoid: he distrusted doctors (he had his blood pressure checked in both arms), curators who hung his paintings, lawyers, and elevators. But he could be extremely generous to fellow artists and other creative types. In his later years he established a foundation, which was to be continued after his death, for the purpose of helping older artists, "mature, elderly painters and sculptors, composers and writers" who have not been successful. Half of his estate was left to the foundation. The other half went to his wife, but she died shortly after he did. Consequently, his children, Kate and Christopher, inherited the estate.

The suit was brought by the executor of Mrs. Rothko's estate. Her executor asked the surrogate court to void the contract that the artist's executors had made with Marlborough three months after his death. In brief (there was nothing brief about the trial, it took four years), he charged that the executors had "wasted the assets of the estate," that they had defrauded the estate through self-serving arrangements. Rothko had named three friends as his executors. Morton Levine, an anthropologist; Bernard Reis, an accountant; and Theodoros Stamos, a fellow painter.

The issues were particularly complex since there were so many different parties involved. Seven sets of attorneys were employed. One old friend of Rothko's reportedly remarked at the start of the trial that "Mark made a lot of money from his paintings, but not nearly as much as the legal profession will."

The main issue concerned the contract negotiated with Marlborough and the reputed dollar value of Rothko's work. The contract was really the third one the gallery had entered into — the first two were with the artist. In 1963 Rothko had sold to the gallery fifteen paintings for $147,667 to be paid out over four and a half years, or an average of roughly $10,000 a piece. By 1969 the prices of Rothko's canvases had jumped one-hundred percent: they were selling for an average of $21,000. Lloyd and Rothko then negotiated a new agreement in 1969, which called for the sale of eighty-seven paintings for $1,050,000, and a few months later, an additional agreement which brought the total to 108 paintings (some were works on paper) for $1,446,000. The prices were based, in part, on what Rothko reportedly received for his work in private sales. In these arrangements, the artist took on an active role guided by his accountant, Reis', advice. Reis was a long-time friend, but his accounting firm was employed by Marlborough for some years. Reis was instrumental in arranging a most unusual third contract.

Regardless of what happened to Frank Lloyd or Marlborough during the next fourteen years (Rothko's life expectancy), the Rothschild Bank would pay the artist $100,000 a year. To protect its investment since this was a sale, Marlborough obtained the rights to represent Rothko for eight years, until 1977. The only exception to this exclusivity was the direct sale by the artist of four paintings a year for which the gallery received a ten percent commission. Thus the contract provided financial security that few living artists attain, irrespective of fads and fashions. Meanwhile, Marlborough had to pledge substantial assets to the bank to cover the guarantee.

These arrangements had run roughly one year when the artist died. In that time, Marlborough had sold twenty-eight works for half of the principal sum.

Shortly after his death, Rothko's executors were faced with the usual estate costs — principally taxes and support of heirs. The executors sold more of Rothko's paintings to Marlborough, as they were apparently obliged to do under the terms of the previous contract for all future sales. Thus in May, 1970, the executors — minus Reis who was sensitive to a possible conflict of interest since he had, at Rothko's persuasion, become an officer of Marlborough — signed a final agreement selling one hundred paintings from the estate for $1.8 million. In short, Marlborough paid almost as much for the second batch of paintings as it had for the first (when adjustments are made for the paper works) even though many of the works in the second batch were already seen and rejected in the previous sale.

How does one judge paintings? One of the main issues in the suit was the value of the executors' sale. Since art has come to be thought of as an "investment," one way of measuring relative value is to use the Dow Jones Industrial Average as a standard. When the 1969 sale was made, the Dow reached a high of 969, but when the 1970 sale was consummated, it was trading in the 660 area. In other words, the blue-chip average lost thirty-two percent of its value. Did that mean Rothko's work had lost a third of its worth? Perhaps.

Richard Feigen, a gallery owner and one-time holder of a New York Stock Exchange seat, remarked that "New York amplifies a boom, as it does a bust. If you have 100 guys making $100,000 a year on Wall Street, you have an art market that is taking off." And conversely, a recession pulls the plug. Who's to hold up prices when they are falling all around? This question of value was the crux of the case and all sides mustered their experts.

Feigen valued the one hundred paintings at $5.5 million. Ben Heller thought the paintings were worth $6.42 million, and with the remainder of the estate, 698 other works that Marlborough was to sell for a fifty percent commission, a grand total of $10.5 million. The New York State Attorney General's office, as a protector of the public beneficiaries of the foundation, was also on the side of the plaintiff — though curiously, the foundation aligned itself with the defense. The state thought the whole estate was worth more than $32 million. The federal government was more modest, evaluating the estate at $16.5 million.

Testimony by the most disinterested party, Peter Selz, a California art historian and one-time curator of the Museum of Modern Art in New York, thought the retail value to be slightly in excess of $4 million. But these were all retail values: the custom of the trade dictated significant reduction for a bulk puchase, up to two-thirds or three-quarters off. Thus Marlborough's price, when translated into retail, amounted to between $5.4 million and $7.2 million. Lloyd had apparently not underpaid if some of the plaintiff's most generous estimates were accepted.

The other significant issue was the commission rate — forty to fifty percent — for the 698 paintings that the executors had placed with Marlborough on consignment. It was high, especially for an established painter of Rothko's stature. But the rate was part of a package and it only became suspect when Theodoros Stamos entered into a contract with Marlborough at about the same time at a significantly lower commission rate. Was Stamos acting in an unprincipled fashion, and did his position as an executor put him into conflict of interests?

Finally, during the course of the trial, Marlborough was enjoined from selling any of Rothko's work in the estate transaction. The gallery was held in contempt by the court when it appeared that some of the paintings had been sold abroad. But confusion resulted from clerical errors in dating invoices on sales in the gallery made before the court order. Documentation by Lloyds of London, the principal insurance broker, cleared up the matter. Many peripheral issues were raised in the case: somehow Marlborough was selling Rothko paintings abroad to a presumed European subsidiary for low prices, then reselling them for prices four to fifteen times higher; somehow Frank Lloyd could control the prices for Rothko's work; somehow international sales were not only instruments of tax avoidance, but were calculated to rip off the estate. What precisely was Lloyd's relationship to Marlborough and to the family trusts that he controlled?

Lloyd's appearance in court — his vagueness — did not help his case. In court he was "suave, angry, petulant, flattering, arrogant, humble, defiant, defensive, apologetic, sarcastic, cheerful and disarming." At the end of four years and almost fifteen thousand pages of transcript with three million words, the surrogate, Millard Midonick, ousted the executors. Finding them negligent and in a conflict of interests, "the acts and failures-to-act of the three exectors were clearly improper." Moreover, the original contract had an "unconscionably low provision as to price and . . . indefiniteness of minimum price provision," wrote the judge in an eighty-seven-page decision. He slapped Lloyd with a $3.3 million fine (though it could be mitigated by return of the estate paintings), deprived the executors of the two percent of the estate each would have been paid for their services, and fined them $6 million. The estate was returned to Rothko's children.

Rothko, with the best of intentions, put his friends in a no-win situation because of his previous dealings. How the court could know the "true" value of his work remains something of a mystery since prices in the art world are notoriously fickle. And to assume that the whole portfolio should be evaluated on the basis of a few high-priced sales is disingenuous. The penalty of $6 million on the executors was outlandish in such dubious circumstances.

Frank Lloyd remained on his Bahama island, out of reach of the disgruntled heirs until 1982. He returned from his island retreat to answer derivative charges stemming from the trial. Lloyd feels he will eventually be vindicated: "We will win, and the art Mafia here will have gained nothing." But the self-imposed exile must have been somewhat bitter to a man who promised himself that after World War II, he would never do anything he didn't enjoy.

# 9. Medicine Men

In her nineties, Gutele Rothschild, wife of the founder of the banking house, consulted a highly recommended physician concerning a number of her ills. The doctor listened sympathetically, but said: "Well, I cannot, alas, make you younger."

"Doctor," said the old lady, "I want only to become older."

## My Son, the Doctor

Close to every Jewish mother's heart, according to cliché, is the desire to see her son become a doctor. Like all clichés, there is some truth in it. No one is sure where the notion got started or why it is true. Apparently, Jewish mothers have prevailed: in the United States there are approximately thirty thousand Jewish physicians, nearly fourteen percent of all physicians in private practice.

Jews do not become physicians only at maternal urging, nor does the medical profession pass only through the mother. Medicine has historic precedents reaching back to the beginning of Judaism. The Jewish physician was a venerated and respected figure, whose services and skills were in great demand by princes and popes. Jewish doctors were sought by rulers from Saladin to Elizabeth I. A Jewish physician attended Charlemagne, and a number of them attended Stalin, much to their chagrin. The papacy made little effort to hide the fact that the popes used Jewish physicians, though canon law forbade Christians from patronizing infidels lest they fall under their spell. Obviously, it was a case of hedging one's bets: better to be cured in this world than deified in the next.

One story — perhaps apocryphal, though frequently repeated in medical histories — was the request of France's King Francis I for a Jewish physician. The King asked the Holy Roman Emperor, Charles V, to recommend one. Charles dispatched his own physician to attend His Most Christian Majesty. When he arrived, Francis started to disparage Judaism and mock the doctor's beliefs. But the physician replied that he had converted to the only true faith, Catholicism. With that, Francis dismissed him immediately and asked for a "real Jewish doctor."

People still seek real Jewish doctors and Jews still pursue careers in medicine with an intensity that gentiles often find incomprehensible. If a Jewish pre-med student cannot gain admission to the school of his choice, he will scour the countryside and, if rejected, apply to foreign schools. The competition is so great that New York State has agreed to sponsor an Israeli institution if it will accept state residents.

The attractions of medicine are of course many: altruism and humanitarianism; awe and respect; pride and a portable profession. Hardly least in the list, though always spoken sotto voce, is money. For ministering to our anatomical needs, the medical profession has contrived to exact no small fee: it is now the most affluent trade in the country. In 1981 the average incorporated American physician earned $80,000.

Gone is the pastoral period of Jewish history when one famous doctor, noted for his unselfish and considerate ways, refused direct payment from patients: he hung out a box for pay-as-you-go contributions. Today, the sentiment is similar to that expressed by Aba, a surgeon of Talmudic times who remarked that "a physician who takes no fee is worth no fee."

The contributions of Jewish physicians to medical science were extraordinary. Building on the legacy of the Greeks and Arabs, the Jews applied empirical and systematic inquiry to the practice of medicine. They even saw the connection between the body and the spirit — how the latter could affect the former. Maimonides thought that sickness was not only attributable to bad habits or excesses, but also to a deficiency in good moral principles. While Acquinas thought that the position of the stars and the possession by demons explained mental illness, Jews approached medicine as a causative science. In medieval times, their Christian colleagues were still waving amulets, uttering incantations, and believing in superstitions.

As in other cultures, early Jewish medicine men combined healing and religion. The rabbis were custodians of the medical arts — both a source of knowledge and the active agents applying that knowledge, frequently taking the role of physician. Eventually, a major philosophical question arose as to the nature of illness: should physicians attempt to cure disease or at least tender relief, or should they rely on God? Was disease a sign of cosmic displeasure, punishment for some transgression against the Almighty? Perhaps healing was not what He had in mind when He first struck down the ill person. It was this ambivalence that was responsible for separating religion and medicine, rabbi from physician. However, the rabbi has remained the traditional healer throughout much of Jewish history. There was a particular benefit from this arrangement since rabbis were charged with enforcement of kashruth, the religious dietary laws, and by extension, the supervision of public sanitation. Jews did not coin the adage that cleanliness was next to godliness (John Wesley, the founder of Methodism did), but a cardinal doctrine of Judaism was to be clean and to care for one's health.

From biblical days, Jews approached problems of health on a trial-and-error basis, devoid of theories and abstractions. One physician who has reviewed the medical achievements of Jews wrote that "ancient Hebrew physicians . . . were pioneers in the field of pathology, preventative medicine, and hygiene. A definite racial trait was evident in their research work in the subject of pathology. Throughout the ages we find the tendency of Jews to be philosophical, to search for obscure causes of the illness of mankind, and to discover new measures for their prevention. They were not concerned so much with the description of the symptoms of diseases as with the mechanisms of their prevention or removal by new methods of treatment."

Jewish doctors were among the first explorers of the New World: Columbus had two of them on his first voyage, a physician and a surgeon. However, the first Jewish practitioner to live in the colonies was Jacob Lumbrozo from Lisbon, who settled in Maryland in 1656 and "built up a lucrative medical practice in Charles County." But for the most part, Jewish doctors were few, usually refugees from the Iberian peninsula or Brazil in colonial times.

The number of indigenously trained Jewish doctors — products of Columbia University or the University of Pennsylvania, the two major medical schools in early America — grew during the nineteenth century. And during the Civil War, there were Jewish physicians on both sides.

The small number of Jews in America in the middle of the nineteenth century (before any large Jewish immigration) did not want to be treated in Christian hospitals, particularly in terminal cases. Patients were often proselytized on their death beds, hardly an auspicious moment and guaranteed to be an intrusion or worse for a religious Jew. Consequently, Jews desired to build their own hospitals. In the middle of the century, there was a reform movement to improve public health and community care in New York City. In the 1850s the Young Men's Christian Association, Children's Aid Society, Roosevelt, St. Luke's, and St. Vincent's hospitals were all founded. In 1852 a group led by attorney Sampson Simson — a student of Aaron Burr and probably the first Jew to be admitted to the New York Bar — established Jews' Hospital in Manhattan. A fashionable charity ball started its initial fundraising campaign, taking in $1,036.14. By 1855 it had opened its first building on then rural 28th Street, between Seventh and Eighth Avenues. The building, in the nature of a four-story brownstone, accommodated forty-five patients and cost $9,000. From the beginning, the hospital was overcrowded. New York's population was half a million, with over ten thousand Jews. Consequently, a very early resolution of the hospital's board was "not to receive any patients other than Jews except in the case of accident." By the Civil War, the policy was changed, and the doors were open to all.

Well almost all. The hospital would not treat unmarried syphilitic women, and men in the same condition had to pay a month's treatment in advance.

In the hospital's first year of operation, the chief resident and attending physician was paid $250 for his annual services, about what a contemporary colleague makes between coffee breaks. He did better the second year; his salary was increased to $500. Private practice, then as now, was more lucrative. Dr. Abraham Jacobi, a political refugee from Germany, came to the United States at about that time and was later to play a prominent role at Mount Sinai Hospital as the country's first pediatrician. Jacobi earned $973.25 in his first year's practice — twenty-five cents for office visits and $5 to $10 for deliveries.

Jews' Hospital moved to Lexington Avenue and 66th Street in 1872, but by then it had changed its name to Mount Sinai. In 1904 it moved again to its present location on Fifth Avenue and 100th Street. Instead of building one large hospital, as was the fashion, the architects designed ten separate low-lying buildings, set off from each other but connected by a series of tunnels. Surrounded by space and facing Central Park, Mount Sinai had the latest amenities: electricity, x-ray machines, and a private pavillion dedicated by the Guggenheims. And within the complex was a two-hundred-seat synagogue. When Mount Sinai opened on upper Fifth Avenue, the daily admission rate was $1.50.

Over the years the hospital expanded, physically and in terms of special departments: a nursing school; a well-baby clinic; radio-therapy, psychiatric, and geriatric departments, and a hyperbaric laboratory were added. Finally in the early 1970s, the classical low profile was radically altered when a skyscraper was erected within its courtyards. This modernistic structure made of cor-ten-steel (steel designed to rust on its surface) hovers over the skyline, dark and foreboding, clashing with the surrounding buildings.

The thirty-one-story tower is the Annenberg Building, the new center for the hospital and the medical school. Its history is a classic example of the potency of Jewish power and money applied to a specific issue. Since the late 1950s, Mount Sinai had begun to think seriously about creating a medical school. The hospital was considered one of the best in the United States: surveys and ratings usually placed it within the top dozen or half-dozen institutions. However, it lacked a comprehensive affiliation with a first-rate university. The limited connection with Columbia University's College of Physicians and Surgeons was not strong enough to be considered an affiliation. Mount Sinai, though not primarily a teaching and research hospital, had a remarkable number of breakthroughs, developments, and serendipitous discoveries. A list of its physicians — Emil Gruening, Arpad Gerster, Carl Koller, Bernard Sachs, Emanuel Libman, Reuben Ottenberg, Leo Buerger, Nathan Brill, Richard Lewisohn, Bela Schick, Gregory Shwartzman, et al. — was impressive.

Today, however, top scientists and researchers prefer hospitals with academic affiliations so they can keep a foot in medicine and research. If basic biological sciences were the key to future medical progress, Mount Sinai would have to offer facilities comparable to those found in teaching and research hospitals. There was the strong impression that the first-rank Jewish doctors were going elsewhere, a result of the decrease in anti-Semitism in academia.

The solution was to build a medical school — no simple undertaking in the best of times and under the most felicitous conditions. At first the board of directors was lukewarm, feeling that it was better to have "a first-rate hospital than to chance a second-rate medical school." A local leader thought that a medical school was a luxury — that it would "loot" community resources better used for more immediate purposes. And finally, organized medicine, whose self-interest could only be diminished by a frontal lobotomy, played an old refrain by insisting that there were already too many doctors.

The opposition soon dwindled as the board of directors got behind the idea. It took ten years of organization and planning — agreements and accommodations with medical and educational agencies, all levels of government, and finally, the Board of Higher Education, since the Mount Sinai School of Medicine became part of the City University. Once the school was established, it became an institution in search of a building. The building would hold the joint facilities of the hospital and the school, plus all the peripheral and paramedical utilities. Initially construction costs were projected at $5 million, but year-by-year, they escalated until they passed the $100 million mark, before construction even started.

Such an undertaking would have caused severe dyspepsia — perhaps even regional enteritis (ileitis), considered a Jewish disease until President Eisenhower came down with it — for a lesser board of directors. Fortunately, the board of directors at Mount Sinai included rich Jews and some of the most persuasive fundraisers in New York City. They undertook to raise $152 million dollars and did so within ten years. The board, according to one close observer, is made up of "guys who really know how to raise money." The sixty member board was sprinkled with nabobs from the world of business and finance: the chairman of the board was Gustave L. Levy, a partner of Goldman, Sachs, investment bankers; Andre Meyer, partner in Lazard Freres, another prominent banking house; a Loeb (Loeb Rhoades); a Lehman (Lehman Brothers); a Lasker (Lasker, Stone & Stern); and a couple of Klingensteins (Wertheim); from the world of whiskey, a Bronfman (Seagrams) and a Rosenstiel (Schenley); and others from real estate, construction, oil, advertising, chemicals, food, and fashion. To start the campaign, Walter Annenberg, publisher, media merchant, and ambassador to Great Britain, gave $1 million dollars to the campaign. His seven sisters also gave $1 million each for a total of $8 million. There were another dozen gifts each for $1 million or more, plus 132 contributions of $100,000 or more. By whatever criteria the campaign is measured, it was a success.

## Sinai in the Slums

Mount Sinai is the centerpiece of Jewish-affiliated hospitals, the exemplar for sixty-three other hospitals, which are connected to the Federation of Jewish Philanthropies. There are "Mount Sinai" hospitals in most of the major Jewish population centers, from Baltimore to Los Angeles. And most of them are inner city institutions contending with the urban problems of crowding, crime, rising costs, and falling income. Perhaps the final irony is that they no longer service the Jews that they were built to serve.

When Mount Sinai in New York City moved to its present location in 1904, the surrounding areas were populated by Jews — rich on upper Fifth, Madison, and Park Avenues, and the middle-class in Harlem. Today, all that has changed: Harlem is populated by blacks and the surrounding neighbors of el barrio are predominantly Puerto Rican. On the hospital's one-hundredth anniversary in 1952, a commemorative report noted that the neighborhood was "an overcrowded, noisy, dirty, polyglot slum." Since then not much has changed. Though some old tenements have been replaced by new projects, the area is still a slum with every indication that it will remain so for the foreseeable future. The streets are chock-full of humanity: women and children hanging out of windows or sitting on fire escapes; older men playing cards or dominoes on the sidewalk; couples sitting in the projects' parks; young men repairing, altering and customizing their "wheels." The two worlds are spheres unto themselves, touching with all the intimacy of car bumpers. Within the hospital there is a commingling of interests, but the segregation is pretty much a fait accompli.

"We're a nonsectarian hospital," commented one of the hospital's surgeons, "but my guess is that ninety-five percent of the attending staff is Jewish. Of course one of the reasons for the hospital, and now the new medical school, is to provide a place where Jews could practice and study. While there may be no discriminatory admission practices now for entrance into medical schools, Jews are still 'outside the club.' They are accepted into the New York Surgical Society, the American College of Surgery and other professional organizations, but you find very few, if any, chiefs of surgery in American hospitals who happen to be Jewish. You may find a handful; however, most of them are in Federation hospitals."

If most of the attending staff at New York's Mount Sinai is Jewish, most of the patients are not. The hospital does not keep religious records, but a substantial majority are not Jews: in the clinics almost all the patients are Puerto Ricans or black; in the private pavillions almost all the patients are Jewish. A decade ago, a study of communal services by the Council of Jewish Federations and Welfare Funds found that two-thirds of those admitted to Jewish-sponsored hospitals were non-Jewish. At present, the ratio is perhaps even more lopsided. The preponderance of non-Jewish patients has created a philosophical and financial conundrum for the hospital administration and the Jewish agencies that contribute funds. How far should Jewish organizations go in supporting medical care for non-Jews, especially when care for indigent Jews is in many ways inadequate? Should Jews come first or are sick people simply sick people? This is a difficult question for Jewish agencies, for funding of public services is intimately tied up with federal and state aid. If the Federation does not maintain its level of assistance, the government agencies are liable to cut back also.

While Mount Sinai has money worries, some of them are self-inflicted. The major expansion — the construction of the Annenberg building — cost $140 million and was an onerous expense. Moreover, the establishment of a medical school was a costly undertaking. Some critics thought that the new tower was a luxury in a period of skyrocketing construction and medical costs, and other critics complained that the school of medicine was redundant — that the Albert Einstein College School of Medicine served the same purpose. Nevertheless, the hospital complex is planning to spend $450 million in renovation in the 1980s.

Though the Mount Sinai Medical Center lost money every year in the 1970s, the physicians and surgeons are making ends meet. Well, perhaps just a bit more than that. New York City is known as a "high-fee town," which is perhaps a none-too-subtle way of saying that rates are set by whatever the market will bear. The chiefs of clinical services — the two dozen or so specialties from anesthesiology to urology — are full-time staff earning close to six-figure salaries annually. In addition, all the physicians on the hospital staff have extensive fringe benefits, from full coverage for any hospitalization to rather complete educational payments for their children. Fringe benefits in industry normally run between 10 and 12.5 percent of the base salary, but the fringe benefits of physicians are twice that, between 20 and 25 percent. In addition, both the heads and the associate heads of hospital departments have private practices that generate substantial monies. The top men can bring in a quarter of a million dollars to the hospital since the institution collects all payments as a quid pro quo.

However, the real money-makers at Mount Sinai are not the one hundred or more physicians and surgeons on the staff, but the twelve hundred doctors with hospital privileges. There is a symbiotic relationship between the institution and this select group: to fill the beds, the hospital relies on these doctors for referrals. These doctors, in turn, have complete access to operating rooms, laboratories, and all hospital facilities. In the words of one staff member, they "give little to the hospital," but "get a great deal." It is these physicians who earn $200,000 or $300,000 a year — especially the ones operating in the specialties — in neurosurgery, and ear-nose-throat, and plastic surgery. Since major surgery usually starts at $1,000 or $2,000, it is easy to see how a busy surgeon can earn his monthly alimony, car, second-home payments and office rent before the rest of the world has finished breakfast. Medical malpractice insurance is costly, to be sure — approximately $20,000 for a general surgeon — but not too expensive for affiliated surgeons.

The American Jewish physician's contribution to health care has been considerable. Literate and well-read, they have written voluminously in medical journals on their studies, experiments, and experiences. At one point, roughly half of all the articles in American medical journals were authored by Jews. Innovation and medical discoveries abounded — from a special knife for cataracts to the Schick test for diphtheria susceptibility. Jewish doctors found the American environment particularly stimulating. While a number of them were developing lucrative practices, others were reformers and crusaders in the public health movement. For instance, Dr. Simon Baruch had developed water therapy at the turn of the twentieth century, believing not only in its internal efficacy but in the benefits of soap and water. At his instigation, the first public baths in the United States were opened on Rivington Street on the Lower East Side. Baruch came to be known as the "Apostle of Bathing," calling for free baths along with free parks.

Before World War I it was relatively easy for anyone to become a physician. The country had 155 medical schools and for the most part, all they required for admission was a high school diploma. Only half of these schools were affiliated with institutions of higher learning. They were graduating approximately five thousand doctors a year, for a population of eighty-odd million. The Carnegie Foundation suspected that much of the medical training was not only substandard but scandalous. The Foundation commissioned Abraham Flexner, a Kentucky physician and brother of Simon Flexner, a noted pathologist and director of medical research at Rockefeller Institute, to examine the situation. Abraham Flexner was also interested in medical education and public health. (Later in his life, he wrote a book on prostitution in Europe.) In 1910 in a brilliant, exhaustive and devastating report, Flexner condemned the way American physicians were trained: the teaching was poor and the facilities were primitive. Flexner's indictment was a watershed in the history of medical training, as states were prompted to close the inadequate and profit-seeking schools.

By 1927 there were only seventy-nine schools graduating doctors, but those that remained provided clinical training and extensive four-year programs. While the quality was much improved, the number of doctors graduating had fallen to nearly half. Before 1929 the average physician was earning $11,000 a year. With the onset of the Depression, doctors' earnings fell almost as fast as the Dow Jones average. At a time when the unemployment rate reached twenty-five percent, doctors' bills went unpaid and health care was postponed. And in medicine, a cry for "protectionism" was heard. The classic way in a free market system is to cut production if supply exceeds demand. There were 125 million citizens in 1933, 40 million more than when Flexner issued his report, yet the country was turning out fewer physicians than in 1910. Nevertheless, the Council on Medical Education of the American Medical Association (AMA) decided that there were too many doctors and ordered cutbacks in medical training.

Up to this point, anti-Semitism in the medical profession was scarce, isolated, and insignificant. But in the effort to reduce the number of questionable medical schools in the twenties and to implement the AMA's proposals in the thirties, Jewish medical school applicants were the first to feel the squeeze. State and municipal universities reduced admissions from nonresidents, while private universities tried to improve their cosmopolitan image by broadening the geographic distribution of the new students. Both moves drastically cut the number of Jewish applicants.

Since Jews lived in a few large cities, they were not welcomed in out-of-state schools. And in the private universities, they became subject to quota systems. Thus, the number of successful Jewish applicants for medical schools from the City College of New York — probably the overwhelming Jewish college in America at that time — fell by one third through the 1930s, but the number of non-Jewish applicants fell only a few percentage points. At Columbia University's College of Physicians and Surgeons, the number of admitted Jewish candidates dropped by nearly two-thirds. At Cornell in 1940, though the medical school had seven hundred Jewish applicants and five hundred non-Jewish applicants, the quota system set the odds at one in seventy for a Jew and one in seven for a non-Jew. In general, Jewish admissions to medical schools dropped by one third because of the AMA's position on the number of doctors the profession could economically absorb.

Jewish physicians were hurt in still another way, for at the behest of the AMA, state boards reduced the number of licenses issued for foreign-trained doctors — Americans who studied abroad since admission to medical schools within the United States was difficult, if not impossible. Heywood Broun had documented some of the prejudicial admission practices in his book *Christians Only* in 1931, but conditions were only aggravated after the book's publication. The AMA policy of limited admission and the university quota system lasted well into the fifties. The final irony of this period of quotas and restrictions came from the attitude of Jewish physicians to Jewish pre-med students. The former saw the latter as competition and also as a potential cause for resurgent anti-Semitism. One observer noted that "it is the common complaint of Jewish doctors that an organized effort should be made to restrict the number of Jewish students in medical schools." This was but another small example in Jewish history of Jews being their own worst enemy.

### In the Mindfields

Over the last few decades, geneticists have found some minor diseases that seem to specifically affect Jews: Tay-Sachs, Niemann-Pick Disease, Torsion Dystonia, Gaucher's Disease, Bloom's Syndrome, and Familial Dyxautonomia. The incidence of these illnesses is not great — most seem to affect Ashkenazic Jewry and non-Jews of Eastern Europe. The most common Jewish affliction is diabetes, striking Jews two to six times as often as the rest of the population. Nevertheless, this does not account for the great reliance Jews have on their physicians.

Jews apparently visit their doctors far more frequently than they visit their rabbis. There is a compulsiveness, a perpetual expectation of illness that undoubtedly gives them the highest patient-doctor ratio in the world. Long ago, the Talmud advised that one should not settle in the city without a doctor. Jews took the message to heart, but remain deeply skeptical of medical science and of personal physicians. This is paradoxical considering their attraction to medical occupations. For the Jew, diagnosis of illness (which the other groups tend to fear since it undermines the illusion of health) is welcome since, in his pessimism "the doctor can only reassure him, because most of the time the patient's imagined cause of pain is far more ominous than his actual condition."

Still, the Jewish patient lacks the blind faith that others have in their physicians — he is the final arbiter. "For the Jewish patient the diagnosis of the cause of pain is too much a matter of life and death. Accordingly, he finds a different solution for the problem. One doctor may make a mistake, but several doctors are less likely to err. Hence he visits not one but several physicians to find the answer to his question."

Thus the Jew is forever appealing his case to a "higher court," forever in search of the "bigger" specialists. "Unlike patients of other ethnic groups, he cannot accept freely the opinion of the expert, for he himself is the ultimate authority ... only the patient knows what is best for him. . . . The behavior of the Jewish patient reflects a value system that has developed throughout the ages and has been transmitted from parent to children, reinforced at times by tragic interaction with a hostile world in which one could depend only upon himself and his family in matters of life and death."

Since World War II the study of comparative social or ethnic pathology has fallen aside, at least until recently, when ethnic consciousness-raising made blacks aware of their susceptibility to sickle-cell anemia and hypertension. Diseases once thought of as distinctively Jewish are now becoming more generalized in the

American population. It is conceivable that within the next two or three generations, American Jews' special somatic ills will disappear. Jewishness will increasingly become a state of mind rather than a condition of the body.

As one hears less of Jewish physical illness, one hears more of Jewish mental problems. Perhaps this change goes hand-in-hand with the shifting status of the Jew in the modern world and especially in America. Besides the normal existential angst that plagues the modern citizen, Jews are more insecure since their "sure sense of self" has come unglued in a secular civilization. Whatever the reasons for the philosophical disarray and mental anguish, Jews were among the first groups to seek relief from psychologists, psychiatrists, psychoanalysts, and psychotherapists. In fact, Jews played a large role in the founding of these disciplines. And they play just as large a role in patronizing them.

No trade, business, or profession is so exclusively Jewish as the field of psychology and psychiatry. Estimates suggest that thirty percent of all psychiatrists are Jews. So disproportionate is their representation that it apparently lends truth to the observation that the development of the mind is not only a Jewish avocation, but a vocation as well. Perhaps psychiatry is today's secular rabbinate. Modern Jewish interest in psychiatry of course started with Sigmund Freud. Freud and his Viennese coterie were, for the most part, Jews. But their Judaism has always been something of a problem for the Jewish world. Unlike Karl Marx, Freud was proud of his heritage and made no efforts to conceal his Jewish identity. But, while he acknowledged his ancestry, he was not religious. However, even acknowledgment was not a simple matter in the Austria of Franz Josef, for anti-Semitism was particularly virulent. So much so that a Jewish friend of Freud, Max Graf, was considering raising his child as a Christian. Freud countered:

> If you do not let your son grow up as a Jew you will deprive him of those sources of energy which cannot be replaced by anything else. He will have to struggle as a Jew, and you ought to develop in him all the energy he will need for that struggle. Do not deprive him of that advantage.

Freud was aware that the acceptance of his theories would come easier if they did not come from a Jew. Heine had remarked a few years before that baptism is "an admission ticket to European civilization." If Freud had converted, there might have been less resistance to his ideas; nevertheless his psychoanalytic concepts were not sympathetic to organized religion. Freud sensed the suspicious attention from his Catholic countrymen. "I do not maintain," he wrote, "that the suspicion is unmerited. If our research leads us to a result that reduces religion to the status of a neurosis of mankind and explains its grandiose powers in the same way as we should a neurotic obsession in our individual patients, then we may be sure we shall incur in this country the greatest resentment of the powers that be."

To some degree, that was precisely what happened. Freud and other psychoanalysts saw in their clincial practices that there were striking parallels between some of their patients' rituals and delusions and the institutional beliefs and practices of Christianity and Judaism. Freud's contribution to psychoanalysis is profound, diverse, and voluminous; perhaps central to his work was the description and explanation of the Oedipal relationship between father and son. This conflict was a key factor in the formation of individual character and Freud related it to a number of human activities — dreams, wit, literature, mythology, art, and religion. The hostility and antagonism between father and son is the core dynamic in family life. Religion is but the projection of family interaction on a cosmic scale. In Judaism, Freud found the perfect example of a "superego" religion in which Jews, through an unconscious sense of guilt, were in a constant state of anxiety for fear of offending the omnipotent Father. Thus they were perpetually trying to propitiate Him by adhering to an unending series of rules and laws.

Freud put the problem succinctly in his last book, *Moses and Monotheism:*

> In the religion of Moses itself there was no room for direct expression of the murderous father-hate. Only a powerful reaction to it could make its appearance: the consciousness of guilt because of that hostility, the bad conscience because one had sinned against God and continued to sin. This feeling of guiltiness, which the Prophets incessantly kept alive . . . cleverly veiled the true origin of the feeling. The people met with hard times . . . it became not easy

to adhere to the illusion . . . that they were God's chosen people. . . . They deserved nothing better than to be punished by him, because they did not observe the laws; the need for satisfying this feeling of guilt . . . was insatiable, made them render their religious precepts ever and ever more strict, more exacting, but also more petty. . . . It [the feeling of guilt] bears the characteristic of being never concluded . . . with which we are familiar in the reaction-formations of obsessional neurosis.

One observer noted that for analysts, Judaism remains "an example of a rigidly compulsive system compounded of elements of guilt, subservience, anxiety, and unconscious resentment toward a nonexistent God."

In brief, Freud saw Judaism as an Oedipal situation on a grand scale. Because Freudians limited the image of God (and by extension, religion) to a murdered patriarch, some critics have called psychoanalysis a "Jewish science." Freud was aware of this criticism and conceivably, it was a strong motive to name Jung, a non-Jew with notably differing concepts, to become the first president of the International Psycho-Analytic Association. Freud knew that his Jewishness would cause conflict, but in a way it was apropos.

"Nor is it perhaps entirely a matter of chance," Freud observed, "that the first advocate of psycho-analysis was a Jew. To profess a belief in this new theory called for a certain degree of readiness to accept a position of solitary opposition — a position with which no one is more familiar than a Jew."

Freud's psychoanalytic observations on Judaism cast doubt on the basic Jewish tradition that suffering is redemptive. Guilt and self-accusation, orthodoxy insists, is preferable to meaningless suffering. Misfortune is a form of punishment and self-condemnation is the price of discovering meaning in a cruel and seemingly meaningless world. Put in this light, one of the main tenets of Judaism appears as a fantasy and a snare. One commentator wrote that it was a "colossal, megalomaniacal and grandiose misreading of a pathetic and defeated community's historic predicament. To this day Jews can be found who delude themselves with the notion that somehow Jewish suffering and powerlessness have a redemptive significance for mankind."

Freud has thus left a highly ambivalent legacy: proud to be a Jew and insisting on identifying himself as a member of the tribe, he was nevertheless irreligious and intellectually disenchanted. He was alienated from any religious practice and could claim that "I do not believe that one supreme great God 'exists' today." Freud sought to describe a system of impersonal forces in nature, on the order of Darwin, that would serve as the key to understanding the human mind. Belief in a monotheistic God led into a cul-de-sac: it did not explain psychological processes but caused a short-circuit that bounced people back and forth between guilt and anxiety.

Freud's psychoanalysis was no intellectual comfort to institutional Judaism, but it did open the floodgates for repressed Jews, among others. Ever since, Jews have labored in the mindfields.

# 10. The Law

No man can be a sound lawyer who is not well read in
the laws of Moses.

— Fisher Ames

## A Nation of Lawyers

"Get a Jewish lawyer, he'll get you off." While this remark is a
tribute to the talents and enterprise of Jewish lawyers, it also im-
plies deviousness, influence, and some unspecified but potent un-
derhanded machination. In either sense, it suggests power and
ability unmatched by other attorneys. The Jewish lawyer not only
gets you off: he does the unimaginable in situations that look all
but impossible. This aura of potency is not cultivated by Jewish
attorneys, nor deprecated by lawyers in general.

The legal profession in the United States started in a very
humble fashion when early colonists had the audacity to think
they could get along without it. One diarist, Gabriel Thomas,
wrote in 1690, "of lawyers and physicians I shall say nothing, because this country is very peaceful and healthy. Long may it so
continue and never have occasion for the tongue of the one nor
the pen of the other — both equally destructive to men's estates
and lives." Of course, the story is totally different today, when it is
almost imprudent to shake hands without legal advice and when
over half the nation's legislators are attorneys. Indeed, the law
may be one of the growth industries in the last quarter of the
twentieth century.

At present, the country has over five hundred thousand attorneys, but by 1985 that number is expected to increase by nearly

fifty percent. Whether the nation is in particular need of seven hundred thousand lawyers is perhaps open to debate: there is one lawyer for every 483 individuals in the country. To look at it in another way — there are over twice as many lawyers as there are bakers — a fact that does nothing to explain why bread is relatively cheap and litigation is not.

Of the five hundred thousand attorneys, it is estimated that over twenty percent of them are Jews, nearly ten times the representation that might be expected. In 1939 it was estimated that over half the attorneys practicing in New York City were Jews. By now the proportion is even greater: perhaps three out of five lawyers are Jews. The last survey of the New York City bar found sixty percent of the city's 25,000 attorneys to be Jewish, eighteen percent, Catholic and eighteen percent, Protestant. Most of the Jewish lawyers — roughly seventy percent of them — are from Eastern European heritages, while sixty-three percent of the Catholics are of Irish descent and fifty-six percent of the Protestants are of British or Canadian origins. It was precisely the inequality of conditions and opportunities that led to the surge of Jews into the legal profession.

Law is something of a Jewish calling, in a sense, the house specialty. Whether under capitalism, socialism, or communism, Jewish lawyers thrive. Not long ago, half the attorneys of Moscow were Jews. No country in the world is overrun with more lawyers than Israel: there is one counselor for every 405 people as compared with Japan, where there is one for every ten thousand citizens. If the United States is beginning to experience a plague of lawyers, Jews have managed to thrive as lawyers because of a legalistic religion and perhaps, in spite of it. The growth in the number of American lawyers is a response to "our consuming individualism, unrelenting contentiousness, and discordant heterogeneity," according to one legal scholar, Jerold S. Auerbach.

Perhaps the creation and development of Jewish law was due to similar conditions, for it not only had to serve as a bridge between tribes, but in the course of three thousand years, it had to contend with a diversity of societies and a multitude of economic systems in the Diaspora. And the codification of the laws in the Bible, commentaries, codes, rulings, and responses constituted the heart of Jewish law — a body of law developed without benefit of a formal political state.

It was the commitment to Jewish law that kept, and keeps, Jews Jewish. It gave them an ethnic identity. The law regulated every aspect of their behavior, causing endless interpretations. Such Talmudic casuistry naturally placed rabbis — the lawyers throughout most of Jewish history — on both sides of an issue. Since the time that Abraham challenged God, Jews have been questioning arbitrary authority. As "the world's greatest virtuosi of the sense of injustice," Jews developed the idea that for justice to prevail, people had to be involved in the decision-making process. Out went the old idea of a Divine Force issuing ultimatums, and in came the notion of a God entering into a covenant with his subjects. It was a revolutionary theological idea, which later would become a revolutionary political doctrine.

Jews played almost no role in the early legal activities of the colonies. Indeed, lawyers were not in demand in colonial times. The trustees of Georgia excluded both rum and lawyers "as being prejudicial to its welfare." While there were a couple of justices of the peace under the British, the first American Jewish lawyer, Moses Levy, was admitted to the bar in Philadelphia in 1778. A graduate of the University of Pennsylvania, he was highly regarded and Jefferson considered him for the post of Attorney General of the United States. While some Jews did study law in the nineteenth century, the number was quite small.

The American Jewish lawyer came into his own in the twentieth century. Some theorists suggest that one reason for the burgeoning number of Jewish law graduates is the fact that Jews had a natural affinity for law. This affinity was derived from their continuous study of scriptures and the law. It was easy to move from the religious to the secular, replacing other-worldly matters with worldly ones. Nevertheless, while some Talmudic scholars may become lawyers, most do not. The supposed transition from the study of *halakah* (religious law) to the writing of contracts and the closing of mortgages is somewhat far-fetched. Another theory holds that Jews are by nature more litigious than gentiles, but there seems to be less to this than meets the eye. No social scientist has yet devised a contentiousness quotient so, until one is invented, judgment may have to be suspended.

The influx of Jews into the legal profession may have a good deal to do with Jewish temperament and tradition. First of all, the law was considered a respectable way to make a living for a first- or second-generation Jew. Not only was the money good, but law afforded an independent existence. It relied on ability rather than connections, merit rather than seniority. Secondly, it appealed to the Jewish predilection for scholarly reflection. Planning, study, respect for the law, using one's head, postponement of gratification — all traits that Jews lived by or could adapt to. Thirdly, the legal profession had a strong philosophical attraction for Jews. As second-class citizens for a millennium, Jews were more conscious of most of their rights and prerogatives — and especially, of the deprivation of those rights. Denial of legal claims, expropriation of poverty without compensation, abrogation of treaties and charters, and moratoriums on loans were part of their history. Inevitably, the Jewish community developed a hypersensitivity to all forms of injustice. What was more natural for the Jews than to react against the loss of rights by learning to manipulate the very systems that were used to deny them equality and humanity?

If this is so, it might be asked why Jews had not turned to the practice of law much earlier in their history. Surely their history is filled with betrayals, discrimination, reneged contracts, revoked rights, and a host of broken promises. Why did Jews wait until relatively recently to use the legal profession as a form of defense and an instrument of retribution? Probably for two reasons: Jewish advocacy in early modern history was in the hands of the rabbis and intellectuals; and in later modern history, in the hands of prominent businessmen. The argument was not carried on at the legal level, but at the theological one in the fourteenth, fifteenth, and sixteenth centuries. As the inquisitional fires died down, and the religious questions slowly receded, Jewish communities were protected, to some degree, by leading Jewish businessmen and financiers — the court Jews of the seventeenth and eighteenth centuries. In brief, the advocates for Jews were not lawyers in the narrow sense of the term, but religious spokesmen

or prominent merchants. Moreover, before the Age of Enlightenment most Western law was concerned with the rights of kings
and states, estates and classes. Individual rights did not evolve
until later, and it was some time before Jews took advantage of
their political and legal emancipation.

Perhaps there is still another important aspect that draws Jews
to the legal profession. Iconoclasm is an old Jewish characteristic — indeed it may be the primary Jewish trait. The breaking of
idols started with Abraham and Moses and has continued in this
day in the secular world with Marx, Freud, and Einstein. The
idols these days are the ideas, concepts, ideologies, traditions, and
customs that are inflexible and unfeeling. So it comes as no surprise to find Jewish lawyers on the cutting edge of change and reform. Obviously, the modern legal profession has the right and
duty to be on both sides of an issue, representing plaintiff and defendant. And so, Jewish lawyers are found in both camps. But
most of their activities are against the status quo. Whether in
structuring a novel business arrangement, breaking ground in
civil liberties, or exercising citizen's prerogatives, Jewish lawyers
tend to advocate individual liberty and personal claims in the
face of big government, the bureaucracies, and big business.

Finally, there is a strong sense of morality and a passion to mor-
alize. Since Biblical times, they have become known as the people
of the law — didactic, pedagogical and sometimes patronizing of
other folks' foibles and failures. This disdain for "lesser breeds
without the law" has caused them endless conflict and ill-will.
Max Dimont, the popular historian of Judaism, wrote:

> [They] are a people born with a pontificating finger, moral busy-
> bodies who are forever telling the world what is right and what is
> wrong. Ever since the days of Moses, the Jews have been swinging
> the club of morality and shouting: Thou shalt not force thy daugh-
> ter into harlotry, thou shalt not commit sodomy, thou shalt not
> murder, steal, commit perjury. They derided the pagan fun of sod-
> omy, naming it bestiality. They denounced as murder the Greek
> custom of killing unsightly children in the name of aesthetics. They
> debunked the custom of holy prostitution labeling it immorality.
> They rejected the idea of divine rights of king and the idea of legal-
> ized torture. They formulated the world's first laws against illegal

search, and were the first to give the accused the right to confront his accusers. Holding their Ten Commandments aloft like a banner, Jews have marched through centuries as though they are conquerors, not the conquered.

Though there has been a veritable explosion of Jewish lawyers in the last couple of generations, it is not because of any overwhelming demand for them. In fact, the legal establishment appears to have shared some of the prejudices and hostilities of the baser elements of American society. Showing the same benighted attitudes, the profession was not a haven from anti-Semitism, or for that matter a retreat from other forms of ethnic bigotry. Perhaps it is not shocking, but in a society dedicated to equality and fair treatment, officers of the court did not live up to their noble roles. Prominent attorneys, sophisticated in other respects, revealed a positively primitive understanding of social dynamics, interpersonal relations, and personal ambitions. Harlan Stone, a future Chief Justice of the United States Supreme Court, was appalled at the influx of Jews into his profession for they "exhibit social tendencies toward study by memorization." Furthermore, they display "a mind almost Oriental in its fidelity to the minutiae of the subject without regard to any controlling rule or reason." The chairman of the American Bar Association Ethics Committee, Henry S. Drinker, mustered all the sensitivity of a falling casebook when he commented that "Russian Jew boys who came up out of the gutter were merely following the methods their fathers had been using in selling shoestrings and other merchandise."

With such sentiments prevailing in the elite law firms, Joseph M. Proskauer described his employment frustration at the turn of the century. "It did not take me many days to discover that the doors of most New York law offices in 1899 were closed, with rare exceptions, to a young Jewish lawyer. Fifty years have elapsed since then and I am happy to record that there has been a distinct improvement in the situation; though it still remains true that generally the Jewish student must qualify twice for such employment."

The exclusionary tactics of the legal establishment have diminished, particularly in the last decade or two. But they have not completely vanished. Jewish applicants for the Ivy League law schools have markedly increased. Jews in large law firms have also multiplied. In the sixties, Philadelphia law offices doubled the number of Jews they employed. A study of fourteen Delaware Valley law offices in 1961 found that of 502 lawyers, 35 were Jewish. Half of these firms had no Jews in them. A second look at the same area in 1969 found Jewish employment had nearly tripled and that only one law firm did not have a Jew. At the partnership level, seven firms still did not have a Jewish partner. In the late sixties, a spokeswoman for the Harvard Law School placement office said "there is no question that the Jewish boy is slower to receive an offer [for employment] than a gentile one. Most law firms doing business with the placement office have an Anglo-Saxon conservative pattern." But present discriminatory practices are rather more passive than active. She continued, "In most cases there is no positive prejudice against Jews, but rather a negative one, that is, Jews will be somewhat slower to get an offer of employment than their non-Jewish classmates." Her views are confirmed in a report in the *Yale Law Journal*, which noted that "gentiles were more successful than Jews in getting good jobs, and in getting jobs of their choice. This was especially true for those in the middle or lower part of the law school class." And this, of course, was reflected in their earning ability. Jews didn't get paid less than gentile colleagues, but tended to end up in less well-paying firms.

Young Jewish college students applying for law school have approximately the same expectations as their Christian peers in terms of job opportunities, advancement, and pay. At that point in time, they have not yet dealt with the realities of the work-a-day world, or at least, the perception of that world as passed on to them by parents and students senior to them. By and large, there are no discriminatory admission practices in the major law schools. In one analysis of four typical law schools, two eastern elite schools, one Catholic and one local, on the average, forty-seven percent of their student body was Jewish.

While there is no problem in obtaining admission to law schools, afterwards students develop a "measured response" to cope with the prejudices of the profession as they see them. On graduation only forty-five percent of the Jews had secured jobs, while fifty-seven percent of the Catholics and seventy-six percent of the Protestants had been employed. It is understood that the large, prestigious, and important law firms have unwritten rules as to how many Jews they will employ, and from which schools they prefer their associates. Consequently, the number of Jewish applicants from the Ivy League schools that are employed in the old and established law firms are not comparable with other groups. And almost no Jewish applicants from the non-Ivy League schools are hired by those same firms.

With this background, it is not difficult to understand the predilection of Jewish lawyers to run their own shops or combine to form partnerships among themselves. The large law factories are not perceived as being predisposed to Jews, though they may have some Jewish partners. None of the major Wall Street law houses are thought of as Jewish firms, though there are one or two Jewish firms that are almost as large and are engaged in securities work. Since the largest law firms do not wish to be thought of as Jewish, preferring to be viewed as politically conservative, socially acceptable, male-dominated, white Anglo-Saxon repositories of corporate power, they are conscious of how many Jewish partners they take in. Consequently, many of them have a "tipping point," the Rubicon that they will not cross. Should the tipping point be crossed, their image may become confused and cloudy to their clients. So there may be a few brilliant Jewish partners, but advancement is controlled. This policy, in conjunction with an "up-or-out" policy — either one moves on to a partnership after six or ten years or one is asked to go elsewhere — the prestigious law firms have not been inundated with job applications from young Jewish attorneys.

Jewish lawyers can be found in all sorts of legal or paralegal positions, on law school faculties, as the house counsel of corporations, in state and federal regulatory agencies, in legislative branches of government, and in public interest law centers. However, most Jewish attorneys prefer a general practice by themselves or with a few partners. It is not simply a matter of avoiding discrimination, for recent federal legislation (the Equal Employment Opportunities section of the 1964 Civil Rights Act, plus the 1972 amendments) goes far to prohibit job discrimination — and who better than lawyers understand the laws. Rather, it is a complicated psychological and cultural phenomenon: Jews fill special niches in the practice of the law, because of their history of isolation and nonconformity.

Primarily, the Jewish lawyer represents the individual against a variety of forces, which either conspire to suppress him or unconsciously step all over him. As a sort of paid ombudsman, the Jewish lawyer helps the powerless stand up to the powerful. Jewish lawyers can be found in every legal specialty, but they have made distinctive contributions to two particular phases of modern law: personal injury litigation and stockholder actions. "These are the areas where they excel, where they make real money, and it's not on the back of anybody else," said Arthur Greenberg, a partner in a small but profitable personal injury firm.

*Personal Injury*

The Woolworth Building in lower Manhattan probably has more lawyers-in-residence than a middle-sized city. This skyscraper, at the time of its completion in 1913, was the tallest building in the city, sixty stories in the 790-foot tower. It is a stone's throw from the legal center of New York: City Hall, the Municipal Building, state and city agencies, and the courts surrounding Foley Square. Into the sparkling gold pseudogothic lobby, an unending river of lawyers carry their polished attaché cases or tattered brown-manila envelopes, sometimes both. Two-hundred thirty-three is no longer the impressive address it was when the building was first opened when President Wilson flicked on all 86,000 light bulbs from the White House, but the offices are spacious, with views of New Jersey and Brooklyn. The firm of Goldfarb and Greenberg took offices in the building in the 1960s when they first set up a partnership practice specializing in the field of torts (personal injury) as trial council to the bar. Both had worked for, and had been associated with, two of the old masters in the field: Ronald Goldfarb with Herman Glaser and Alfred Julien, and Arthur Greenberg with Alfred Julien.

"The field of personal injury really expanded in the forties and fifties," said Greenberg. "A dozen or so lawyers developed this area of law, and most of them were Jewish. Emile Zola Berman, Aaron Broder, Jacob Fuchsberg, Harry Gair, Herman Glaser, Alfred Julien, Joseph Kellner, Charles Kramer, Moe Levine, Harry Lipsig." For the most part, they came from humble backgrounds and did not graduate from the eastern elite law schools. In fact, Harry Gair never even went to law school.

"Practically every Jewish trial lawyer I know," remarked Ronald Goldfarb, "is a product of schools other than the Ivy League. Not many Jewish kids could get into those schools a while back, so the majority went to New York University, New York Law, Brooklyn Law, Fordham. The curricula are all pretty much the same now, but at one time Harvard, Yale, Princeton and Columbia taught a more esoteric form of law. In New York the schools stressed more of the practical and procedural aspects — what to do in court and how to pass the bar exams."

The nature of the law school attended was but one element that set off many Jewish attorneys from their gentile colleagues. "We didn't grow up in the country club set and we had few social contacts," Goldfarb said. "We had no entree into large law firms; prejudice limited working for banks and insurance companies; we commanded no estate business since our families didn't have any and we had no significant corporate connections. The practical solution to making a living was to work in the community, to be concerned about an individual's problems."

The image of the Jewish lawyer representing the underdog, that victim of fate, is not wholly inaccurate. In a sense, he has become the conscience of the community, raising issues of public policy and social needs — often long before the state legislatures or the Congress come to grip with these issues. The recent spate of consumer legislation was, in a way, derived from the protection garnered by the public on a case-by-case basis.

"It was only through a legal action that a wronged citizen could obtain any satisfaction over the reputedly flammable child's pajamas which went up like a Christmas tree even though the garment met the trade association standards; the blood transfusion which gave the patient hepatitis; or the brake system of a car which doesn't operate properly," said Goldfarb. Naturally, the field of personal injury, product liability, and medical malpractice are not pursued by the Wall Street firms and the law factories. Since they represent the car manufacturer, the hospital, the trade association, the bank, the drug company, the railroad, and the insurance company, to accept a tort case would put them in an awkward position indeed. It is not the kind of conflict of interest that they welcome. Consequently, regardless of how clear-cut and clean the case may be or the potential of the award from, say a major airplane accident, which would run into millions, the legal establishment will not participate except as counsel to the defendants.

This leads to a dichotomy of legal functions: the private citizen and his attorney fight the powerful corporation and its counsel, with a staff of a hundred or more. However, the seeming imbalance has not precluded a redress of grievances. "We out-lawyer them," said one attorney who preferred anonymity. "It's as simple as that."

Not quite. While the power of the corporation and institution can be awesome in legal talent, money, and time, in some ways, the powers-that-be are on the defensive since public opinion is running against them. Not that the business world has divested itself of any of its corporate responsibilities or defenses or suddenly developed a taste for altruism. They are as hard-nosed and toughminded as ever — and ever mindful of being thought the patsy for nuisance claims and other harassments. And perhaps that is as it should be. What has changed is the development of individual rights and protections, the safeguarding of the citizen by making the producers of goods and services responsible for their products.

For a while it has been illegal to sell snake oil as a cure for lower back pains, the common cold, and flatulence. In the last few years, it has become unlawful for pharmaceutical companies to peddle sophisticated drugs or devices without thoroughly testing them, having them appraised by independent tests, and getting the approval of the Food and Drug Administration. And even then they can be held liable if some untoward consequence develops years later. This interpretation of product warranty and liability is one of the most beneficial areas of law for the citizen. It gives him a chance to get even — not in a vengeful way, for tort law seeks to compensate for wrongs and not to punish — for the unintentional harm done to him.

Recovery in personal-injury cases has created more controversy than any other legal development and the subject is still evolving. Personal-injury cases are spoken of disparagingly in some legal circles: the attorneys who take them are called ambulance chasers and the clients who institute them, blackmailers. The former are accused of champerty — getting a piece of the award though they are not a party in the dispute — and the latter are denounced for perjury — lying on the witness stand in an attempt to extort money. The usual comment runs something like this: "Personal-injury actions are notoriously a source of both intellectual and literal corruption, because there is often nothing to them but money." Of course, the same may be said of most legal matters — they deal explicitly with the gamut of property claims, in other words, money. Historically, the law's chief concern has been the division of old wealth or anticipating claims on new wealth. Personal rights and individual liberties have arrived only recently. The only way to attempt to compensate the individual for the loss of those rights, in the words of one law journal, "the denial of a foot, a feeling, or a function," is through monetary damages.

Modern Jewish lawyers have succeeded in developing and extending the old English proofs of negligence. The idea behind civil liability, or tort law, was to compensate for harms rather than punish for wrongs. Of course, the first step was to prove that harm and injury was the result of negligence. Early in the game, a fundamental rule was laid down that still guides the litigation process. Was the accident or incident a result of someone's negligence? How do you prove it?

A man was walking down a London street, minding his own business when a barrel of flour fell on him from an upstairs window. The judge, in deciding the issue, put it succinctly, *"res ipsa loquitur,"* the thing speaks for itself. That is, barrels of flour don't descend from the sky by themselves. Moreover, no other explanations are useful in explaining the accident. Finally, this kind of accident doesn't happen unless somebody is at fault. Since the defendant was in sole control of the situation that caused harm, while the plaintiff was in no way a contributor to the accident, the defendant is at fault.

Of course, most personal-injury actions are far more complicated than the original flour barrel incident, for every step in the legal syllogism is fraught with qualifiers and conditions.

"The image that some critics of personal-injury cases have is that of a greedy attorney with his hand out, not so much practicing law as mendicancy. The reality is otherwise," said Greenberg, reflectively, while working at his large, curved desk. In the fashion of Blanchard and Davis of West Point's winning football team a generation ago, Greenberg is Mr. Inside and Goldfarb, Mr. Outside. Greenberg prepares the briefs, researches the problems, manages the office, and on specific occasions, tries cases. Goldfarb, a former track enthusiast, also does research, but prefers the trial work and spends most of his time in court. Handsomely clad in dark blue, he keeps pacing around the office, uncertain as to whether the habit comes from his athletic background or from his days in court.

The immediate anguish and personal trauma of most personal injury cases are gone, receding both in memory and time, when the courts are finally ready to hear them. Most cases are never adjudicated but are settled either before a court date or while the trial is in progress. But the trial attorney must be ready to go all the way should no settlement be forthcoming.

"Many wrongs are not worth pursuing," said Greenberg. "There is either no liability, or even when it exists, it is not substantial enough to warrant legal action. You must remember that litigation is time consuming and an expensive process to the litigants and their lawyers. We simply can't pursue cases unless there's real harm and merit involved. Since accidents and injuries know no favoritism with regard to social or economic status, there are many people who, if not for the contingent fee, could not afford to pay a lawyer for his time and efforts to right wrongs. We can't run the meter, in the way a firm on retainer or a hired house can. Needless to say, we don't get paid if the case fails."

While the injured and their lawyers have no doubts about its merits, the contingency fee is a sore point in the legal establishment ("a boil on the backside of the law," in the words of one law-yer). And there have been rumblings in various state bar associa-tions to do away with it, to ban it by canon. Perhaps some day they will succeed, but at the present time, it is the only mecha-nism that allows the public and the consumer a toehold so they can redress injury in an insensitive world.

Other countries are bemused by the contingency fee arrange-ment, but are slowly incorporating it into their legal systems. Even in Great Britain, where it is an accepted technique, there is a feeling that the United States may be making too much of a good thing. One English magazine has written:

> Greed is as human as eating; and demanding gigantic damages for real or imagined injury as American as apple pie. That is no acci-dent: true to its country's entrepreneurial tradition, the American law industry has devised a splendid marketing aid to increase its turnover, the contingency fee, which rewards the lawyers with a fat slice — typically, 30% of any damages they get for their client, but nothing if they lose. No sale, no commission. What could be fairer than that? And if once you accept that law is not merely the rare-fied dignity of the supreme court but also a commodity to be sold like popcorn or hairdressing, can you complain that its practioners indeed go out and sell. . . . To staid Europeans, the idea is shocking. But is it in fact harmful?

Personal-injury cases often have a way of raising a question of tort to a public policy debate. One such case that Goldfarb and Greenberg participated in dealt with the issue of personal safety in a housing development. A nine-year-old girl was accosted by a teenager on the grounds of a project of fourteen high-rise apart-ment houses. She was returning home for lunch from a nearby school when the teenager, who also lived in the project, dragged her to the roof and proceeded to rape her. He then threw her from the roof: she hit the pavement below and died instantly. The firm represented her estate in a nonjury trial against the project for failing to provide adequate police protection. They contended that in a large development of fourteen apartment houses, with a prior history of numerous criminal occurrences, a single guard was inadequate to provide reasonable security. The judge thought so also and found for the plaintiff. The court awarded

$135,000 consisting of $35,000 for wrongful death and $100,000 for pain and suffering. The housing authority was obliged to review its security arrangements and beef-up its guard patrols in all its projects. The case would not stop future crimes, but it might make incidents less likely — especially since the case set some precedents and is widely cited by other lawyers in similar cases of inner-city crime.

The judge in this case was trying his last cast before retiring: the late Samuel Liebowitz was a remarkable gentleman who had brought much honor to the ranks of Jewish attorneys as a defender of the rights of the dispossessed and downtrodden. He was well versed in defending the underprivileged from his days as trial counsel to the Scottsboro Boys. Liebowitz had lost none of his sympathy for society's victims, and in his last case wrote:

> The issue here is obvious. What obligation did the defendant, Housing Authority, owe to its tenants to protect their lives, safety and property in the circumstances here shown? I am informed by counsel for defendant that provision of an adequate police force in its various projects would have been an excessively heavy economic burden. My response to that argument is that it is high time that they assumed that burden. What system of mathematics can we use to balance financial limitations with the torture suffered by this young soul during her half-hour ordeal?

Liebowitz has passed from the scene, but he left a remarkable record defending the underdog, a legacy that was passed on to the next generation of lawyers.

Medical malpractice is one of the fastest growing areas of personal injury, for the public has recently overcome its reticence in facing medical authority. While physicians and surgeons believe that there are far too many malpractice suits, the number is likely to grow dramatically. The American Medical Association, in its professional liability survey, indicated that for every patient filing a medical malpractice suit "there are probably ten times as many who never become aware of the fact that they have legitimate fault claims" under the present system.

Goldfarb and Greenberg have been and are trial counsels in a considerable number of medical malpractice actions. "It has gotten so that because of our research on behalf of a client we sometimes know more about human anatomy and physiology in specific instances than the doctors we face in court," said Goldfarb.

The veritable explosion of medical malpractice suits has brought forth complaints from physicians and escalating premiums from insurance companies. Some doctors refuse to practice and some insurance companies refuse to write this kind of insurance. And negligence attorneys are accused of ripping off the system, taking advantage of physicians, and bilking the carriers. According to Ronald Goldfarb:

> This assumption that doctors are sitting ducks and juries will make unconscionable awards is somewhat paranoid. In a medical malpractice case the claim basically is that the doctor or hospital passed a medical red light, that the care given was below a standard established by the medical community itself. The trial lawyer, through necessity, must depend on the expertise, opinions and testimony of physicians to inform the jury and court where a colleague deviated from normal and accepted medical standards. It is the medical profession, as well as the conscience of the community, that attempts to right a wrong when committed. The consumer of medical services is entitled to the same reasonable prudent care as a consumer of any other service or product.

The Jewish attorneys who were in the forefront of developing liability protection are now finding themselves caught in the center, besieged both by an aroused public that is demanding greater societal protection through some sort of governmental legislation and by business, the health industry, and insurance companies that are finding judgments intolerable and premiums inordinately expensive. Personal-injury lawyers have been on the cutting edge of the drive for personal rights under the tort system. But their future function may be limited as government strives for a new solution to some very old problems.

## Contra the Corporation

In the affluent eighties, it is hard to recollect or even imagine the hard times of the legal profession in the thirties. Today the average lawyer in private practice is earning an income in excess of $55,000. But back in 1933, the median income of Manhattan lawyers, presumably among the best paid in the nation even then, was below $3,000. In fact, fifteen-hundred New York attorneys were ready to take the pauper's oath in 1934 to qualify for work relief. It would be inordinately difficult to find an attorney applying for food stamps in contemporary America.

During that period, another group of lawyers arose — most of them Jewish — who were also destined to cut out a piece of the legal firmament for themselves. Sons of immigrants, they were far removed from the elitist bar. When the New Dealers took the helm of the country, the American bar was divided into two parts: in the words of Karl Llewellyn, a legal scholar, there was the "blue-stocking bar" and the "catch-as-catch-can bar." The Jews, the Italians, and the blacks, of course, belonged to the latter. From the wreckage of the Great Crash and the subsequent Depression, some of these lawyers started to pick through the pieces. And some of the pieces were particularly foul. A number of America's largest corporations were being run as vest-pocket businesses for the sole enrichment of the senior executives. Ferdinand Pecora, as counsel for the Senate Committee on Banking and Finance, uncovered a cesspool of corporate boondoggling and buccaneering in the highest echelons of capitalism. There seemed to be an untold amount of nepotism, insider trading, securities corners, excessive compensation, gratuitous bonuses, and general trafficking in corporate assets. The stage was set for the major reforms of the 1933 and 1934 securities acts.

Through the use of a little-known technique — the minority stockholder suit — these attorneys evolved a way to make corporate managers accountable to the fractional and separated owners of the company. These suits were not frontal attacks on capitalism. The attorneys who undertook them — Milton Paulson, Milton Pollack, and Abraham Pomerantz — were not out to destroy the system, but rather to cleanse the economic body. Nevertheless, their suits did not win them popularity among their professional colleagues. Such litigation was regarded by the respectable bar as a form of harassment, dismissed as a nuisance. In brief, "strike suits," were tantamount to legal blackmail. Of course the blue-stocking bar was charged with defending the allegedly erring corporations — Chase National Bank, National City Bank, American Can, and Coca Cola.

The stockholder suit developed along two lines: the derivative suit and the representative or class-action suit. In the former, the stockholder bases his case on the wrongs suffered by the corporation at the hands of its officers. The suing stockholders derive power from the corporation, since ostensibly it is unable to cure itself with its present officials. In the class-action suit, the stockholder sues because he and a like group of shareowners have been dealt with unfairly. In this instance, the wrong is direct, so the corporation is sued. In derivative cases, the stockholders gain only in the sense that the offending officers have to reimburse the corporate treasury. All shareholders stand to gain, but the gain is only nominal. In representative suits, just the single class of stockholders (say, the preferred or the class B) participate in the recovery of funds, not the corporate treasury.

But in either case, the lawyers stand to reap vast rewards. While the shareholders may recover only $1.25 a share, as in a 1976 settlement against International Telephone and Telegraph (ITT), the lawyers hit the jackpot. When ITT settled with the sixteen thousand stockholders representing twenty-two million shares over the merger with Hartford Fire Insurance (the shareowners of Hartford Fire were being reimbursed for any federal tax liability that they were subject to, though they were originally assured that the 1972 exchange would be tax-free), the lawyers received a windfall fee of $3.5 million. The suit did take nearly four years to settle, but the remuneration seems adequate.

Litigating stockholder suits may well be one of the most remunerative of law practice. Settlements, whether agreed to out-of-court or adjudicated, almost invariably come to seven or eight figures. Naturally, the plaintiff's attorneys are handsomely rewarded from any recovery. And perhaps rightly so, since at one time the bar considered it pariah's work. At one time, judges allocated between twenty percent and thirty percent of the "benefit" to the lawyers representing the plaintiff. While the pay is not exactly on a pro bono publico level, the work does render a substantial public service. One federal judge remarked that "vindication of rights under the federal securities law would seldom be accomplished were it not for the class-action device."

Thus the combination of three elements leads Jewish lawyers into one of the most creative and sensitive areas of modern capitalism: stockholder litigation. As an outsider in the legal profession, discrimination and prejudice put the Jewish attorney in a position to attack both his elitiest colleagues and the corporate establishment. Not only was there something terribly satisfying in working against the power structure, but one was extraordinarily well-paid if successful at it. One victorious case could gross more than a lifetime of reading contracts, filing government forms, and divorcing spouses. Perhaps last but not least — there were real wrongs involved, the classic situation of the strong and the rich ripping off the weak, the poor, and the ill-informed. The cases were highly remunerative, true, but they also appealed to the deeply ingrained Jewish sense of justice. In the pursuit of stockholder litigation, they were cleansing the Augean stables of capitalism. The dean of stockholder suits, Abraham Pomerantz, has had his bellyful of capitalism and now is a confirmed socialist — perhaps one of the richest socialists in the United States.

"Stockholder work," said Pomerantz, "is an enlarged game of twenty questions. You have to have a dirty mind; it's a prerequisite in this business. If you were to stay up at night counting corporate shenanigans rather than sheep, you couldn't dream up the half of it." Pomerantz has played the game with extraordinary skill. Besides the innumerable cases against individual corporations, he has taken on the whole mutual fund industry. He has forced them to roll back their management fees, claiming them to be excessive, thus saving the public nearly $50 million. In return, his firm received legal fees of $2.4 million. He subsequently attacked the practice of give-ups, the designation of part of a brokerage commission to agents who actually sold shares; and interpositioning, using an unnecessary broker in a transaction. The former practice has now ceased, while the latter is much diminished. Though Pomerantz may be unduly sour on capitalism, his activities attacking corporate mischief, malfeasance, peculation, and perjury have made him wealthy. He may not be the highest paid attorney in the land, but his reputed annual salary of $350,-000 puts him in a select group of those that are.

With the explosion of stockholder suits in the seventies — upwards of a thousand actions annually — the impetus was not very different from that of the thirties. However, the reasons for the suits are somewhat different. To be sure, defrauding the corporation by its officers is still an occasional pastime of some unscrupulous managers. Other litigation is inspired by corporate ignorance of the innumerable Securities and Exchange Commission regulations or by sheer stupidity.

Other corporations have been sued for bribing foreign government officials and not informing the stockholders of their actions. These are run-of-the-mill actions or 10b-5 suits. Rule 10b-5 of the Securities Act of 1934 covers a multitude of potential sins with regard to the purchase and sale of securities. It outlaws any device or scheme to defraud, any untrue statements of material fact or omission of such facts, and any act or practice in the course of business that is fraudulent or deceitful.

There has been a substantial change in stockholder suits in recent years caused by new problems, and they have taken on a new complexion. Two issues in particular are at the source: campaign gifts and bribery of foreign officials, purchasing agents, or intermediaries. Some of these suits are brought by public interest law groups, interested in corporate reform rather than corporate cash.

Many stockholder actions are, of course, concerned with cash. One of the most significant cases was the Eisen matter. Morton Eisen, a shoe salesman and dabbler in the stockmarket, sued a brokerage house that specialized in odd-lot trading. He claimed that odd-lot broker Carlisle & Jacquelin overcharged traders, since it was customary to charge an eighth or one-quarter of a point ($0.125 or $0.25) per share more than round-lot trades of one hundred shares. His suit was brought on behalf of two million odd-lot traders from 1962–1966. The odd-lot differential was exorbitant, he maintained. Defendants retorted that even should the case prevail on its merits, there was simply no way to repay all those who were overcharged. Consequently, a class action was an impossible vehicle in this situation.

personal injury action — that is on a contingency basis. Lawyers shared in the proceeds if they won, but gained nothing if they lost. In recent court rulings in some federal circuits, the victorious plaintiff's counsel have not come away empty-handed but rather have been rewarded in the more conventional terms in their profession — on an hourly basis. Instead of, say twenty-five percent of a two million dollar settlement, judges are making awards on the basis of the number of hours employed on the case. Usually a far less remunerative figure results. Thus the risk remains the same but the potential for reward is reduced. While these tendencies reflect judicial thinking, they seem contrary to the recent trends to make corporations and fiduciary institutions more accountable through litigation. Deterrence to venality and criminality are lessened if it becomes more difficult to bear down with meaningful pressure. Governmental action is usually too little and too late: the Securities and Exchange Commission brings injunctive relief, but that hardly hits errant businessmen where they live — in their pocketbooks.

Instead of considering stockholder litigation as a destructive mechanism that undermines the system — a theme widely heard in financial circles — it is rather a cathartic procedure for businesses that forget or ignore ethical considerations. Jewish attorneys have led in the battle to protect shareholder rights in the face of corporate interests that are hostile to private individuals. Milton S. Gould, a prominent attorney, writing in the *New York Law Journal,* commented that "any historian of the development of our profession in the 20th century should recognize that it was the very exclusion of these men [lawyers for plaintiff stockholders] from the ranks of the established lawyers that transformed them into the skilled and intrepid *condottieri* who have done so much to keep American business on the level."

# 11. Tithes That Bind

The inboard engine on a transatlantic flight suddenly caught fire, and the pilot asked each passenger to 'do something religious' in accordance with his or her own faith. A Moslem bowed toward Mecca; Roman Catholics prayed over their rosaries; Protestants sang hymns. And a Jewish passenger went from seat to seat soliciting funds for research to prevent future engine fires.

First, high degree, than which there is no higher, is that one who takes hold of an Israelite who has become impoverished and gives him a gift or a loan or goes into partnership with him or finds work for him, in order to strengthen his hand so that he may be spared the necessity of appealing for help.
— Maimonides, "The Eight Degrees of Charity"

The manner of giving is worth more than the gift.
— Pierre Corneille, *Le Menteur*

## The Funding Fathers

Never before have so few raised so much for so many. The Jewish fundraising machine is wondrous to behold. When lubricated and in gear, it is the envy of competitors, both here and abroad. It not only uses every fundraising technique in the textbook, but has invented numerous ploys to extract that extra dollar. The techniques range from appealing to the most profound Jewish instinct of charity to using the most flagrant and cynical panhandling techniques of the schnorer. It pulls out all the stops, from pathos to bathos, and cashes in on every emotion. Maurice Samuel, a noted Jewish writer, remarked that a fund drive could best be described as "mixtures of public spirit, imaginative kindness, publicity-hunting, social pressure, cajolery, professional slickness, sentimentality, Jewish loyalty, high-pressure salesmanship, advertising stunts and nostalgic echoes of forgotten pieties . . . a perpetual tug of war between educational effort and a surrender of techniques." Of course, it is all polished technique by now, but the extremes are forever surprising.

Since much of the monies raised goes to Israel, Middle East tension is a catalyst for giving, and open conflict brings generous donations. Each of Israel's four wars brought forth an avalanche of wealth — some of it donated spontaneously, the rest barely pump-primed by the fundraising machine. Before the start of the Yom Kippur War in 1973, contributions were running significantly behind the previous year — by about fourteen percent. Within one week after the war started, American Jews had donated $100 million in cash to the United Jewish Appeal (UJA) and the Israel Emergency fund. And as might be expected, the year was not only a record one for donations, but it doubled all previous annual drives. Americans contributed $477,470,000 in 1973, and lent the state of Israel over $502 million through the purchase of bonds.

Money poured in from the most unexpected places as well as the more common ones. A national telethon produced $1 million an hour for a brief period. (For the first few days of the war, according to Israel's Minister of Finance, the late Pinhas Sapir, the conflict was costing $8 million an hour.) Thirteen dollars in pennies came from a child's savings bank, a one-time citizen of Germany sent a year's worth of reparation money, while the kids who parked cars at the World Series games sent in their $160 from car jockeying. An elderly woman gave all her money — $30.69, while a Wall Street broker dropped a $1,000 check into a collection box opposite the New York Stock Exchange. Another woman, about to leave on vacation, contributed her traveler's checks and canceled her trip.

There was the same phenomenon in the preceding war in 1967: on the day the fighting started, a luncheon at the Waldorf Astoria found pledges running at $1 million a minute for the first fifteen minutes. On that first day, Chicago raised $2.5 million and Atlanta, over $1 million. Within the first week of the Six Day War, the UJA's Israel Emergency Fund raised $90 million. Some people contributed in kind, mostly securities, but one man sent the deeds to two of his service stations.

And along with the cash and checks came letters — poignant, compassionate, determined, and full of prayers. From the Jewish Theological Seminary professor who sent a check for $23,000 and a note, "you have it all now," to the associate dean at a Catholic University who wrote: "We are willing to help in any way you feel feasible — to answer phones or lick stamps. I would be willing to go to Israel to relieve a man for other duties. You know, the world stood silent while the Six Million went into the gas chambers, but I do not intend to remain silent while millions of the survivors are flushed down an oil well."

Wars, of course, bring out the best as well as the worst in mankind. But the gush of money, the impetuous generosity due to hostilities are the climax of highly orchestrated campaigns, long in preparation. The Jewish establishment views them as something more than exercises in fundraising, though all the major Jewish organizations are dependent on the flow of funds for their budgets. It would be naive to assume that they do not have a vested interest in their success. However, they view the work of philanthropy as educational and proselytical: it is a chance to convert Jews, or at least to recapture Jews that have wandered from the fold. Judaism, along with all other major religions in the United States, is finding that the houses of worship are not drawing the faithful, as attendance slips year by year. It is doubtful that more than thirteen percent of the adult Jewish population is active in their synagogues on a regular basis. Therefore, it becomes necessary to reach Jews in some other fashion if there is to be some communal cohesiveness.

Philanthropy has come to serve as the nexus, the center that gives a focus to communal existence. One student of the phenomenon has noted:

Fundraising is often the only medium of affiliation by Jews with Jewish agencies or institutions. In short, fundraising personnel in most Jewish agencies are expected to help raise the money necessary for the preservation and improvement of these institutions and services which represent for these agencies the means for Jewish survival; and to raise the money in ways which encourage and develop the kind of identification among Jews which themselves might lead to Jewish survival. Fundraising is thus a way of inducing the continuity of the Jewish group, its institutions, its services, its values, and its traditions, and enhancing their effectiveness in improving the quality of Jewish life.

Moving from the general to the specific, the guidelines for raising substantial amounts of money change from group to group, from the hard sell of card-calling to the subtle pressures of a coffee klatch. Substantial amounts of money are not raised at the Sunday suburban breakfast, but presolicited by pledges before a meeting, dinner, or community event. The pledges are looked upon as a floor, not a ceiling, for donations.

Paul Zuckerman, a Detroit businessman, a past chairman of the UJA, and head of the fundraising arm of the Jewish Agency of Israel, stresses the need for careful homework to see what the prospective donor is really worth. "It is important to rate to get the most," Zuckerman said. "In every city there are men who have always been the pacesetters in terms of giving and working, they are not giving as much as they can. We must have the courage to take a look at what they are really worth and ask for that amount," he stressed.

There are rules to this game as in any other. When out for big trophies, a safari is the preferred hunting party. Zuckerman continued: "It is an accepted principle that one man should never go alone to solicit a major gift. It is too easy to say no to one man, especially if he is a friend or neighbor. When two or more go, it is no longer one Jew asking another for a gift — it is the entire community, it is the Jewish people." Naturally, the more guns, the better the chance for game, so overseas solicitors are frequently brought in for the attack. Israeli ministers, Russian emigres, and famous Jews are all utilized in landing the prominent quarry. Thus a prospective contributor is overwhelmed "when a national leader, an Israeli and a respected local leader call on a man, then quite literally the world Jewish community is calling on him," Zuckerman emphasized. Obviously, it is difficult to turn aside this concerted attack — and most subjects really don't want to, since this attention is flattering.

What makes Jewish fundraising organizations so successful is the simple fact that they really work at it. Since all Jewish wealth is far from apparent, the first step is to make visible monies that have kept a low profile. To this end, the UJA established a project to discover the "paper millionaires." Researchers scan the public records for prospective Jewish candidates, looking for stock market successes, notable business deals, or substantial financial transactions. Once they find out a potential donor's interest, and his friends and associates, they hold meetings with him or plan trips to Israel.

"This project does not only raise money, it literally makes Jews out of men we weren't reaching before. There are already instances of men going from $200 to $75,000, from $5,000 to $15,000 and higher. Quite clearly, we are talking about more than money when we talk of increases like that; we're talking about changing the essence of man, making him a valuable community asset," said Zuckerman.

Removing anonymity to raise a contributor to the status of a "valuable community asset" can also be done through bestowing some sort of encomium or prestigious office. "If we honor a man, give him a position of leadership, then I sincerely believe he has a responsibility to live up to it," he remarked. In some instances it works the other way. When, in good times, donors start to give more money, they then want recognition. One old joke has it that one steadfast contributor gave $1,000 annually, always anonymously, although he was able to afford more. Finally, he was persuaded to ante up $10,000. He was asked if he still wished anonymity. "Of course not," he replied, "what do I have to be ashamed of now?" Anonymity is one of the sure signs of an unplumbed donor. Rather like the tip of the iceberg, the anonymous pledge is a sign of far greater resources.

Jewish fundraising agencies are very thorough in analyzing the business world by its components. By looking at "natural relationships," the fundraisers have defined over a hundred different trade and professional groups. In fact, Jewish fundraisers were the first to look to the business sectors for money: from dentists to dresses ("popular priced and better") each division is fine-combed for nuances of annual changes.

Another device of Jewish fundraising is card-calling, a technique that works for Jews but for almost no one else, or at least nowhere near as successfully. A testimonial dinner or a community happening is staged. But before the event, the sponsoring organization prepares a series of pledge cards based on their research, past donation, and present prospects of the guests. The guests are aware of the circumstances and know full well that after the baked Alaska and the prominent speaker, their names will be called and a donation requested. Naturally, the public nature of a dinner with one hundred or five hundred friends and business associates exerts the maximum amount of peer presure. And it would seem that in order to subject oneself to this potentially humiliating and possibly mortifying experience, a donor must be willing to contribute fully. Though a crass and tactless exhibition, it does raise money. This modern-day form of potlatching differs from the more primitive variety by presenting a positive end, one that benefits the community-at-large. It is not a negative exercise to see who can destroy the most goods, but a competition to publicly out-give one's neighbors. Whether the saving grace of a socially desired end outweighs the questionable means seems debatable however successful.

The man who developed card-calling to a high degree is Joseph Willen, a consultant to the Federation of Jewish Philanthropies. In fifty years of fundraising, Willen has helped raise in excess of a billion dollars. He defends the technique and its social value. "Card calling is the hallmark of conspicuous giving. Some people say conspicuous giving is bad but spending the money — conspicuous consumption — that's all right. Conspicuous charity has a lot more value than driving round in a Rolls Royce," Willen has said. The idea for card-calling originated with Lawrence Marx in the 1920s — Marx was president of the textile house Cohn Hall Marx Company. Marx took the idea to Felix Warburg, a partner of Kuhn Loeb & Company, reportedly to give it some social class. Since its inception the technique has flourished and today it is one of the main tools of Jewish philanthropy.

The UJA campaigns and the Federation drives do not always

get the biggest fish in their fundraising nets since the bulk of their monies go for the daily facts of life: food, clothes, rent, vocational training, immigrant assistance, salaries, and other mundane activities. The heavy hitters are more interested in capital improvements. Sponsoring building programs for libraries, laboratories, class rooms, nursing homes, or hospitals are more conspicuous contributions. In short, a capital program feeds an "edifice complex," assuring "present prestige and future immortality" in the words of one observer.

The special appreciation that Jews have for education gives it a high priority in any organized philanthropy. Capitalizing on this sentiment, the UJA established an exclusive "club" to benefit Israel's schools — the Israel Education Fund (IEF). Since 1964 the Fund has raised millions largely from American sources to establish a series of combined academic and vocational schools in development areas in Israel. What makes the Fund exclusive is its search for the ultimate donors — it will not take small- or medium-sized contributions. Indeed, all donations below $100,000 are politely refused and directed to its parent, the UJA. Thus the routine gift is somewhere between $100,000 and $500,00. "Jews want to give to education," remarked Eliezer Shmueli, the Israeli Deputy Director-General of the Education Ministry who supervised the Fund. The IEF cultivates big donors with an air of exclusivity and an intensive capital-building program that the wealthy love. The irony of this snob appeal is further compounded by the fact that the prime purpose of these development schools is to use "education to break down social barriers," in the words of the Deputy Director-General. Whether or not the seventy-nine completed schools of the IEF accomplish this mission, the Fund has earned itself a niche in the annals of fundraising.

## Dues Time

Perhaps the Jews did not invent taxation — a feat generally credited to the ancient Egyptians — however they were among the earliest civilizations to levy tribute to support political and religious classes. It was commonplace all over the ancient world to take a tenth of a man's property or produce. These "first fruits" probably originated with the tribute that conquerors levied on new subjects as well as old residents.

Early Hebrew tribes had their cornfields, vineyards, and flocks subject to the tithe for the king. Indeed, the tithe can be regarded as one of the earliest prerogatives belonging to the divine right of kings. (The tithe was not only the earliest manifestation of divine right but one of the longest lasting royal tributes: in Western Europe it lasted until 1936 when it was abolished in Great Britain by an act of Parliament.)

The first fruits were brought to the house of God to maintain and support the nascent religious establishment. Some of the contributions found their way into a corner cupboard or small room. These rooms, termed "Cells of Silence" or "Chambers of Whispers," were depositories for the poor — the food stamp centers of their day. Gifts of produce were left, anonymously, and were later picked up, also anonymously. These "Cells of Silence" were an advance over the usual biblical assistance program to the impoverished — to leave a corner of the cultivated land unharvested for the use of the poor.

While the tithe was not a Jewish invention — indeed its use predated Judaism — Hebrew tribes took to the concept very early in their development. The patriarch Abraham gave one-tenth to Melchizedek, king of Salem, apparently as spoils of war. Isaac was probably the first Jew to give a tenth of his earnings. When the practice became common is impossible to say, but the concept received a Hebrew name, *Ma'aser,* a derivative of *asarah,* ten. The Talmud recognized the function of tithing and placed limits on its application. A tenth was the minimum contribution, though very generous individuals could donate up to a fifth of their income — twenty percent.

Through the ages, rules and regulations formalized the practice of tithing. First of all, every Jew was subject to it for "as for him who does not distribute his tithe with an open hand, his prayers will not rise up to heaven."

Indeed, everyone is to give to the poor — even the poor who are the object of charity. There are a few exceptions: it is not obligatory if the donation deprives the family of basic sustenance. Nor is it a necessary act for an orphaned young lady if by doing so, her dowry would be reduced below the marriage level and thus lower her chances of matrimony. *Ma'aser* funds should be segregated into one or more boxes if the charity is for more than one purpose. Yet though the tithe and the giving of a tenth of income is ingrained in tradition, there appears to be no word in Hebrew or Yiddish for outright gifts to charity.

Judaism has approached the problem of assisting others from a different point of view. Charity, as is commonly understood today, is derived from the idea of Christian love and natural affection for fellow men and women. Its modern application of alms-giving, benevolence, or bequest did not become commonplace until the sixteenth or seventeenth century. The Jewish idea of the tithe has other roots — not out of love but out of duty, a moral imperative. Regardless of whether one personally likes and admires the recipients, Jews are duty-bound to contribute to alleviate suffering. And since Jewish history had sufficient suffering to go around, giving became institutionalized. "For the poor shall never cease out of the land; therefore I command thee, saying, thou shall open thine hand wide unto thy brother...." (Deuteronomy 15:11) It was a religious obligation to assist the impoverished, the helpless, the homeless, and all victims of malevolent fate. To do so was a righteous or just act, in Yiddish, *tzedaka.*

"Charity begins at home," an expression of prior claims by the family does not apply to *Ma'aser* money. Of course the old saw is frequently a dodge, an excuse not to give at all. While it is up to the donor's discretion whether to tithe money, there are some prohibited beneficiaries. After placing the donations in the various *Ma'aser* boxes (*pushke*), the proceeds should go to the truly needy as quickly as possible. It is permissible to loan oneself some funds on a short-term basis, but only if the object of the donation is not present. *Ma'aser* monies should not go to educating your own children, to marriage brokers, to pay rabbis and other religious functionaries, or to build synagogues. One's relatives may be beneficiaries of the tithe funds, but preference must be given to those who devote their time to study the holy books.

Perhaps the quaintest tradition associated with *Ma'aser* money is the oath preceding the gift. Ever mindful of setting precedents, the benefactor utters an oath stating that the gift is not to be taken as one.

Within the last generation or two, the *pushke* boxes have gradually disappeared, while the act of charitable contributions among Jews has undergone a revolution. Leo Rosten's mother had twenty-two boxes for household giving. Today, the tin can of the Jewish National Fund might be the only one left in a Jewish family. However, Jewish charitable donations have increased dramatically, whether measured in current or constant dollars, as well as in percentage of disposable income. And the sophisticated developments of fundraising have brought about social and legal changes in the Jewish community. Outright charitable gifts and bequests to major Jewish organizations and agencies are today the usual form of donations. The voluntary pledge has replaced the poor box.

Heretofore, a promise to donate to a charity was unenforceable under common law, though enforceable under Talmudic law. A promise was not a true contract since money had not changed hands in return for the promised goods and services. If a Jew had reneged on a promise to a Jewish institution or cause he could be charged in a religious court of rabbis, the *Beth din*. But he could not be sued in a secular court since it was against a long Jewish tradition — on pain of excommunication — to have religious matters settled by outsiders.

In the 1960s a significant move away from the traditional practice now gives pledges the force of contract. Though religious organizations are somewhat reluctant to sue members or friends, preferring to use peer pressure, there is now sufficient legal grounds. Charitable agencies have come to rely on their annual campaigns and plan accordingly. The years of large endowments by a few fat cats or "social service barons" are past. Long-term planning can only be effective with enforceable pledges. The crux of the legal basis for enforcing pledges lies at the very heart of fundraising techniques: "A person's pledge is given in consideration of pledges by others, and these mutual pledges support the enforceability of each." Perhaps this is a legal way of describing "peer pressure"; no doubt that it is an updated version of the social contract. Consequently pledge cards are worded so that the donor pledges "in consideration" of other people's pledges.

In 1969 a Michigan man pledged $25,000 for himself and three members of his family for a synagogue building campaign. Since he was the building committee chairman, his pledge was all-important in setting the tone. It is tacitly understood that on accepting the chairpersonship of any fundraising campaign, the chairperson will make a "sacrificial gift." In the Michigan case, the pledge card was never filled out — only an appended paper was attached to the cards. Differences arose between the would-be donor and the synagogue, and the latter sued for the pledged sum. Though the lower court ruled for the synagogue, the appellate court reversed the decision on a technicality: the cards had not been filled out properly and it was moot as to whether the appendant paper could be deemed a contract in a secular or religious court. So while the pledge was not enforceable in that situation, the secular courts are increasingly enforcing pledges of religious contributions.

The fundraising revolution of the last few decades is not wholly a Jewish phenomenon but an American development with roots in the seventeenth century. If one discounts the fundraising effort undertaken by Columbus in the Spanish court to finance his journey, the first purely American effort took place in 1641. Harvard College was short of money so it sent three clergymen to London to solicit so that the college could, among other things, "educate the heathen Indians." The clergymen were at first quite successful and raised £500. Though they were not able to provide movies, slide shows, foreign dignitaries, and guest speakers, they did provide the first in a long river of paper with a promotional pamphlet entitled "New England's First Fruits." Eventually, the fundraisers fell out of grace, the expedition was decried as fradulent, and one of them ended up on a scaffold. It was an ominous start.

In the eighteenth century, that protean American, Benjamin Franklin was asked by a clergyman to give both money and advice in order to build a church. Franklin, ever to the point, remarked: "I advise you to apply to all those whom you know will give something; next to those whom you are uncertain whether they will give anything or not, and show them the list of those who have given; and lastly, do not neglect those whom you are sure will give nothing, for in some of them you may be mistaken." As for personally donating, Franklin was freer with his advice than his money and turned the good Reverend down.

If soliciting in London for Harvard was the first systematic attempt at fundraising in America, two centuries were to pass before the New World came to the assistance of the Old. The tide reversed itself when Americans provided relief for the Irish in the famine of the 1840s. Local fundraising efforts dot American history but it was not until the Civil War that a national campaign was launched to solicit funds from the public. The task was undertaken by the dubious patriot, Jay Cooke, selling government bonds for country and commission. But the concept of national solicitation for Jewish charities was imported from Great Britain. In Liverpool the idea of centralized campaigns through a federation developed in the 1870s. By 1895 a Jewish federation was formed in Boston and in 1896 one in Cincinnati.

American generosity has been one of the country's strong points — a fact noted by many foreign visitors from De Tocqueville to Churchill. One prominent historian, Arthur M. Schlesinger, Sr., wrote that "this philanthropic streak in the national character, an index of the pervasive spirit of neighborliness appeared early and has ... reached fabulous dimensions. It is another of the distinguishing marks of the American way."

Not all Americans see these "distinguishing marks" in such an appealing or positive fashion. Critics of organized philanthropy view it as a tax dodge for the shrewd and an exercise in egomania for the powerful. Moreover, the techniques and methods employed are divisive, embarassing, antisocial, crass, and sado-masochistic. And all too frequently the donations perpetuate and institutionalize bureaucratic agencies of dubious distinction — self-serving sinecures. John Steinbeck reflected some of this feeling when he wrote:

> Perhaps the most overrated virtue in our list of shoddy virtues is that of giving. Giving builds up the giver, makes him superior and higher and larger than the receiver. Nearly always, giving is a self-

ish pleasure, and in many cases is a downright destructive and evil thing. One has only to remember some of the wolfish financiers who spend two-thirds of their lives clawing fortunes out of the guts of society and the latter third pushing it back. It is not enough to suppose that their philanthropy is a kind of frightened restitution, or that their natures change when they have enough. Such a nature never has enough and natures do not change that readily. I think that the impulse is the same in both cases. For giving can bring the same sense of superiority as getting does, and philanthropy may be another kind of spiritual avarice.

## Social Service Barons

Organized Jewish philanthropy at the turn of the century had to meet the pressing requirements of a vast East European migration. Jews needed basic social services — health care, primary education, hospitals, and settlement houses. Until World War I, Jewish philanthropy was largely domestic in nature. The older established community of Western European descendants, predominantly German in background and Reform in persuasion, assisted the new immigrants of Eastern Europe, largely Russian and Polish in origin and Orthodox in tradition. By and large, American Jews did not extend help overseas except for special circumstances — such as to aid the survivors of the Kishineff massacres of 1903 and the Russian massacres in 1905. Those pogroms "made American provincialism impossible."

Before World War I, the limit of overseas relief was $1.5 million to victims of the Balkan War of 1912. World War I galvanized American Jewry since three-quarters of the world's Jews lived in the belligerent nations. Furthermore, hostility to the Jews was apparent on both sides of the battleline. "Whereas other unfortunate poeples, such as the Belgians and the Serbs had one enemy before them, these millions of Jews had two — the one in front and the other behind."

By the time of the Armistice in 1917, American Jewry had raised $63 million for both European and Palestinian Jews. Indeed, hardly a month after the war began, Henry Morgenthau, then ambassador to Turkey, cabled the American Jewish Committee that "the Jews of Palestine were facing a terrible crisis," and he called for aid of $50,000. The Committee put up half that sum and the other half was provided by the Committee for General Zionist Affairs and Jacob H. Schiff, the prominent banker.

In the 1920s philanthropic drives reverted to aiding local causes. Overseas aid, administered by the American Joint Distribution Committee, went to Jewish communities in Europe. Jews in Palestine received next to nothing — only what the incipient Zionist organization could raise. In a sense, the Zionists were persona non grata in the councils of American Jewry in the twenties and thirties. The Establishment figures, the heavy hitters for generating funds, for the most part directed, controlled, and administered the major Jewish agencies: the American Jewish Committee, the Joint Distribution Committee, local welfare funds, the Council of Jewish Federations and Welfare Funds, National Refugee Service, et al. These prominent men were termed the "social service barons:" Schiff, Felix M. Warburg, Julius Rosenwald, Arthur Hays Sulzberger, Herbert and Irving Lehman, Henry Morgenthau, Cyrus Adler, Lewis H. Strauss, and Sol Stroock. Zionists characterized them as "one great philanthropic holding company with interlocking directorates."

Their interests and considerable fortunes were attuned to traditional charities at home and abroad. Broad philosophic differences separated them from Zionists: they were asssimilationists, believing that Jews could integrate, be accepted by non-Jews, and play a role in American democracy; they believed in a laissez faire economy, industrialism, and commercial activity. And naturally they believed in success and the surety of their opinions. Zionism was at once alien to them, counterproductive to improving general conditions of Jews except perhaps in Palestine, and tinged with a messianic, rural socialism. There were religious differences as well: the "barons" were Reform Jews for the most part who took their Judaism in small spoonfuls. The Zionists were perhaps even less religiously oriented, but had a consuming faith in the manifest destiny of Jewish history. There was a mysticism attached to Zionism that went against the grain of rational businessmen.

Throughout the twenties and thirties, the Zionists tried to insinuate themselves into positions of leadership, to capture the decision-making processes so that they could control the sluice gates. They entered into "pacts of glory" with the "philanthropic oligarchs" and attempted to run joint campaigns, but the Zionists felt they were selling out "the purity of the Zionist political ideal." The Jewish Establishment, on the other hand, felt that a Jewish state was too physical — they preferred the concept of a national homeland, one that did not require national sovereignty, a majority of the population or too much space.

In 1941 Louis Lipsky, a former president of the Zionist Organization of America, looked back and commented on the "influential group of Jews who are anxious to keep American Jewish life loyal to isolationist, assimilationist ideas, who are always limiting the Jewish interest, always avoiding Jewish identification, always seeking to have Jewish life adjust itself to the fears and negations arising out of an everlasting apology for Jewish existence."

A later observer wrote that the heads of the local welfare funds were successful business leaders since that seemed sufficient recommendation for leadership in Jewish affairs.

> Unlike most European Jewries, in which spiritual leadership was accorded mostly to scholars of Jewish lore, American communal dominance — especially in the power to disperse philanthropy — gravitated into the hands of those willing and able to "set an example" by making a large contribution to the local philanthropic fund. As often as not, moreover, this oligarchy of wealth and power was devoid of Jewish education or even Jewish sympathies.

The ideological conflict continued right up to World War II. It was in the nature of fundraising in that period (and to some degree even now) that a few individuals were responsible for the majority of monies donated to any given cause. It was not uncommon for two percent of the donors to contribute half of all the funds raised.

Obviously with non-Zionist fat cats controlling the major Jewish organizations, the Zionists despaired of getting a fair break. Rabbi Abba Hillel Silver, a leading Zionist and head of the United Palestine Appeal noted:

> [American Jews] choose rather to listen to their omniscient and infallible philanthropic mentors who counselled them to give all aid

to the Jewries of Eastern and Central Europe, but only a pittance to that visionary project of impractical idealists in Palestine. One must be realistic, they argued — and what greater realist in the world is there than a successful Jewish banker or broker, and who can question his unerring judgment.

The gathering war storms of the late 1930s, compounded by anti-Semitic outbreaks in Central Europe, the Austrian capitulation to Germany, the restrictive attitudes of the British to Palestinian immigrants all intensified the need to increase the Palestinian donations. In 1939 a newly reconstituted United Jewish Appeal gave the Zionists proportionately more money from UJA campaigns in addition to greater support and stature. From 1940 onwards there was a veritable explosion of Zionist sentiment in the United States of the "maximal, Herzlian" variety. Membership in the Zionist Organization of America jumped from 43,000 in 1940 to 250,000 in 1948, and suffrage rights in the World Zionist Congress rose nearly five-fold.

With the threat to Jewish existence, the purse strings were untied. In the United Jewish Appeal campaign of 1940, over $14 million were collected — $3 million of which went for Zionist purposes. Every year thereafter, funds for Zionism increased dramatically up to the establishment of the state of Israel of 1948. Compared with the history of early Zionist efforts, the results were impressive. In the period from 1901 to 1929, $14 million were sent to Palestine from the United States, $8 million in 1930 to 1939, but over $200 million from 1939 to 1948. These pre-Israel funds generated by Zionists were impressive not only in themselves, but also compared with other fundraising efforts. Of course, analogies are not really appropriate since Zionism is not quite equivalent to a medical problem, a university, a hospital, a cultural center, or even to a religious enterprise. It is sui generis. But it does give an idea of UJA's 1948 campaign to know that it collected approximately four times more than the American Red Cross that year.

One observer of the Jewish scene remarked that Jews were "possessors of a belligerent generosity." The same might be said of Americans in general: they give away approximately as much as American corporations distribute in dividends. Even in the midst of the last recession, 1980 and 1981, Americans were still giving money away at a rate of $54 billion a year.

Marshalling $54 billion a year is no mean job, particularly in a time of worldwide business recession, an energy crunch, global inflation, high unemployment, and general economic uncertainty. Most charitable contributions are from individuals (seventy-nine percent), followed almost equally by bequests (eight percent) and foundations (eight percent), with the remainder coming from corporations.

Religion is the major recipient of charitable donations, accounting for forty-three percent of all dollars given. Almost all religious donations come from individuals. Even though church attendance keeps falling, and is now down to two out of five adults on a regular basis, religious donations have doubled in the last decade. Religion is followed by health and hospitals, education, social welfare, and arts and humanities, in that order.

Jewish congregations in the 1970s received a per capita donation of $30 per year. This puts Jews at the bottom of religious philanthropy — an anomaly since Jews as a group are more generous than other sectarians. The reputation of Jewish generosity is not undeserved, but the philanthropic picture is confused by all the additional aid that is channeled to nonreligous purposes such as social services and assistance to Israel.

If total Jewish giving is consolidated then the figures are wholly different and very formidable. But it remains true that on a strictly religious level Jews have not given congregational support a high priority. Indeed, it is a sore point in Jewish circles. A number of critics feel that Israel is draining too much money from the domestic American scene. "Many Jewish educational institutions at the local level of the typical Diaspora community are living on ancient methodology and on a starvation budget. They cannot compete — no matter how meritorious their claim — with a request made in great earnestness and with deep felt sincerity by the Prime Minister of Israel to 40 or 50 very rich men who are made privy to some of the vital needs of the state," commented Philip M. Klutznick, former president of the B'nai B'rith.

In fact, there has been something of a capital freeze on new construction outside of Israel since 1967. In other words, the battle for priorities continues. In the twenties and thirties, the Zionists made little progress; in the forties they reversed the field and have dominated Jewish fundraising efforts ever since. As long as the Jewish state is threatened, whether the perception be real or imagined, Jewish assistance is likely to be weighed heavily in Israel's favor. Consequently, nearly three out of four Jewish dollars raised in the United States goes overseas.

It is hardly news that there is a strong correlation between American Jewry's support and the danger level to the state of Israel. For instance, the sales of Israel bonds jumped over 27% in 1956 after the Sinai campaign, 140% after the 1967 Six Day War, and 86% after the Yom Kippur War.

Similar jumps in donations are noticeable in community campaigns though only a portion of the monies raised eventually go to support Israeli organizations. Jewish consciousness is raised in these times with the specter of the "final solution" branded on the collective Jewish mind. In 1956 Jewish community campaign funds jumped eighteen percent, but more significantly it reversed a downturn in donations that had peaked out in 1948, the year of Israel's birth. Thereafter, donations remained relatively flat until the 1967 war, when not only did the regular campaign perk up but a separate emergency drive brought in more money than the ordinary campaign. So successful was the "emergency" effort that it was perpetuated though the ostensible emergency had passed. Emergency funds are somewhat like extraordinary tax levies — organizations and officials become addicted to their salubrious effects.

So while direct religious congregations averaged out to $30 per individual Jew in the seventies, the total Jewish philanthropic contribution was about $150 per head. Some Protestant denominations receive greater per capita donations: the Presbyterian Church had an average gift of $176, the Seventh-Day Adventists, $454. However, the more populous churches such as the Methodists and the Baptists raised only two for every three dollars the Jews raised.

These figures tell only part of the story. As a group, Jews are less religious than their Christian counterparts if church membership is used as a criteria of religiosity. On the national level, almost fifty percent of the Christian population are members of their respective churches. For Jews, the figure is only forty-two percent. If Jewish religious adherents were proportionately as dedicated as the Christian population, the nineteen percent gain would undoubtedly unlock substantial monies. It is a fact which has not escaped the fundraising establishment.

## Pair Bonding

You can't tell the baseball players without a scorecard nor a Jewish organization without its abbreviation or acronym. The old saw that three Jews make for four political parties is nowhere so true as in the official and unofficial structure of the Jewish world. Bifurcation seems to be the name of the game for there appears to be an endless number of national organizations. They all don't raise money — it just seems that way. How much overlapping, duplication, and sheer waste in this prodigious amount of people, time, and money is anyone's guess and is likely to go unrecorded until there is a budget crises. That, however, does not appear on the horizon.

Federation and Welfare fund campaigns supply the bulk of the Jewish establishment's maintenance and operating needs for the affiliated agencies. Separate campaigns are run for capital costs and endowment drives — usually in association with a local agency. Organizations that wish to partake of Federation beneficence must forgo independent fundraising drives. However, the two-hundred Federations from city to city have somewhat different guidelines and local needs vary. Each Federation decides for itself how its funds will be used — how much will go to the UJA, how much to local hospitals, community centers, homes for the aged, and parochial schools. Consequently, there are numerous supplementary fundraising drives, some sponsored by Federations, some run solely by local agencies. In addition, there are independent campaigns for national and international causes such as drives for Hadassah, Hebrew University, Brandeis University, City of Hope, and National Jewish Hospital.

New York City occupies a special niche for the fundraisers: there is so much concentrated wealth that separate agencies run their own campaigns. The Federation of Jewish Philanthropies of New York (FJPNY) and the New York UJA have their own distinctive drives. New York is also a source of frustration for, unlike Cleveland or Los Angeles, it is not well organized for fundraising purposes. Besides the very real affluence, there is a considerable amount of Jewish poverty, not exactly terra desideratum. In Cleveland, four out of five Jewish families contribute to the Federation campaign. By contrast, in New York only one out of four families contributes. But at the same time New York UJA received 864 donations of $10,000 or more in 1973, fully half of the campaign receipts came from less than one percent of all contributors. Not only do fewer New Yorkers give compared to other large cities, but the average contribution per family is less than half of the national average. The latter situation is undoubtedly due to the general attempt to milk the New York cow, but the returns also diminish because New York has become the most heavily taxed metropolis in the country. But nowhere else in the country do you receive a sprinkling of $5 million gifts, and a fistful of $1 million contributions. Federation and Welfare funds and the Israel Emergency Fund receive the largest portion of the Jewish community campaigns, but it is only a part of what has been termed the "Jewish Gross National Product." Indeed, the Jewish GNP gives a rather concise view of the sources of funds raised for all Jewish communal services. Excluding some special capital projects, income and costs roughly balance each other. For instance, in 1978, $475 million was raised in fundraising campaigns and almost $400 million was distributed to the various agencies. The difference is attributed to shrinkage (not everyone who pledges actually gives), plus the administrative costs in conducting the drives. Welfare Fund contributions have fallen from the record year of 1974, when over $660 million were raised. Estimates of the total level of official Jewish income in 1976 reached $2.8 billion.

Jewish fundraising has produced remarkable results: from 1939 through 1976 approximately $6.9 billion has flowed through the various campaign coffers. How much of those funds have found their way abroad is difficult to judge for the percentages vary from year to year, but recent budgets call for overseas distribution of between seventy-five and eighty percent of their funds — a considerable increase from the pre-1973 war level. The balance of the monies are used to service a whole range of Jewish community services: religious education, health centers, hospitals, homes for the aged, youth camps, community relations, defense agencies, and family services. Not all beneficiaries are treated equally. In Jewish population centers of forty thousand or over, nonlocal agencies receive a majority of the funds. In cities where Jewish populations are small — five thousand or less — most of the raised funds go out of the area since there are no "developed networks" to perform the full range of services as in larger suburban centers. Thus there are distinct variations in community services and distinct disadvantages for Jews living in sparsely populated Jewish areas. Even when the cities are comparable in size, community services may not be, since priorities differ.

Only slightly less impressive than the fund drives are the campaigns to sell Israeli bonds. The bonds appealed to those who would not or could not give their funds away as charitable gifts. All American charities are blessed with favorable tax laws that allow individuals to contribute to "religious, charitable, scientific, literary or educational" nonprofit organizations. Such gifts are deductible from taxable income. Deductions ease the pain of giving since an individual in the thirty-three percent tax bracket finds every dollar donated is costing him only sixty-seven cents and in the fifty percent bracket, the dollar costs only fifty cents. A further tax break exists when a taxpayer donates appreciated property, most commonly securities, since he is not obliged to pay a capital gains tax on the appreciation while he is allowed to deduct the appreciated property from his taxes.

Bonds, however, do not enjoy any tax advantages in and of themselves. Americans buying Israeli bonds must pay taxes on interest received, plus they must declare any capital gain or loss. Some purchasers have donated the bonds to cover pledges, and thus become eligible for a tax deduction if the recipient is a nonprofit institution.

The initial idea for Israeli bonds sprung from the collective brow of the late Henry Montor, perhaps the leading Jewish fundraiser in American history, Sam Rothberg, the general chairman of the American operation of the State of Israel Bonds, David Ben-Gurion, and Golda Meir. Ben-Gurion called a conference in Jerusalem in September, 1950 to see if the state could raise money outside the usual philanthropic channels. After the founding of Israel it looked like future fundraising drives would be anticlimactic. After all, what could one do for an encore?

At first the Israeli bond idea seemed somewhat bizarre since Wall Street was unsympathetic and would not have any part of it. The financial world did not expect very much and thought that sales of $10 million could be considered successful.

"Wall Street couldn't understand Jews and their simple relationship to Israel," remarked one observer. In 1951, the first year of the program, Israeli bonds had a 3.5% coupon, not enough to draw money from the moon, but respectable in relative terms. First year sales amounted to $52.6 million, far in excess of Wall Street estimates. Jews were buying bonds — many of them sure they would never recoup their funds — without even getting a small wall plaque in return.

The success of the first few bond drives gave Israel a greater standing in financial circles and made it easier for her to borrow money since banks always prefer to lend money to people and states who have already borrowed some. Israeli bonds were never sold in the usual fashion, that is through underwriters, syndicates composed of investment banking houses. Instead, they were sold directly to Jews where emotion counted far more than yield, risk, and negotiability.

On the face of it, Israeli bonds may not look like an investment vehicle. After all, the state is surrounded by intense hostility, it is militarily vulnerable, its natural resources are limited, its economy heavily taxed and overextended, and its balance of payments in a perpetual deficit position. If the Prudent Man Rule for trusts was applied ("considering the probable income as well as the probable safety of the capital"), Israeli bonds would not likely pass muster. Nor do the bonds look terribly attractive compared with other debt instruments. The municipal market aside, in an inflationary era when United States government issues are sold to yield twelve and fourteen percent; certificates of deposit, commercial paper, letters of credit are in the same range; and investment grade corporate paper have coupons of twelve and fifteen percent, the yields are approximately two or three times greater than the Reconstruction and Development Issue which yields an "effective rate of approximately 4% per annum, compounded semi-annually." Nevertheless, they do sell well for they do have saving graces. While the bonds issued to individuals have a limited negotiability and are only redeemable at maturity, they can be used as legal tender in Israel for tourist expenses and can be given to Israeli institutions as gifts. The proceeds can be paid out in Israeli shekels, a considerable fillip since the shekel has been sharply devalued against the dollar in the past few years. Israel will also purchase any bond from the estate of a bondholder.

The state of Israel has total control over the proceeds — unlike the situation with the UJA funds which are partially controlled by the American agencies that raise them. Nearly half of the bond funds are used for housing, followed by community facilities such as schools and hospitals, with telecommunications the third major allocation. The remaining bond money is used for the country's infrastructure: roads, port development, irrigation, and agriculture.

In the first twenty-seven years of bond sales (1951–78), Israel has sold $4.2 billion of bonds and has redeemed $1.5 billion. Some two million individuals have bought them plus scores of institutions, banks, foundations, and pension funds. Anyone buying $25,000 of Israeli bonds is eligible for membership in the Prime Minister's Club. Bond officials see the bond program as viable for another twenty-five years. "It will be another generation before yield overwhelms emotion," remarked one spokesman.

Though the well of Jewish charity may never run dry, there are a number of economic facts in the American constellation that cast doubt on any massive increase in help. The American economy is not in the best of health. The back-to-back recessions not only left industrial output running far below potential capacity, but a towering structure of debt and deficits that Americans are having a hard time coping with. Most of the Jewish-American community, as with Americans in general, are finding their earnings and resources squeezed and their priorities up for reexamination. The fundraisers will have to devise some new stratagems if they are to separate the citizen from his shekel.

# 12. The Poor: Where the Jewish Money Is Not

The greatest of evils and the worst of crimes is poverty.
— George Bernard Shaw, *Major Barbara*

If the rich could hire others to die for them, the poor could make a nice living.
— Yiddish proverb

## The Invisible People

Jews have been so busy "making it" that this preoccupation is close to a *deformation religieuse*. Or so it seems. So ingrained is the general perception that Jews are rich, that only very recently did anyone realize that there was a sizable gap between perception and reality. Tunnel vision had focused on Jewish affluence to the exclusion of other conditions.

Therefore, it comes as a considerable shock to find that Jews are also among the least affluent group in American society. The images of stark and grinding poverty that come to mind — Appalachian hillbillies, Indians on reservations, Chicano wetbacks of the Southwest, black teenagers in Watts, and Puerto Ricans in Bronx's Hunts Point — are not Jewish in connection or countenance. Only in history can one imagine Jewish poverty — the huddled shtetl immigrant frozen in a sepia daguerreotype at the turn of the century. But the present day images of opulent three-day country-club Bar Mitzvahs, the conspicuously decorated suburban villa, the ostentatious vacation trip to Tel Aviv, or annual migration to Florida all crowd out the unappetizing vision of previous poverty. It is hard to get a fix on today's poor Jew. Indeed, for a long while he was the invisible man, forgotten by sons and daughers, the Jewish establishment, and society at large.

Of the 5,900,000 American Jews, probably six hundred thousand of them are living at or below poverty levels. Poverty, of course, is as much a personal feeling about oneself as it is an economic and cultural phenomenon. Lots of people are broke but not poor, while countless others feel that they are impoverished regardless of their net assets and bottom-line considerations. Thus the condition is as much a state of mind as it is a wiggle on the Consumer Price Index. The federal government's recent syntactical change in its official prose from "poor," a perfectly serviceable word, to "non-resource persons," an obfuscating invention, doesn't change the image or the reality.

For official purposes, poverty is determined by what a family spends on food. Since food is presumed to cost one-third of a family's income, the government multiplies the cost of an economy food budget by three to find the basic poverty line. In 1981 a nonfarm family of four was considered to be below the poverty level if its income fell below $8,450 — a single person lived below the poverty level if his or her income fell below $4,310.

The poor are always with us, or so the Biblical injunction warns, but in the last two decades the United States has made significant strides in improving their lot. In 1959 twenty-two percent of the country's population was thought to be poor. A great effort was then made to raise that submerged fifth of the population by the Kennedy-Johnson "war on poverty" and a host of social welfare reforms. This extraordinary shift of benefits and income through Social Security, unemployment insurance, food stamps, Medicare, Medicaid, public housing, and a number of other local programs succeeded in transferring enough money to push a full ten percent of the poor above the poverty line. Since the early seventies, the figure has remained rather fixed: only twelve percent of the nation's population is considered poor.

This does not mean that there has been a massive redistribution of wealth in the United States. On the contrary, all recent evaluations indicate that the economic and social status of the country has remained relatively fixed since World War II. It does mean that more money is now pumped into the poorest sector of the nation. In the last decade, there has been an explosion of transfer payments: 1966 federal transfer payments (social welfare expenditures) equaled $37 billion, but in 1978 they were in excess of $240 billion — a tenth of the Gross National Product. However, the war on poverty and the growth of transfer payments has had little effect on poor Jews.

How poor are Jews in relative terms? There are different ways of looking at poverty. At the national level, a little more than thirteen percent of Jewish households probably fall below the poverty line. This is roughly comparable to the number of the nation's families classified as poor. But it is surprising considering the fact that the Jewish median income is so much higher than the national average. To put it another way, there are a lot of poor Jews — more than one would expect from their collective high level of income.

Jews are also poorer compared to most ethnic groups. In 1969 a Census Bureau report on ethnic origin found that Irish, English, German, Italian, Polish, and Russian groups had less of their populations living in poverty than Jews did. Only the Spanish-speaking ethnic groups had higher poverty rates. This is a curious anomaly: Jews are both the richest and almost the poorest group in American society.

This comparison of Jews with ethnic groups has only partial validity: in a strict sense, Jews are not an ethnic group, but a religious body, found in each national community. But the comparisons do serve as a broad gauge of income accomplishment. The report on ethnic origins was the only one the Bureau ever did, for they found that there was too much inconsistency in follow-up interviews. Where people first reported they were of one ethnic origin, on subsequent interviews, they changed their responses. Thus it is imperfect information at best, but on a mass, national scale it does give a general idea of economic accomplishment.

Another way of measuring poverty is to look at New York City, the city with the largest Jewish population in the world. New York Jews constitute eighteen percent of the city's population and twenty-one percent of the national Jewish population. Of the 1.2 million New York Jews, fifteen percent, or 184,200, Jews are poor or on the fringe of poverty, while another five percent are living on incomes between poverty and the Bureau of Labor Statistics' Lower Income Level: a total of 245,600 Jews in the city, or one out of five, are potential welfare clients.

Though potential welfare clients, relatively few poor Jews queue up for the dole. The war on poverty, when it was gathering steam in the sixties, was not intended to better Jewish conditions, but to aid blacks, Hispanics, Indians, and Eskimos. In fact, for a variety of federal programs that assist minorities, the usual definition of minority is Indian, Negro, Oriental, Spanish-speaking, or any other foreign language minority designated by state agencies. The planners, politicians, bureaucrats, and social workers simply assumed that Jews, ipso facto, were not poor.

In New York City the mayor established a Council Against Poverty to distribute government funds. Poverty areas that were to receive funds and make provisions for special programs were designated. Designations were based on three criteria: the number of persons receiving welfare assistance; live births in hospital wards; and juvenile delinquency offenses.

With such criteria, Jewish poverty was not apparent. Since many poor Jews are old and half of them live alone, their juvenile delinquency rates and birth rates were — almost by definition — absurdly low, a veritable Catch-22 situation. And the number of Jews receiving welfare assistance was also minimal since they traditionally avoided government aid, considering public assistance a confession of failure and incompetence and a source of shame.

One of the strongest Jewish values, moral rectitude, has proven to be a destructive double-edged sword. Jews have felt that receiving benefits from state agencies was equivalent to perpetuating a form of fraud. Furthermore, benefits are equated with "relief," the demeaning handouts that passed for welfare before the major social security legislation of the 1930s. Moreover, this ancestral baggage was compounded by belief in the American credo of self-sufficiency — no real citizen would accept public charity except in the most dire circumstances. The presumed stigma of poverty is an affront to their pride. Finally, the American system of public assistance is designed to require near-destitution, one must crash to the bottom of the social class before help is extended.

Thus, on many levels, Jews would not partake of government programs. The idea that they had contributed to these programs in the form of taxes, insurance, and social security payments, that they had "paid their dues," did not affect their sensibilities. For example, in Los Angeles, when there were eight thousand Jews receiving public assistance in one area, there were ten thousand more who were equally eligible but not availing themselves of this support.

Jews have been invisible in numerous social welfare programs for some very practical reasons as well. Initially, community poverty corporations held their elections on the Jewish sabbath, effectively disenfranchising Jews. Though this was eventually rectified, Jews were not properly represented. In some areas of New York City, they were threatened by other minorities — forced to stay away from programs and projects. Jews were "viewed as intruders who were 'hustling-in' and boarding the gravy-train that is the poverty program."

In many inner-city areas, poor Jews constitute a minority within a minority. The predominant minority, whether black, Puerto Rican, or central European ethnic, tends to regard all Jews as affluent, each possessing a secret bundle or a slum tenement. The reality is otherwise, of course, for many Jews are even more destitute than the base figures would indicate. Strict religious beliefs in American society impose some burdens and cultural proclivities and communal patterns impose others. For orthodox Jews, particularly members of the Chassidic community, following the dietary laws of Kashrut is bound to add a premium to their food bills and a few points on their personal consumer price index. It is probably no exaggeration that *Glatt* (certified) kosher food costs between five and ten percent more than standard supermarket fare.

Moreover, the truly orthodox communities do not believe in birth control or limiting the size of the family. In Williamsburg, the home of Chassidism in New York, the average family has over six children, compared with the average Jewish family of two children. These communities are doubling in size every ten years. As if raising additional children were not burden enough, these Jews, putting little faith in secular education, send their children to parochial or religious schools instead of taking advantage of the free public schools.

Orthodox religious communities also prefer to live together and so cluster around their rabbis and their synagogues, taxing themselves to support their spiritual leaders. There are additional costs for poor Jews, especially the medical and health expenses that go with an aging population. Though perhaps insignificant in general terms, these costs do add up, creating a greater burden on poor Jews than on other poverty-stricken minority groups that are younger and healthier.

What does the explosion of transfer payments mean to Jews? Have they partaken of the administered riches? Will they have another crack at the "gravy train?" The prognosis is not particularly bright for a number of reasons. First of all, Jews were slow to get on board. For this delay and negligence, the blame must be laid squarely on the Jewish establishment. Their interests and concerns before the 1970s were elsewhere — indeed, everywhere but with their poor constituents.

Jews are blessed — or cursed, depending on one's view — with a global empathy, a world view of morality that places them in the front lines of innumerable causes; some related to Jewish interests, some not. From the civil rights movement for blacks to ecological crusades, from consumerism to proabortion and women's liberation, Jewish leaders and organizations take up the fight. Occasionally, they are found on both sides of the issue — liberal Jews were for the legalization of abortion while orthodox members were against it. Jewish hyperactivity for morality and social justice often leads them far afield.

Until recently, Jewish poverty was not an "issue": the Jewish agencies assumed that such poverty either did not exist, or if it did it was on such a modest scale as to be only of lesser interest. The American Jewish Committee admitted that the "Jewish community did not recognize the relevance of this phenomenon to its own people."

Faced with the growing realization of poverty among Jews, Jewish agencies found that they were short on demographic data. For years, the Jewish establishment had taken a strong position against a religious census as part of the great national surveys every ten years. The feeling was that such a census was inherently mischievous, that it would be open to misinterpretation and might lead to conflict. One observer noted the curious corner that Jews had backed themselves into: "We have the paradox of a self-conscious group allegedly given to excessive introspection extremely hesitant in undertaking a systematic process of self-examination."

This position was paradoxical in another sense as well. In the effort to fight discrimination and prejudice, there was a concerted attempt to remove the questions of religious preference from college and university admissions, job interviews, employment applications, or any situation in which the information could lead to discriminatory practices. If the information was not available, so the thinking went, it would be infinitely more difficult to take an anti-Semitic attitude. It was later realized that this lack of such information hindered the implementation of enlightened policy: it was impossible to know how minorities were, in fact, treated in large corporations, state bureaucracies, or professional schools. Social wisdom, in its next phase, called for a reversal: to ensure equal opportunity it was necessary to monitor minority hiring. Back came the questions. Progressive Jewish policy called for support of "affirmative action."

This change in attitude paralleled a subtle shift in social philosophy. Previous generations paid homage to the melting pot: the essence of Americanism was a fusion of differences. Whether this fondue democracy ever existed is highly debatable, but it was felt that publication of religious affiliation data would "have a negative effect on our underlying democratic philosophy of equality of our heterogeneous citizenship and intensify the consciousness of differences among religious and ethnic groups." The way to peaceful Americanization was, in brief, to submerge differences; the way to social strife was to emphasize diversity. This bland recipe, if it was ever fully subscribed to, would have turned out a very vapid stew. Happily, diversity and ethnicity not only became fashionable, but were increasingly viewed as strengths in the body politic.

Another objection to a body count was the feeling among Jewish organizations that it would open a Pandora's box. One interagency memorandum from the postwar period saw a "religious question in a census . . . an entering wedge for demolition of the separation of church and state in the United States. If the federal government introduces it, it is likely to be followed by the state and local governments with the result that the idea of classifying people by religion would become a part of the American consciousness, whereas up to the present time the effort of all men of goodwill has been to efface such lines of demarcation in official fields."

Finally, religious identification might loose unspecified fears that the data would be manipulated to the detriment of Jews and Jewish interests. The memorandum continued: "That such a question would open the way for various correlations between the statistics of religious affiliation and other data in the census and that such correlations may be made by ignorant or malicious people in such a way as to produce conclusions that might be invidious to various religious groups."

If the Jewish establishment felt that it would be bad social policy to have an official census question on religious affiliation, they could not get away from the fact that without some solid demographic information, the government would be making social, economic, and political decisions in a vacuum. For instance, previous estimates of Jewish population were based on either voluntary head counts by communal organizations or on school absences on Yom Kippur (before it became a school holiday in school districts with heavy Jewish populations). Thus the Council of Jewish Federation and Welfare sponsored the National Jewish Population Study. Published in 1972, it was based on scientific sampling and complete interviews of 7,550 Jewish households. For the first time, a relatively complete statistical portrait of American Jews emerged. Up to then, the number of Jews had always been an educated guess.

## A Numbers Game

Jews were among the first explorers and colonists in the New World; in fact, the first Jew to come to America was Columbus's interpreter on the first voyage, Luis de Torres. Though de Torres was baptized the day before the expedition set sail, Columbus undoubtedly brought him along for his linguistic talents, not his theological views.

The Jewish "Mayflower" brought to North America from Brazil the first substantial group of Jews — twenty-three of Dutch ancestry — who were fleeing the Inquisition in 1654. They were not welcomed in New Amsterdam, and the governor, Peter Stuyvesant, wanted to send them away, complaining that they were a "deceitful race" worshipping the "feet of Mammon." However, in what must be the first instance of Jewish commercial pressure in North America, the Jewish refugees communicated with Stuyvesant's employer, the Dutch West India Company, which had a few Jewish stockholders, and the refugees were allowed to remain. Profit triumphed over prejudice.

Both the Dutch and the British restricted Jewish activity in America, but the Jewish community continued to expand. By 1700 there were roughly 250 Jews in the colonies — a significant number of them in international trade and commerce. A Jew might not be able to hold public office, serve in the military, or carry on a profession, but restrictions were modified in overseas commerce as the English wished to encourage mercantilism.

And as always, international commerce provided natural advantages and a salubrious climate for Jews. It diversified risk and circumscribed local controls, evaded arbitrary taxes, and allowed Jews to take advantage of overseas connections with other Jews. Jewish traders were active in sending native raw materials to, and importing finished products from, England. They were represented in the infamous triangle trade: exchanging African slaves for West Indian sugar and molasses, which in turn was exported to New England to produce rum. The trade was completed by shipping the rum to Africa. Jews had no significant monopolies in international trade, but they started a number of sugar plantations, were particularly active in the ginger market, and attempted early to corner the market on whale candles.

By the American Revolution, there were appoximately twenty-five hundred Jews in America, located mainly in the cities, and employed in a variety of trades. Shopkeeping was probably the main Jewish occupation at that point.

In the eighty-odd years between the Revolution and the Civil War, the character of the country changed rapidly due to industrialism and expansion. The Jewish population rose from a couple of thousand to 150,000 in 1860. Migrating from Germany and Central Europe, the new arrivals turned their energies to the internal markets of the United States, away from the colonial concern with international trade. With a vast country to explore and exploit, Jews took to peddling, merchandising, cotton farming, real estate speculation, and finance. The developing country needed the occupational specialties of Jews: moneylending, distribution, shipping, commodity financing, clothing manufacturing, and retailing.

Individual Jewish immigration continued after the Civil War: together with the natural increment of newborn, the Jewish population reached 280,000 by 1880. Shortly thereafter, the influx of Jews took on new dimensions as whole communities fled Eastern Europe. Up to 1882 Jews "hardly came to this country at all," reported one newspaper. Or so was the popular impression. The new influx came from Russia predominantly, due to a series of harsh new statutes — the May Laws — that forced Jews to move to the cities from the country. In addition, the Odessa pogrom of 1871 was a warning of things to come and a stimulus to emigrate. However, under Alexander II, 1855–1881, Jews were well treated and relatively content — some even referred to that period as "a golden age."

The tolerant and reformist policies, at least in Russia, accounted for a very modest Russian emigration of a thousand people a year. But with the new Czar, Alexander III, oppressive and discriminatory policies and reactionary administrators returned. Russian emigrations rose to twenty thousand, then fifty thousand to one hundred thousand annually — seventy percent of which were Jews.

In 1880, the 280,000 Jews in the United States constituted 0.56 percent of the general population. By the time of the new immigration laws of 1924, effectively ending free immigration, the Jewish population had grown to 4.5 million, or 3.91 percent of the total. To look at the immigrations in another way, eight percent of the immigrants in the late nineteenth and early twentieth centuries were Jews.

Some found their new home uncongenial and returned: almost a quarter of European Jews returned from the 1880s immigrations, but that figure continued to fall to less than one percent after World War I. The immigrants came with a tightly knit family structure. Almost as many women came as men, with more women in child-bearing years. Within a relatively short period of time, the waves of immigrants caused the United States to have the largest Jewish community in the world.

After 1925 the Johnson Act controlled immigration, fixing quotas on the basis of the 1890 census and limiting the total to 154,000 annually. The year was important since it tilted the two percent allotment of foreign-born (as a percentage of previous national immigrants) toward northern and western Europe, the older immigrants. Southern and Slavic Europe was not yet as heavily represented. Thus the new immigration laws effectively reduced Jewish arrivals so that by 1940 half of American Jews were born in the United States.

Before World War II, the majority of Jews lived in Europe, twice as many as the number that lived in the United States. After the Holocaust, twice as many Jews lived in the United States as in Europe.

Of the 14.4 million Jews in the world (compared to 580 million Catholics and 590 million Muslims), America accounts for 5,900,000 or forty-one percent of world Jewry. Jews in the United States make up 2.7% of the population compared to twenty-three percent (49 million) Catholics and thirty-four percent (72 million) Protestants. Many Americans — nearly two-fifths of the citizenry — are not affiliated with any religion.

Nearly sixty percent of the Jews in the nation live in the northeast, though the area's relative share appears to have declined recently. The north-central region contains 11.9% of the Jewish population, the south, 15.8% and the west, 14.3%. In terms of national averages, Jews are overrepresented in the northeast, underrepresented in the north-central region and the south, and almost par for the population in the west.

To put it another way, Judaism is an urban, or increasingly suburban, religion. Over seventy-seven percent of the Jewish population live within the fourteen largest cities or county agglomerations. Almost all the rest of American Jews live in cities or towns. There are relatively few rural Jews.

Jews have a very low birthrate and as a group, are perilously close to zero population growth. While the rest of the country has also reached this point, the Jews were there first. The average Jewish family contains 2.76 people (2.98 if non-Jews living in Jewish households are included). This compares to a national average of 3.6 individuals. Furthermore, American Jews are an aging community. There are more old Jews, 65 and over, proportionately speaking, than in the general population, and increasingly fewer young people. And increasingly, Jewish youth are marrying out of the faith: over nine percent of all Jews are intermarried, with recent intermarriage rates running as high as thirty percent, compared to only 3.5 percent in 1957.

The picture, then, is of a somewhat older community compared with the overall citizenry, a mature society plagued by low fertility and with no prospects for internally generated growth.

In common with most ethnic or religious groups, five out of six households are headed by males, but that figure is declining with the increase in divorce. Most household heads, fifty-eight percent of them, are first generation Americans, twenty-three percent are foreign-born, and nineteen percent are second-generation or later. This generational spread is interesting, for while it does not determine what Jews do for a living, it is a substantial influencing factor. On its face, it shows that a majority of all Jewish households had a direct bridge to a foreign ancestry with a predominantly European value system.

If the immigrant generation's main concern is surviving in a foreign country, the first generation's goal is financial success and the second generation's tends to be social status. Perhaps this generalization explains the drift away from problems of poverty. A community attempting to succeed, with a fierce determinism that only a one-time disenfranchised, pariah people can generate, is not worried about the poor — only about staying away from poverty. Once the federal government stepped in with social legislation in the thirties, Jewish defense agencies moved progressively away from considerations of basic sustenance. A number of observers have voiced concern over the leadership and policies of the Jewish defense agencies. Gut issues of survival are no longer paramount. They "have been so preoccupied with ecumenical duties and checking survey statistics on anti-Semitism that they have not always taken adequate care of these Jews with real life problems. Other Jewish social agencies have also not developed adequate programs to help a minority of Jews caught up in the fall out from the urban crisis."

Indeed, rather than face the dissolution of the inner cities, these agencies "had become so much a part of the urban non-Jewish establishment while currying favors from it that they could no longer stand up for Jewish rights with proper vigor." It was natural to assume in the fifties and sixties that American opulence was permeating all levels of society. After all, the boom of the sixties was the longest in the annals of American business history. It was fashionable in economic circles to pay lip service to the trickle-down theory. This financial Pollyanna hid the reality of an aging Jewish population sinking further into poverty.

While surveys of income are far from complete, there is an unmistakable trend toward worsening conditions. In 1956, 13.6% of Jewish families had poverty incomes. In 1972 that figure had risen to 15.1%, and one in five Jews could qualify for welfare. Adjusting that figure for double-digit inflation has assuredly not improved the situation.

While the plight of the Jewish poor worsened, Jewish defense agencies were otherwise engaged. The problems they addressed themselves to were not trivial, but perhaps more essentially middle-class concerns: for instance, affirmative action, suburban integration, ethnic relationships, discriminatory practices against executive Jews, punishment for juvenile offenders, Christian-Jewish interaction, Jewish culture, Soviet Jewry, and Israel. Such interests, valuable though they may be, were not concerned with the bread-and-butter conditions of the growing number of poor Jews. And the poor remained not only invisible, but silent as well.

In fact, Thomas J. Cottle, an observer of the poverty scene, saw no improvement in the condition of the aged poor in the last decade. Moreover, the Russian emigres toward the end of the seventies threatened to start a new wave of "nouveau Jewish poor." Only the reduced flow of Russian Jews — a tragedy in iself — has kept the picture from becoming grimmer.

As a result of this indifference, New York City's poor Jews have received the very short end of the stick in city poverty funds. New York had designated the Council Against Poverty and the Community Development Agency to serve as the official administrator to the city's poor. But Jewish representation among the council was "minimal." The "fair share" formula set up by the council for poverty areas — based on welfare assistance, live births, and juvenile delinquency — excluded the Jewish poor more effectively than if they had been deliberately designed to exclude them.

The late start in accepting welfare has cost the Jewish poor dearly: they received approximately one percent of all the city's poverty money funneled through the Council Against Poverty. In 1975 the city granted to the Metropolitan Council on Jewish Poverty (an umbrella agency belatedly established by the Federation of Jewish Philanthropies) $475,000 or twenty-five cents per Jew or two dollars per poor Jew. Since that budget allocation was made before New York's fiscal crisis, future largess is not probable.

On the national level, Jews are not a minority group according to the guidelines for federal benefits. Since they are not members of black, Spanish-speaking, American Indian, or Eskimo communities, they are not eligible for poverty programs designed to service minority groups. Thus they are excluded from a series of federal programs to alleviate abysmal conditions like theirs.

Indeed, when the issue was brought to the attention of the federal government, it agreed that Chassidic Jews experienced overwhelming prejudice and discrimination. However, the Small Business Administration ruled that Chassidic Jews did not qualify as a "socially and economically disadvantaged group" despite their poverty. Consequently, Chassidic Jews were barred from minority small-business programs, since the group is essentially a religious community. In the constitutional interest of separating church and state, Chassidic businesses' interests could receive no assistance from programs designed to help the poor.

The prognosis for Jewish poverty is somewhat grim. While tending to the flowers in other gardens, the Jewish front lawn has become patchy and full of crab grass. Jewish organizations, so poised to take positions on a multitude of issues, find that one of the fundamental problems of keeping body and soul together for a substantial part of its constituency has passed it by. It is indeed ironic that such a highly developed community with organizations dedicated to many different projects were so myopic or insensitive to basic needs. To be sure, Jewish organizations administer a variety of programs to individuals and communities, but the revealed poverty calls into question whether Jews really take care of their own. Have not the priorities been badly scrambled in recent years?

Belated recognition of Jewish poverty has left the Jews who had not escaped the ghettos of the inner cities frozen out of official funding. And the problems are worse since the Jewish population is an aging one. Presently, one out of nine Jews is over sixty-five, but in twenty years, it will be one out of six Jews. Since the aged constitute half of the poverty population, there will be a larger number of poor Jews in the immediate future.

# 13. Conclusion: Affluence and Anti-Semitism

Jewish economic success is invariably spoken of in reciprocal terms — it is always accomplished "in the face of anti-Semitism." To some degree, this general platitude has it all backwards. It was and is anti-Semitism that accounts for Jewish success. This perpetual threat to Jewish existence has caused Jews to excel in order to succeed and survive. The threat has, at times, been all too real. Even in pacific surroundings, Jews tend to overestimate the adverse opinions of non-Jews to a remarkable degree. No doubt Jews are somewhat mistaken when it comes to appraising the feelings of their neighbors. Perhaps this is an all-too-human defense mechanism, a consequence of ages of hostility. It may well be that this defense mechanism has not only saved them, but made them a nation of overachievers.

Presently, there is enough anti-Semitic feeling to be a cause of concern, not only to Jews, but to a liberal, tolerant democracy. However, though there is such sentiment, it does not necessarily portend a pogrom. In recent years, Jews have developed a new set of worries. Rather, it is the Old Worry but in a new set of clothes. The new worries have to do with their new levels of wealth. The hoary anti-Semitic belief of tying Jews to mercenary motives originated with the downfall of the Jews at the beginning of modern history. But it remained a subsidiary theme: deicide — the death of Christ — continued as the cardinal anti-Semitic myth. If the Jews were guilty of deicide, it made all else conceivable and every act against them possible. They were disenfranchised and forced to deal with the detritus of the economy. They were condemned to low status, petty trades, and a parasitical existence. In brief, theological anti-Semitism placed the Jews in a position of utter contempt in the eyes of host nations.

Today there is a subtle shift in the nature of anti-Semitism. Theological antagonisms are not quite passé, but they are ebbing. The subsidiary theme — accusations of the Jews as universally greedy and motivated by gross materialism — have surfaced. While the new anti-Semitism, attacking the role of Jewish money and influence, arose in the last century, it is only within the last generation or so that fantasy is confronted with fact. When the charge against Jews concerning their use of wealth and money were first fabricated, there was virtually no substance to the allegations. Today, the charges harbor the same prejudicial motives, but now there is some truth to the presumption of affluence.

If most people believe that Jews have more money than other people, is that belief simply recognition of contemporary fact, or does it arise from an ancient grudge? Does the recognition of reality nurture some prejudicial sentiments?

The new anti-Semitism seems rooted less in religion or contempt, and more in envy, jealousy, and fear. Anti-Semites' perception of Jewish economic success is far greater than the facts warrant, and the old shibboleths and buzz words of dominance and control are regurgitated. Consequently, Jews are now subject to a new kind of racism, anti-Semitism due to affluence.

So while old fashioned anti-Semitism can still be aroused — can still be malicious — this secular age has relegated religious antagonisms to the back burner. The new racism reflects contemporary problems: the concern with money, income distribution, employment, resources, property, and ownership. And the old syllogisms of the Jew as economic man (deceitful, cunning, and greedy) appear in new guises. At one time the Shylock image was based on the idea that Jews were unable to countenance the existing economic customs, that they lived by different rules and marched to a different drummer. Today, Jews are charged with being too successful because they abide all too well by the modern spirit of capitalism, too powerful because they utilize all the tools of leverage in a democracy.

It is contemporary Jewish wealth and status that is the new target of the anti-Semites and the cause of Jewish insecurity. Jews have finally worked themselves into the position of "haves" in this world just as the "have-nots" are beginning to make themselves heard.

Jews are heavily represented in the top income brackets. Estimates suggest that the top five percent of society gets sixteen percent of all income and that the top twenty percent, the highest fifth, gets forty-three percent of all income. Consequently, many Jews, along with everyone else in the top brackets, are earning and amassing wealth far beyond their comparable numbers. As long as the beneficent sun of economic growth shed its light, however unevenly, on all aspects of society, the maldistribution was tolerated and accepted.

But a new problem arose in the seventies and became manifest in the eighties, which seems destined to remain with the West for quite some time. Industrial economies are faced with conditions that have hampered luxuriant growth and its trickle-down philosophy. Stagnation, unused plant capacity, high unemployment, natural resource shortages, and inflation are now part of the formula. In the past everyone was able to get a little fatter, especially the middle and the upper classes. Today, increasingly lean times may well mean social conflict and confrontation over an income pie that is not expanding as fast as before. For the Jews, this conflict may harbor potent germs of anti-Semitism.

# Sources and Notes

# Sources and Notes

*1 Introduction*

PAGE

4 Baron's observation is in *Economic History of the Jews,* by Salo W. Baron, Aradius Kahan and others, edited by Nachum Gross (New York: Schocken Books, 1975), p. 48. The contributions to this book of essays were originally published in the *Encyclopaedia Judaica.*

5 Drumont was one of the most notorious French anti-Semites of the nineteenth century. When asked "Why do you attack Jewish financiers and not all financiers?", he replied: "My God, it is not the financier in the Jews that arouses my hatred, but the Jew in the financier!" Quoted in Albert Memmi, *Portrait of a Jew,* translated by Elizabeth Abbott (New York: The Viking Press, 1962), p. 158. Drumont's remark about anti-Semitism being an economic war is quoted by Memmi on page 121.

6 All of these disparaging comments were collected by A. A. Roback in *A Dictionary of International Slurs* (Cambridge, Massachusetts: Sci-Art Publishers, 1944), pp. 185–205. His analysis of these proverbs and linguistic scapegoating can be found on pages 272–279.

8 Andrew M. Greeley, before assuming his new role as novelist, was with the National Opinion Research Center. His study, *Ethnicity, Denomination, and Inequality* (Beverly Hills, California: Sage Publications, Inc., 1976) deals with many religions and ethnic groups besides this summary note on Jews on page 39. Black conservative economist Thomas Sowell studied the income and earning ability of nine groups in *Ethnic America* (New York: Basic Books, Inc., 1981). His observations on the Jews are on pages 69–90.

*2 Success and Survival*

9   The only survey of religion by the government was conducted by the Bureau of the Census, "Social and Economic Characteristics of Major Religious Groups," March, 1957 (unpublished).

10  For a detailed breakdown of income figures of the National Jewish Population Study, see Fred Massarik and Alvin Chenkin, "United States National Jewish Population Study: A First Report," *American Jewish Year Book 1973* (New York: American Jewish Committee, 1973), pp. 264–306. The study was based on a survey of 7,550 Jewish households in 1970. National income figures are published annually in the *Statistical Abstract of the United States.* Specific income figures for ethnic groups were published by the Bureau of the Census in "Income in 1970 of Families and Persons in the United States," *Current Population Reports,* Series P-60, No. 80. Also see the Bureau of the Census, "Characteristics of the Population by Ethnic Origins, November, 1969," *Current Population Reports,* Series P-20, No. 221. The surveys of the National Opinion Research Center are based on a composite sample of twelve surveys from 1963 through 1974 with 17,700 respondents. The results are summarized in Greeley, *Ethnicity, Denomination, and Equality,* pp. 26–29.

14  This conflict between the old and the new rich is examined by Ben B. Seligman, *The Potentates* (New York: The Dial Press, 1971), pp. 336–338. The "Jewish-cowboy connection" was first coined by G. William Domhoff, in "Fat Cats and Democrats," *Ramparts,* June 1972, p. 41.

15  The sources of the tabulated figures are the National Jewish Population Study and the Department of Commerce. Observations on Jewish blue-collar workers are made in Marshall Sklare, *America's Jews* (New York: Random House, 1971), pp. 61–69.

16  This point about the "agrarian ritual" is well noted by Amos Elon in *The Israelis* (New York, Chicago, San Francisco: Holt, Rinehart and Winston, 1971), p. 145.

17  For an analysis of the Jewish labor force, see Herbert Bienstock, "The N.Y. Job Market and Its Implications for the Orthodox Jewish Community," *Jews and Manpower,* ed. Marvin Schick (New York: Council of Jewish Manpower Associations, 1975). Also Herbert Bienstock, "The Economic Scene and Implications for New York's Jewish Community" (U.S. Department of Labor, October, 1975).

18   For a fuller discussion of class consciousness, see John C. Goyer and Peter C. Pineo, "Minority Group Status and Self-Evaluated Class," *Sociological Quarterly,* Vol. 15(2) (Spring, 1974), p. 205.

19   Simon Kuznets provides a masterful analysis of the economic constraints faced by immigrants in his pamphlet, *Economic Structure of U.S. Jewry: Recent Trends* (Jerusalem: The Hebrew University of Jerusalem, 1972), pp. 10–27.

21   The number of millionaires is cited in Moses Rischin, *The Promised City* (Cambridge, Massachusetts: Harvard University Press, 1967), p. 53.

22   This passage is from Michael Gold, *Jews Without Money* (Garden City, N.Y.: The Sun Dial Press, 1946), p. 301.

23   The *Fortune* article was reprinted in a hardcover edition by Random House, but it first appeared as "Jews in America," *Fortune,* January, 1936. Adolph Hitler, *Mein Kampf,* translated by Ralph Manheim (Boston: Houghton Mifflin Company, 1943), pp. 308–310, is the comparable translation from the original.

26   The notion of a high economic profile was developed by Nathan Glazer and Daniel Patrick Moynihan, *Beyond the Melting Pot,* 2nd ed. (Cambridge, Massachusetts: MIT Press, 1970), p. 151.

27   This second *Fortune* article was written by Charles G. Burck, "A Group Profile of the Fortune 500 Chief Executives," May, 1976.

28   Stephen D. Isaacs of the *Washington Post* claimed that this was the case in the early seventies. See his *Jews and American Politics* (Garden City, New York: Doubleday & Company, Inc., 1974), p. 49.

## 3 *A Monetary Imperative*

29   The quotation is from Leon Poliakov, *The History of Anti-Semitism,* trans. Richard Howard, Vol. I (New York: The Vanguard Press, Inc., 1965), p. 156.

30   There is, of course, much controversy over evolution — and not just from the Christian fundamentalists who disavow it. In the scientific community, hereditary traits are the subject of great curiosity. On the one hand, R. C. Lewontin has written that "natural selection of the character states themselves is the essence of Darwinism. All else is molecular biology." And sociobiologist Edward O. Wilson has noted that a "key question of human biol-

ogy is whether there exists a genetic predisposition to enter certain classes and to play certain roles." Citing the work of G. Dahlberg, he writes that it may be that a single gene is responsible for success and an upward shift in status; and that "it can be rapidly concentrated in the uppermost socioeconomic classes. . . . The hereditary factors of human success are strongly polygenic and form a long list, only a few of which have been measured. IQ constitutes only one subset of the components of intelligence. Less tangible but equally important qualities are creativity, entrepreneurship, drive, and mental stamina. . . . The influence of genetic factors in the adoption of certain *broad* roles cannot be discounted." Edward O. Wilson, *Sociobiology,* abridged ed. (Cambridge, Massachusetts: Belknap Press, 1980), pp. 278–279.

31   The list of Nobel Laureates was compiled by the Swedish Information Service. The American Jewish Committee has prepared another list: "Nobel Prize Winners of Jewish and Part Jewish Extraction."

33   For a closer view of the German hyperinflation see my book, *The Dying Dollar,* rev. ed. (Chicago: Playboy Press, 1975), p. 32.

34   The report of the U.S. Industrial Commission of 1901 is cited in Nathaniel Glazer, *American Judaism* (Chicago: University of Chicago Press, 1957), pp. 80–81.

35   These figures of educational achievement are cited in the *American Jewish Year Book 1973,* and in the *Statistical Abstract of the United States.* Greeley has written in *Ethnicity, Denomination, and Inequality* that "given where they 'start out' in terms of educational background, the Jews and Catholics make the most of their opportunities," p. 21.

37   This point on ecclesiastical celibacy is made in Ernest van den Haag, *The Jewish Mystique* (New York: Stein and Day, 1969), pp. 14–18.

38   On the composition of college faculties see Andrew M. Greeley, "The 'Religious Factor' and Academic Careers: Another Communication," *American Journal of Sociology,* Vol. 78, No. 5 (March, 1973), pp. 1247–1251.

39   A survey in 1899 found that three out of four Jews in the labor force were self-employed. Robert Gutman, "Demographic Trends and the Decline of Anti-Semitism," in *Jews in the Mind of America,* by C. H. Stembler and Others (New York, London:

Basic Books, Inc., 1966), p. 366. The quotation on the development of economic skills comes from Thomas Sowell, *Race and Economics* (New York: David McKay Company, Inc., 1975), p. 120.

42  Miriam Beard wrote an interesting essay on the economic roots of anti-Semitism, in addition to commenting on some of the actions of Benjamin Franklin. See her "Anti-Semitism — Product of Economic Myth," in *Jews in a Gentile World,* ed. I. Graeber and S. H. Britt (New York: Macmillan Publishing Company, Inc., 1942), p. 375. Sombart's views on capitalism and Judaism can be found in his *The Jews and Modern Capitalism,* trans. M. Epstein (New York: Collier Books, 1962), pp. 187–237. Quoted from Karl Marx, *A World Without Jews,* trans. D. D. Runes (New York: Philosophical Library, 1959), pp. 37–41.

43  The Jewish role in commerce, trade and finance is explored at the start of Sombart's work, as noted above. For the role of sex see Sombart, p. 226.

## 4  The Bankers

46  For a review of Jews in banking, see Baron, Kahan, and others, *Economic History of the Jews,* pp. 211–225.

47  The hoax of the century is covered in many books, but it is summarized in Edward H. Flannery, *The Anguish of the Jews* (New York: The Macmillan Company, 1965), pp. 191–193.

50  The quotation is from a feature story in *Business Week,* November 10, 1975.

51  For a fuller discussion of the Lehman-Goldman, Sachs relationship see Stephen Birmingham, *Our Crowd* (New York, Evanston, and London: Harper & Row, 1967), pp. 331–333.

52  The Lehman story was examined in both *Dun's Review,* October, 1974, and *Financial World,* July 31, 1974, as well as in *Business Week,* November 10, 1975.

55  The first recent look at bank holdings was undertaken in a congressional *Staff Report for the Subcommittee on Domestic Finance of the Committee on Banking and Currency,* 90th Cong., 1st sess., 1967, pp. 5–10. Another look at institutional investors was provided by the Senate Committee on Government Operations, *Disclosure of Corporate Ownership,* Document No. 93–62, 93d Cong., 2d sess., 1974, pp. 1–12. The quotation on nominees is from the previous Senate study, p. 5. The most recent examination of bank holdings ap-

pears in the Senate report by the Committee on Government Operations, *Power to Vote Stock of Large Corporations Concentrated in Twenty-One Institutions*, 94th Cong., 2d sess., 1978.

56   For a critical view of Leasco's operations, see Abraham J. Briloff, "Whose 'Deep Pocket'?" *Barrons* July 19, 1975. Another informative review of the battle was provided by Douglas V. Austin, "How Not to Take Over a Bank," *Bankers Magazine*, Winter, 1970.

58   *New York Times*, February 6, 1969.

60   Prejudice in banking was most recently examined by Steven Slavin and Mary Pradt, "Anti-Semitism in Banking," *Bankers Magazine*, July–August, 1979.

61   Among all the books and articles on Swiss banking, one of the most informative is by a native, Hans J. Bar, *The Banking System of Switzerland*, 2d ed., rev. (Zurich: Zurich Buchdrukerei Schulthess & Co. AG, 1957).

62   The "lost millions" were documented in *The Financial Times*, April 15, 1964, and the *New York Times*, March 14, 1964.


## 5   The Business World

64   For the social history of the wealthy German Jews see Birmingham, *Our Crowd*, p. 48. A broader view of the immigration process can be found in Bernard D. Weinryb, "Jewish Immigration and Accommodation to America" in *The Jews*, ed. Marshall Sklare (New York: The Free Press, 1958), pp. 4–22.

65   The quotation on peddling is from Abraham J. Karp, ed., *Golden Door to America* (New York: The Viking Press, 1976), p. 149. The number of millionaires is cited in a book on the Internal Revenue Service: Gerald Carson, *The Golden Egg* (Boston: Houghton Mifflin Company, 1977), p. 60.

68   Nostalgia is discussed in Glazer and Moynihan, *Beyond the Melting Pot*, p. 172.

70   The study of the representation of Jews in business schools was first made in *Business Week*, January 24, 1970. More recently, Steven Slavin and Mary Pradt reported that on average, fifteen percent of all business school graduates are Jewish, but at Columbia University and New York University, Jews constitute a third of the graduates. The *Bankers Magazine*, July–August, 1979, pp. 19–22. Slavin also looked at bias in employment practices in

"Bias in U.S. Big Business Recruitment," *Patterns of Prejudice*, September, 1976.

71   The quotations are from: Charles Lindbergh, in a speech at an American First rally in Des Moines, Iowa, September 11, 1941; General George Brown, in a speech at the Duke University Law School on October 10, 1974; Spiro Agnew, in a television interview on May 12, 1976. The number of Jewish organizations were counted by Will Maslow, *The Structure and Functioning of the American Jewish Community* (New York: American Jewish Congress, 1974), p. 12.

72   *Business Week*, January 26, 1976, and the *Wall Street Journal*, February 12, 1982.

73   The quotation is in Isaacs, *Jews and American Politics*, p. 49. The *New York Times'* skittishness was reported by Gay Talese in *The Kingdom and the Power* (New York: World Publishing Company, 1969), pp. 92–93. Also, it is noted in the work of David Halberstam, *The Powers That Be* (New York: Alfred A. Knopf, 1979), pp. 208, 216–217.

75   Hollywood's Jewish antecedents are described in Seligman, *The Potentates*, pp. 259–267.

81   One of the major international oil companies, Shell, was founded by an English Jewish trader and broker, Marcus Samuel. Samuel imported seashells from the Far East and used them as the symbol for the new oil company he and a Dutchman started in 1906 — Royal Dutch/ Shell.

82   The Amoco battle was retold in *Forbes*, July 15, 1977.

84   Hess' peccadillo was reported in the *New York Times*, April 16, 1976.

85   Friedman's comments on his trip were printed in the *Wall Street Journal*, June 28, 1977.

## 6 *International Finance*

86   There have been any number of books and articles on OPEC and the energy crisis in the last decade. They are too extensive to cite. However, for an overview of OPEC, see Jean-Jacques Servan-Schreiber, *The World Challenge* (New York: Simon and Schuster, 1981). The book was written at the height of OPEC's power, before the 1981–1982 oil glut became apparent.

87   The first projections of petrodollar surpluses were overwhelming. See Adrian W. Throop, "Economic Consequences of the OPEC

Cartel," *Business Review* (Federal Reserve Bank of Dallas: May, 1975), pp. 1–10.

88 Early in 1981 it became clear that the development plans were excessive. The lowering of world oil prices in 1982 assured Western banks that OPEC producers would become net borrowers before long, the *Wall Street Journal,* February 19, 1982.

90 On the independent nature of national boycott lists, see the *Economist,* November 21, 1981. For an explanation of the mechanics of the boycott, see Walter Guzzardi Jr., "That Curious Barrier on the Arab Frontier," *Fortune,* July, 1975. Also, see the *Wall Street Journal,* June 26, 1976.

91 King Faisal is quoted in Marvin and Bernard Kalb, *Kissinger* (Boston: Little Brown, 1974), p. 8.

92 Before publication of corporate names, Richardson's point was valid, the *New York Times,* October 10, 1976. After publication the compliance rate fell, but the logic of his statement still held, the *New York Times,* October 22, 1981.

93 For the Bechtel case see the *Wall Street Journal,* January 11, 1977.

95 For an interesting view of American complicity in OPEC's rising prices, see V. H. Oppenheim, "The Past: We Pushed Them," and Theodore H. Moran, "The Future: OPEC Wants Them," *Foreign Policy,* No. 24 (Winter, 1976–1977), pp. 24–77.

96 The development of the Arab capital market has been slow compared to their rapid flows of revenues. See Michael Prest,"Arab Banking and Finance," *Middle East Economic Digest,* October 8, 1976, p. 31. The lack of professional financing skills was noted by the *Economist,* November 21, 1981.

97 The *Wall Street Journal,* March 6, 1975.

98 The French spokesman was quoted in the *New York Times,* February 12, 1975. The *Business Week* comment was in the March 15, 1976 issue.

99 For the complete content of the memorandum, see the *Wall Street Journal,* December 12, 1975.

104 Aspects of the indictment can be found in the *New York Times,* April 9, 1975, and the *Jerusalem Post,* May 27, 1975. According to Hank Messick in his book *Lansky* (New York: G. P. Putnam's Sons, 1971), the "International Credit Bank of Switzerland remains Lansky's private financial institution." This was written before the scandal and subsequent closing of the bank.

105 The Tzur case was summarized in the *Jerusalem Post*, May 27, 1975.

106 For a review of the case, see Richard Karp, "Sleeping Watchdogs: How the American Bank & Trust Company Went Broke," *Barrons*, December 20, 1976.


## 7 Crime

113 Judaism as a source of crime prevention is a point developed by Jackson Toby in "Hoodlum or Businessman: An American Dilemma," *The Jews*, ed. Marshall Sklare, p. 550.

114 David Singer discusses the absence of self-analysis in "The Jewish Gangster," *Judaism*, Vol. 23, No. 1 (1974).

115 The $300 million net worth of Lansky is reported in Hank Messick, *Secret File* (New York: G. P. Putnam's Sons, 1969), p. 185. For a fuller description of Lansky's activities, see Messick's *Lansky*. Benya Krik appears in Isaac Babel, *The Collected Stories* ed. and trans. Walter Morrison (New York: Criterion Books, 1955), p. 213.

116 Lansky's observation on casino attendance is quoted by Sidney Zion, "Once a Jew, Sometimes a Jew," *Harpers*, August, 1972. For the rationalization of criminal business practices, see Joseph Epstein, "Browsing in Gangland," *Commentary*, January, 1972. See also, Messick, *Secret File*, p. 185, for Lansky's relationship with the government.

119 Wolfson's takeover attempt was described in *Business Week*, May 24, 1969. Wolfson is quoted in the *Wall Street Journal*, April 22, 1969.

120 For background on the Supreme Court problem, see the *Wall Street Journal*, April 22, 1969, and May 5, 1969.

122 Black's business life was examined in the *Wall Street Journal*, February 14, 1975. For the merger and acquisition activity of Black, see Stanley H. Brown, "United Fruit's Shotgun Marriage," *Fortune*, April, 1969.

123 For the finances of the company, see the 1975 Annual Report of the United Brands Company. Black's talents were as "an asset manager, and whether he knows a banana tree from a potted palm is largely irrelevant. His ability lies in uncovering value on a large scale, getting control of it, and putting it to work uncovering more assets," Stanley H. Brown observed in his *Fortune*,

April, 1969 article. For a history of United Fruit Company, see Thomas P. McCann, *An American Company*, ed. Henry Scammell (New York: Crown Publishers, 1976).

124    The banana cartel was revealed in "Banana Split," the *Economist*, December 25, 1975.

127    The quotation is from Harry Levinson, "On Executive Suicide," *Harvard Business Review*, July, 1975.

129    For background on Bergman, see the *New York Times*, January 21, 1975.

132    Bergman's financial machinations are explicitly revealed in the seven volumes of the New York State Moreland Commission on Nursing Homes and Residential Facilities, published in 1975 and 1976. For the "eyes and ears to the Jewish community," see the Moreland Act Commission Report 3, *Political Influence and Political Accountability*, pp. 39–42.

136    Dr. Fleck's summary of Bergman's activities is in Moreland Act Commission Report 3, p. 46.

138    Bergman's net worth was reported in the *New York Times*, January 23, 1975.

## 8  *The Art World*

141    Martin Buber is quoted in Abram Kanof, *Jewish Ceremonial Art and Religious Observance* (New York: Harry N. Abrams, Inc., 1969), p. 28.

142    A "semitic lack of talent for the figural arts" is a comment by Abram Kanof.

143    This paradoxical comment on Jewish art is made by M. Sgan-Cohen, "The Jewish Experience in Art," *Art in America*, May, 1976. Chagall is quoted in Albert Memmi, *Liberation of the Jew*, trans. Judy Hyun (New York: Orion Press, 1966), p. 197.

144    Harold Rosenberg's opinions were published in the art column of the *New Yorker*, December 22, 1975.

148    The information concerning Sidney Janis was obtained by the late Ruth Marossi-Krefetz through personal interviews.

158    The reticent Rothko was interviewed and quoted by Selden Rodman in *Conversations with Artists* (New York: Capricorn Books, 1961), pp. 93–94.

159    For the business side of the Marlborough Galleries, see the *Wall Street Journal*, December 31, 1968.

161   For the forces arrayed against Lloyd, see Grace Glueck, "The Man the Art World Loves to Hate," the *New York Times Magazine*, June 15, 1975.

162   Some interesting background notes to the case can be found in Leah Gordon, "The Rothko Estate in Marlborough Country," *New York Magazine*, August 20, 1973.

163   For a critical view of the Rothko case, see Augusta Dike, "Unpublished Aspects of the Rothko Law Suit," *Art International*, January 20, 1975. For a more favorable view of the estate's actions, see Lee Seldes, *The Legacy of Mark Rothko* (New York: Holt, Rinehart & Winston, 1978). Also, see Paul Gardner, "The Ordeal of Kate Rothko," *New York Magazine*, February 7, 1977.

165   The surrogate's decision can be found in the *New York Times*, December 10, 1975.

## 9 *Medicine Men*

167   Fred Rosner provides some historical notes in "Jewish Contributions to Medicine in the United States," *New York State Journal of Medicine*, August, 1976.

168   For income figures and comparisons, see Gerald Krefetz and Philip Gittelman, *The Book of Incomes* (New York: Holt, Rinehart and Winston, 1981), p. 167.

169   The philosophical problem of religion and health is discussed by Harry Friedenwald, *The Jews and Medicine*, Vol. 1 (Baltimore: The Johns Hopkins Press, 1944), pp. 5-6. The quotation about ancient Hebrew physicians comes from Solomon R. Kagan, *Jewish Contributions to Medicine in America (1656-1934)* (Boston: Boston Medical Publishing Company, 1934), p. xxvii.

171   For background on Mount Sinai Hospital, see *The Story of the First Fifty Years of the Mount Sinai Hospital — New York 1852-1902* (New York: Mount Sinai Hospital, 1944), p. 3.

172   For the immediate issues concerning the proposed medical school, see George James, "Early History of Mount Sinai School of Medicine of the City University of New York," A Report Prepared for the Macy Conference on the Founding of New Medical Schools, New Orleans, December 12-15, 1971.

173   A description of the neighborhood can be found in Joseph Hirsh and Beka Doherty, *The First Hundred Years of the Mount Sinai Hospital of New York, 1852-1952* (New York: Mount Sinai Hospital, 1952), p. 284.

176   The prolific authorship of Jewish physicans is mentioned in

Lawrence Bloomgarden, "Medical School Quotas and National Health," *Commentary,* January, 1953.

177 For an analysis of the quota system, see Bloomgarden in the preceding note.

178 The quotation is from Jacob A. Goldberg, "Jews in the Medical Profession: A National Survey," *Jewish Social Studies,* Vol. 1, 1939. These diseases are under intensive study by the recently formed National Foundation for Jewish Genetic Diseases in New York City.

179 For an unusual approach to ethnic sensibilities, see Mark Zborowski, *People in Pain* (San Francisco: Jossey-Bass Publishers, 1969), pp. 120–121, 135.

180 Freud's views are quoted in David Bakan, *Sigmund Freud and the Jewish Mystical Tradition,* trans. Katherine Jones (New York: Vintage Books, 1955), p. 68.

182 Richard L. Rubinstein wrote of Judaism as a rigidly compulsive system in *The Religious Imagination: A Study of Psychology and Jewish Theology* (Indianapolis: Bobbs Merrill Co., 1968), p. 12. Sigmund Freud's comment on the first advocate of psychoanalysis can be found in *The Collected Papers of Sigmund Freud,* Vol. V (London: Hogarth Press, 1955), pp. 174–175. The quotation on redemptive suffering was written by Rubinstein, *The Religious Imagination,* p. 175. Freud's comment on the existence of God is in his *Moses and Monotheism* (New York: Vintage Books, 1955), p. 166.

*10 The Law*

184 Thomas's quotation is in Leon Huchner, "Jews in the Legal and Medical Professions in America Prior to 1800," American Jewish Historical Society Reprint, November 22, 1914.

185 The survey of the New York City bar is published in Jerome E. Carlin, *Lawyer's Ethics: A Survey of the New York City Bar* (New York: Russell Sage Foundation, 1966), p. 19. American contentiousness is examined in Jerold S. Auerbach, "A Plague of Lawyers," *Harper's,* October, 1976.

186 For some historical notes on the Constitution and the Bill of Rights, see Edmond Cahn, "The Jewish Contribution to Law," *Jewish Frontier,* May, 1961. One recent study did lend some support to this theory of litigiousness. An analysis by sociologist Edmund Doherty of Wayne State University found that in a large

city hospital the group most likely to sue doctors for malpractice were middle-aged Jewish white-collar workers. A summary of the report appeared in the *Wall Street Journal,* January 11, 1977.

187 It is no coincidence that Jewish interest in justice is responsible for forty percent of the membership of the American Civil Liberties Union (ACLU). However, the defense of the Nazis to speak and march in Skokie, Illinois cost the ACLU considerable Jewish support. For details, see Jim Mann, "Hard Times for the ACLU," the *New Republic,* April 15, 1978.

188 The quotation is from Max Dimont, *The Indestructible Jews* (New York: New American Library, 1971), p. 382.

189 These prejudicial statements by some of the legal elite are revealed in Jerold S. Auerbach, *Unequal Justice: Lawyers and Social Change in Modern America* (New York: Oxford University Press, 1976), pp. 107, 127. Proskauer's observation is in Erwin O. Smigel, *The Wall Street Lawyer* (Glencoe: The Free Press, 1964), pp. 44–45. The American Jewish Committee released a study on exclusionary tactics in 1970.

190 Though the report is from the 1960s, it is not clear that there has been any noticeable change. For the complete report, see John Young, "The Jewish Law Student and New York Jobs — Discriminatory Effects in Law Firm Hiring Practices," *Yale Law Journal,* Vol. 73, No. 4, March, 1964.

191 Hiring practices are further discussed in Albert I. Goldberg, "Jews in the Legal Profession: A Case of Adjustment to Discrimination," *Jewish Social Studies,* Vol. 32, No. 2, April, 1970.

195 The comment on intellectual corruption is made by Martin Mayer, *The Lawyers* (New York, Evanston, and London: Harper and Row, 1966), p. 259.

197 The *Economist,* March 6, 1976, found "greed as human as eating."

198 For Liebowitz's decision, see 305 NYS. 2d 801. The conclusions of the American Medical Association are cited in "Medical Malpractice," the *Center Magazine,* August/ July, 1975.

205 Rosenfeld explained the consequences of the decision in "The Impact of Class Actions on Corporate and Securities Law," *Duke Law Journal,* Vol. 1972, No. 6.

206 Gould wrote in the *New York Law Journal,* February 13, 1976.

*11   Tithes That Bind*

209   For Jewish synagogue attendance, see the National Jewish Population Study in the *American Jewish Yearbook 1973,* p. 301. Sixty percent of the respondents said that they were "not at all" active in temple or synagogue, 26% responded as "slightly," 6.6% said they were "quite" active, while 6.3% said they were "very" active. For the benefits of fundraising, see Charles S. Levy, "Fundraising: Design for Human Service," *Journal of Jewish Communal Service,* Vol. L, No. 2, Winter, 1973.

210   For the techniques of raising money, see Paul Zuckerman, "The 1972 Campaign: Large Cities," Paper read before the Fortieth General Assembly of the Council of Jewish Federations and Welfare Funds, 1971.

213   The Israel Education Fund is described in the *Jerusalem Post,* June 3, 1975.

214   Jewish tithing is explained in Joseph Oppenheimer, *Ma'aser: The Precept of Tithing* (New York: Shengold Publishers, 1971), p. 44.

215   On charity, see Leo Rosten, *The Joys of Yiddish* (New York: McGraw Hill Book Company, 1968), pp. 416–418, and "Charity" in *The Shorter Oxford English Dictionary on Historical Principles,* 3rd rev. ed. (Oxford: Clarendon Press, 1956).

216   On enforceable pledges, see Daniel J. Elazar and Stephen R. Goldstein, "The Legal Status of the American Jewish Community," *American Jewish Yearbook 1972,* p. 65.

217   The Michigan case is Congregation B'nai Shalom v. Martin, 382 Mich. 659, 173 N. W. 2d 504 1969.

218   For the origins of American giving and Benjamin Franklin's advice, see Scott M. Cutlip, *Fund Raising in the United States* (New Brunswick: Rutgers University Press, 1965), p. 3ff. Steinbeck's comment is quoted in Cutlip, *Fund Raising in the United States,* p. 477.

219   For some early twentieth-century examples of Jewish fundraising, see Henry H. Rosenfelt, *This Thing of Giving* (New York: Plymouth Press, 1924), p. 12.

220   The antagonisms between the Jewish-German bankers and the Zionists are amply discussed in Samuel Halperin, "Ideology or Philanthropy? The Politics of Zionist Fund Raising," the *Western Political Quarterly,* Vol. XIII, No. 4, December, 1960.

221   The quotations come from the previously cited article.

222   Possessors of a "belligerent generosity" is a phrase from Roger

Kahn, *The Passionate People: What it Means to be a Jew in America* (New York: William Morrow and Company, 1968), p. 186.

223 The quotation is from an article of Philip M. Klutznick, "The State of Israel and the Diaspora," *Reconstructionist,* September, 1973.

226 A summary of Jewish revenue raising and expenditures can be found in the *American Jewish Yearbook 1980,* pp. 150–158.

## 12 The Poor

232 The figure of six hundred thousand (10.17% of all American Jews) is probably a conservative one, considering that some estimates go as high as one million. Moreover, six hundred thousand is below the national level of 12% to 13% of the population living in poverty. The 1957 Bureau of the Census survey showed 13.6% of Jewish households living in poverty, while the National Opinion Research Center in 1962 found 15.3%. In 1971 the Jewish Telegraphic Agency reported nearly eight hundred thousand Jews living below poverty levels. At the end of the seventies, not much had changed according to Thomas J. Cottle, "Impoverishing the Poor," the *New Leader,* February 26, 1979. For national poverty figures, see the *Statistical Abstract of the United States.*

233 The statistics of the National Jewish Population Study indicated that 13.3% of Jewish households had incomes below $4,000 while the 1970 Census found 14.6% of the nation's families subsisting on comparable incomes. Some ethnic comparisons, though over a decade old, help place Jewish poverty in perspective:

| Ethnic Origin | Median Income | Rank | Percent Below Poverty Level | Rank |
|---|---|---|---|---|
| Jews | $12,630 | 1 | 13.3 | 4 |
| Russians | 11,554 | 2 | 4.5 | 10 |
| Polish | 8,849 | 3 | 5.3 | 9 |
| Italian | 8,808 | 4 | 6.1 | 8 |
| German | 8,607 | 5 | 8.6 | 7 |
| English | 8,324 | 6 | 8.6 | 6 |
| Irish | 8,127 | 7 | 10.5 | 5 |
| Other | 7,671 | 8 | 15.4 | 3 |
| Not Reported | 7,264 | 9 | 15.6 | 2 |
| Spanish | 5,641 | 10 | 24.3 | 1 |

Sources of the above table are: U.S. Bureau of the Census, "Characteristics of the Population by Ethnic Origin, November, 1969,"

*Current Population Reports,* Series P-20, No. 221, p. 22; the National Jewish Population Study, *American Jewish Year Book 1973,* pp. 288–291.

234    For potential welfare clients, see a report by Blanche Bernstein, Richard Schwartz and Bahk Sang of the New School for Social Research published in 1972, "New York's Jewish Poor and Jewish Working Class," which suggests that 15.1% of the Jewish population of the city is poor or near poor. A 1974 study by the Human Resources Administration of the City of New York found that one out of every five Jews in New York are "potential welfare risks." For the distribution of poverty funds, see Jack Simcha Cohen, "Jewish Poverty Issues" (New York: Metropolitan New York Coordinating Council on Jewish Poverty, 1975).

236    For the belated realization of poverty, see Ann G. Wolfe, "The Invisible Jewish Poor," *Journal of Jewish Communal Services,* Vol. 48, No. 3, Spring, 1972.

237    The Jewish paradox of an analytical people avoiding self-examination is suggested by H. H. Lurie, "Jewish Social Research," *Freedom and Reason,* ed. S. Baron, E. Nagel, and K. S. Pinson (Glencoe: The Free Press, 1951), p. 384.

238    The quotations are found in Lurie, "Jewish Social Research."

240    The report that Jews "hardly came" is from the *New York Evening Post,* January 7, 1905. For a review of Jewish migration, see Priscilla Fishman, ed. *The Jews of the United States* (New York: Quadrangle-New York Times Book Company, 1973), p. 35.

243    On moving away from issues of basic sustenance, Bertram H. Gold, Executive Vice President of the American Jewish Committee in an address on December 13, 1971. The quotation on "ecumenical duties" is from Paul Weinberger, "Conflicts and Consensus Around Jewish Welfare Fund Allocations," *Jewish Social Studies,* Vol. 34, No. 4, October, 1972. Finally, a rabbi accused the defense agencies of currying favors from the non-Jewish establishment: see Eugene B. Borowitz, *The Masks Jews Wear: The Self-Deceptions of American Jews* (New York: Simon and Schuster, 1973), p. 58.

244    The late start was costly indeed. The city's annual $40 million antipoverty program, according to a report of the city comptroller in 1977, was distributed inequitably. Tens of millions of dollars "went to the wrong neighborhoods because the Council Against Poverty allocated the funds on the basis of old formulas,